MODEM NATION

MODEM NATION

The Handbook of Grassroots American Activism Online

Charles Bowen

TIMES BUSINESS

RANDOM HOUSE

To the wise, wonderful women of my family:
Pamela, Peggy, and Kathy

Acknowledgments

This book exists because of some special people. First, thanks to my editor, Tracy Smith, whose insights and support made what could have been a torturous journey for me a joy. Thanks too to my friend, editor Mike Roney, who was this project's first booster. As always, I appreciate the help and encouragement I've received for the past dozen years from my agent, Katinka Matson of Brockman A ssociates Inc. And finally, thanks to my good friend, writer James E. Casto, who started it all when he said, "Hey, Bowen, why don't you write something about computers and politics?" See there, Jim? I *was* listening.

Contents

PART I

POLITICIANS, PARTIES, AND POLICY

Chapter 1

Introduction

When Bill Clinton took up residence in the White House in 1993, he found a phone system that was straight out of a 1940s black-and-white movie. Calls had to be transferred by operators pushing plugs into holes in a switchboard! As much as running mate Al Gore had talked up the nation's new "information superhighway," it was pretty apparent that the digital blacktop couldn't be found anywhere near the Clintons' new front door. In fact, *candidate* Clinton and his team of yuppie technocrats had run the campaign with a computer communications system that was far more sophisticated than the one the new president inherited to run the country.

In the months that followed Inauguration Day, the federal government's executive branch learned about new technology at the same time that much of the public did. New computers were installed in the White House. Electronic mail addresses were set up for the president, the vice president, and the cabinet. White House forums were established on CompuServe and America Online, to allow computer users around the world to chew the fat with Clinton's new cyber-savvy staff. Al Gore could be seen typing at a keyboard on C-Span as he participated in a national electronic real-time conference. (Not all historic events are especially great photo opps.)

Ever wonder why everyone now knows about the Internet? Because, in recent years, the federal government turned its not inconsiderable attention to this global computer network. The White House now has a "home page" on the Internet's World Wide Web. So do the Senate and the House of Representatives and most of their members—

3

Democrats and Republicans, liberals and conservatives, Libertarians, Socialists, and independents. And candidates—are there ever candidates! Four years ago, the idea of politicking in cyberspace was a novelty; today, for any serious contender for national office to *not* be represented in cyberspace would be like deciding not to stump in any cities that begin with "C."

WHEN WILL CYBERSPACE SPEAK?

Cyberspace is suddenly all grown up and ready for its first presidential election. What will its presence do to the process as we have known it?

The exact effect is hard to predict. Today's modem-linked community of computerized citizens—we'll call it the Modemocracy—is like a bright, strong, troublesomely lazy schoolboy who is full of potential but very easily distracted. Being grown up is not necessarily being mature.

Right now, the Modemocracy represents only about 10 percent of the entire electorate. To some observers, the Net as a political force is about as influential as television was during Eisenhower's campaigns. TV's impact on the elections of 1952 and 1956 was a far cry from the power it gained in the 1960 race. Many mark the Kennedy–Nixon debates as the beginning of the Television Age.

From all indications, it won't take a decade for online voters to confer the same kind of power on cyberspace. As author/columnist Nicholas Negroponte points out, statistics about the digital population often aren't reliable. Negroponte runs the media center at the Massachusetts Institute of Technology and spends much of his day thinking about our networking future. The Net is growing, he says, at 10 percent per month overall and, in some places, at 10 percent per week. He adds, "We also currently have such a strong generational divide . . . it may take a couple of years before the demographics of the Net are in sync with the world at large." A couple of years. The Cyber Age may break the tape before the millennium's final sprint.

For now, should we follow the suggestion of Dr. David Lytel, the White House's Internet specialist, and view the Net community simply as "an extremely well-off neighborhood" whose political clout so far is largely untapped?

Lytel, who manages the White House's online activities—including that new Web home page—is frankly *un*impressed with the computing electorate he has seen so far.

"What passes for political discussion online comes out in the real world as just noise," Lytel told a recent gathering at the Digital World Conference and Exposition in San Jose, California. "The biggest problem with the Net for a political medium is the curious resistance of 'netheads' to do anything more than send electronic mail to people in authority. It's like drunks who look for the lost car keys under the street lamp because the light is better there, even though they lost them elsewhere."

Lytel (and most other Net watchers) says we should look for 1996's candidates to campaign on the cyberspace networks. They'll be mostly "borrowing the image of modernity that the Net conveys without ever really engaging the Net community," he grumbles. The acid test for any online presence for candidates, Lytel believes, will be whether they can "take mild partisans and turn them into wild partisans who will actually do something off-line on behalf of their candidate."

Whether this leap into action will occur in the current election year is anyone's guess. It probably is just a matter of time until the Modemocracy awakens as a full-fledged political animal, but no one knows *when* the electronic community will advance to organized political action, rising above "e-mail storms" and online petitions, which, according to Lytel, are essentially ineffective. "Getting 50,000 or 80,000 people to hit the Enter key on their computers doesn't represent much commitment on their part," he says, "and legislators know this."

WHO SPEAKS FOR CYBERSPACE?

Assuming this new, untested, sleeping cyberspace constituency does become a political force, who will be its representative or spokesperson or acknowledged leader? One thing is for certain. If Bill Clinton thinks he has favorite-son status in the cybersphere simply by being the first president plugged into the Internet, he has not been reading his e-mail.

Nor has he been taking into consideration the network king, Newt Gingrich. Arguably, the gentleman from Georgia was America's first Net-smart politician. For years now, conservative Gingrich, while regularly quoting his favorite futurist, Alvin Toffler, and singing the praises of Internet resources, has warned his Republican colleagues not to allow the Democrats and liberals to beat them in staking out the new and ever-expanding electronic electorate. And somebody's been listening—*a lot* of somebodies have created Internet sites with names like The Conservative Connection, Conservative Generation X, and The Right Side of the Web. And, after leading the GOP revolution of 1994 with his "Contract with America," Gingrich has kept the spotlight steadily focused on telecomputing. For instance, among the recent projects of the Progress and Freedom Foundation, a focal point for Gingrich's "Renewing American Civilization" course, is "Cyberspace and the American Dream." Built around something called "A Magna Carta for the Knowledge Age," the project proposes in-depth discussion of the role of computer communications and related topics (a key suggestion: disband the Federal Communications Commission).

Some observers insist that the Web would lean to the right even *without* Gingrich, for demographic reasons. The overwhelming majority of the Modemocracy in the United States is white, middle-class, and male—traditionally, the traits of our society's most conservative segment.

And then there's the Rush Limbaugh Factor.

When George Bush was in the White House and few of us had even heard of Newt Gingrich, Rush Limbaugh was urging listeners to his daily national conservative radio show to drop him a line via something called "e-mail." Many Americans learned from Limbaugh what electronic mail was all about. And hardly a day went by when he didn't report on the air something provocative he had found on CompuServe. In fact, Limbaugh was so electronically linked that he even met his wife-to-be by modem. (Their relationship started when she complained to him electronically about something she had heard on his show.) Nowadays, Rush Limbaugh, as The Right's Pied Piper of cyberspace, is praised and vilified on more sites around the Internet than Bill Clinton.

But this doesn't mean The Left is left out. Besides a growing collection of anti-Rush and anti-Newt pages that communicate varying degrees of seriousness and civility, the Internet has a rising tide of sites with names like Turn Left and The Liberal Link, as well as pages produced by traditionally liberal organizations such as the American Civil Liberties Union and Amnesty International.

WHERE POLITICS IS ALWAYS A LOCAL AFFAIR

Weaned in a world of physical dimensions, we find it a little difficult to get our minds wrapped around the concept that, for all practical purposes, cyberspace is *boundless*. *No one* is left out because there's no "out" out there. For the tens of millions around the world who log into it every day, the Internet has no "front" or "back" (nor any "top," "bottom," "inside," "outside," "beginning," or "end"). Every electronic visitor starts at a different site and travels an individual trail to discover his or her own favorite features. There is no manual of standard operating procedures, no *correct* way. Some pioneers in this peculiar wilderness find this absense of guidance unsettling; they drive themselves nuts trying to map it all. Others, feeling strangely liberated by the vastness they have entered, take a decidedly Zen-like posture: where there are no roads, you're never lost.

In keeping with its boundlessness, the Net may signal a return to grassroots politics on a huge scale. Tip O'Neill, one of Gingrich's predecessors, wasn't talking about cyberspace when he said all politics are local, but he certainly could have been. The Net may be global, but all of us have it at *our* fingertips, running on *our* screens, delivering the pages *we* choose. Cyberspace is a highly personal mass experience.

It also is a great equalizer in terms of how we influence each other. The cybersphere has no town square, no communal watering hole, no assembly hall or convention center for addressing—or joining—the masses. When we browse the Web, all the sites we come across are viewed through the small window of our computer screen. People who have an axe to grind—politically or otherwise—depend on grabbing us through visually attractive screen displays. And, whether funded from the substantial coffers of a political party's national committee or the meager resources of a graduate student, each page we see occupies the same amount of space on our screen. Theoretically, each page has the same chance of capturing our imagination or gaining our support, regardless of the clout behind it.

We say "theoretically" because, in reality, online activists do have some clout. Literally and figuratively, they have *connections*. Their strength comes from a new spin on that most time-honored of political tools: word of mouth. The Web is held together, socially as well as technically, by "hypertext links"—cross-references that function like the "see also" section in an encyclopedia article. With a computer, you don't have to turn paper pages to find and read the see-also's. Instead, you use your mouse to click on the links (usually, pictures displayed on your screen, or words in a different color or typeface) and—*poof!*—you are automatically transported to the related material or feature. It is quite common for an active website to provide links around the Net to scores of related pages that have been produced by other people and organizations. These links enable politically like-minded people not only to advertise each other's sites, but also to provide the cyber-based "transportation" for getting there.

It works like this. Suppose you've discovered a page of material about domestic violence, with data on outreach programs, shelters in major cities, advice to victims, and so on. Also on the screen are links to other features that the page's creator thinks you'll be interested in—perhaps sites devoted to gun control, law enforcement, crime and punishment, women's health, child care issues, and more. Click on a link and away you go. At that next site, you might find new links—say, sites for discussions of liberal issues, congressional representatives' voting records or public statements on domestic violence or maybe a database of pending related legislation.

Exploring the Net by click can be digitally addictive. You've heard of "net surfing"—clicking on links by whim and intuition, then gliding the globe on the wave of your own curiosity? The Web is where the concept was born. Hypertext links yield some pretty mind-stretching, globe-striding leaps. One moment, you're reading an electronic newspaper out of Raleigh, North Carolina. Two clicks later, you're cozied up to a page produced in Oslo, Norway. The time it takes ranges from seconds to a minute or two (depending on, among other things, how many other computer users around the world currently are clicking in to the same online neighborhood).

DO WE BECOME CYBERSPACE CONNOISSEURS OR NETHEAD BIGOTS?

The nature of data surfing—clicking into a site on the "recommendation" of the previous one—keeps Web users on a path of special interests that is not necessarily straight but is certainly narrow. "Web browser" programs, the generic name for software for traveling the Internet's World Wide Web, usually have built-in "hot lists" or "bookmark" features for automatically saving the addresses of sites you discover. (Many Web page addresses are ridiculously long, like

http://falcon.cc.ukans.edu/~cubsfan/antirush.html,

and would be a pain to manually type in each time you wanted to visit.) After a few weeks of poking around these parts, your online destinations will often become increasing specific. Instead of drifting through hundreds of thousands of resources at random, you've collected and narrowed down your favorites to two or three dozen that you might visit daily. (In the back of this book, we have provided you with an alphabetical listing of the Web addresses we have discussed.)

Each new Net citizen tends to recreate the Internet in his or her own image, narrowcasting data to satisfy current interests and personal opinions. This self-imposed digital tunnel vision has some psychologists wondering whether the Net is nurturing a narrow-minded, static population.

It is "more efficient to be parochial," declares Robert Kraut, a professor of social psychology involved in an ongoing Carnegie Mellon University study of 50 families using the Internet for the first time. At the same time, Kraut acknowledges that a network life also "gets you to come across people and interests that you wouldn't have simply by being in your small location with your previous identity."

Ultimately, will the Net become primarily *global* or *local*? "The jury's still out," says Kraut. Everything is too new and is changing too fast to make accurate predictions. Some analysts, like Professor Negroponte, wonder whether the term "parochial" is even applicable to the Net. Many of the terms we use to define ourselves—"cosmopolitan," "backwoods," "regional," "international"—are rooted in a physical, geographical world in which we have the ability to move about in person and interact with others. Transport that communication to a plane where physical distance is no longer a barrier to the mingling of cultures and ideas—where Joplin, Missouri, is just a click away from Japan, Jakarta, and Java—and the terms begin to change or lose their meaning. You even have to wonder: Will other labels (liberal, conservative, internationalist, isolationist) also be altered when they are transplanted online?

John Perry Barlow on Future Politics

"Culturally, I'd prefer to hang out with the Clintons, but ideologically I have nothing in common with them," says Internet philosopher John Perry Barlow.

Names on the Net

"They believe in the power of government. The only thing government can do with this [cyber] space is to screw it up, and that only temporarily."

Republican Barlow, best known as the lyricist for the late, great Grateful Dead rock band and cofounder of the Electronic Freedom Foundation (EFF), also muses, "I don't believe there will be a federal government left on this planet in fifty years. There won't be a need for it."

It's one thing to say such things online at midnight, or maybe in the pages of *Wired* magazine, but Barlow was saying them in Washington, to the faces of people who are in the business of federal governing.

Covering last summer's meeting between the Newt Gingrich-influenced Progress and Freedom Foundation and the EFF board of directors, Rex Nutting of United Press International reported: "The software pioneers, civil libertarians and hippies at EFF charmed and challenged congressional staffers and think-tankers with their practical and philosophical views about how computer and communication technologies are transforming American and global business, politics and culture."

Barlow told the wire service how he met with Gingrich and found they were in surprisingly close agreement on most issues, other than the war on drugs ("The bourbon and football culture has declared war on the marijuana and Frisbee culture"). Barlow believes the true split is not between Democrats and Republicans, but between authoritarians and libertarians, and there are plenty of both in each party.

"IT'S TRUE! TRUST ME!"

Cyberspace messages raise a very fundamental concern, especially in the political sphere: Are they true? How can we tell if they're not?

In what we still charmingly call the "real world," most of us—some more grudgingly than others—acknowledge that the news media at least *want* to be fair, accurate, and objective. That is why professional journalists have established certain baselines to use in their pursuit of accuracy. For instance, it's important for reporters and editors to routinely consider the *source* of incoming information, to seek *confirmation* from other verifiable sources, and, more importantly perhaps, to *question the motivation* for the data's publication in the first place.

No such baseline exits on the Web, because most of what appears there is not contributed by journalists. Everything you access may *look* pretty much the same (printed words on the screen), but the information available on the unregulated, global Internet comes in far more flavors than you'll find in any newspaper or magazine. There is some "real news" ("real-world" news media are beginning to show up on the Net, as we'll see in a later chapter), but there also are opinions, advertising, predictions, outright fabrications, hate mail, poems, put-ons, parodies, pornography, and manifestos from every corner of the world, all stirred together within a dizzying whirlpool.

Real-world journalists are trained to work in just this kind of murky depth; they were wading in these waters long before the Internet came into being. Every day, they fish out facts from the rivers of daily events and serve them to us on the evening news and in the morning paper. They pass judgment on the day's hordes of rumors and happenings, decide which ones deserve our audience, and process them through increasingly finer grids to test for accuracy and newsworthiness.

On the Net, though, we all work without a net. No one's looking out for us, screening the cranks before they get to us. It's exciting. Information comes at us from all sides, as it does to a reporter or an editor. Official government reports stand shoulder-to-shoulder with

Is there a "home page" in your future?

In the spring of 1995, it was bandied about that an estimated 5 million World Wide Web users had already created introductory home pages, and that the number would double every 57 days. A qualified computer industry insider figured that, at that rate, there will be one website for every person in the world by 1999.

A Home Page in Every Home?

quirky newsletters of vague origin. Beautifully constructed screen displays tell the damnest lies in the prettiest forms; everywhere, the half-truth is the coin of the realm.

Technological naysayers, alarmed at this confusion of news and rumor, say the great edifices of the Information Age are destined to tumble with the erosion of accuracy. A world in which no one guards the gate, they warn, will devolve into the New Dark Ages. Their anarchy anxiety is discussed at length in a later chapter; for now, let's just note a more optimistic view of these developments. As data consumers, we are beginning to evolve into being *our own gatekeepers*. We've grown up in a nation in which the concept of "Buyer Beware" has become so ingrained it could be engraved on our currency. We make a parlor game out of nit-picking the flaws in our films and TV shows. Political commentators on television and radio have created a new buzzword by doing "reality checks" of political advertising. This book applies to the Net some of that same show-me tradition.

The first part of the book's mission is to convey the depth and breadth of political and social activity in cyberspace. Hundreds of sites have arisen from national parties, elections, and superstar candidates as well as from extensions of the day-to-day operations of federal, state, and local governments and international agencies. And the story would be incomplete if we stopped there. Other sites are devoted to consumerism and activism, what we might call "the little-p politics" of issues and causes that have characterized so much of the past half-century. These diverse, often grassroots movements, united in a shared desire for the empowerment of the individual, seem quite at home in the Web's ego-centricity.

It would be impossible—and of questionable value—to simply list every conceivable political site on the Net. The number changes daily, there's much repetition, and, frankly, many of them aren't worth the time it would take you to visit. Therefore, in preparing this book, we've exercised some discernment in selecting what sites to highlight. All those we do feature we have visited personally, choosing them because we think they have something to show you. They are original, imaginative approaches to the subject, or are newsworthy in and of themselves, or are well-established gathering places for people of like minds. Because the Net is a dynamic, unfocused, ever-evolving medium, there's no guarantee that all the sites we saw yesterday will still be there tomorrow. We have tried to spotlight the Net pages that seem likely to have a greater staying power and can serve as starting points for your own exploration.

The second part of the book's mission is to persuade you to be discerning as you travel the Internet. We shall remind you from time to time that both the beauty and the beastliness of the Net is that it is unregulated. This freedom allows rapid deployment of data, but no prerequisites exist for publication, and there are no promises of fairness, accuracy, or honesty. If we are indeed evolving into being our own gatekeepers, we need to realize that the most important attitude a well-wired citizen can adopt when cruising the Net is a healthy skepticism of what he or she finds there, whether the contributors are traditional news services, government agencies, or special interests.

ABOUT THOSE SPECIAL INTERESTS

White House Internet specialist David Lytel says the political efficacy of communicating via the Internet generally "is vastly, wildly, hugely overstated" and that online groups "emphatically do not wield terrific economic and political power." However, he does acknowledge that today's Net is especially powerful in at least one area—service to special interests.

"What *does* work," he says, "is where there's an effective lobbyist on the other end . . . [who] provides accurate and timely reporting on what's happening in the legislative process so that attention can be focused to the right legislators and the right time from the right people."

"Special interests" is a term that regularly gets a political beating, but it also has a kinder, gentler side, especially online. From their very beginning more than 15 years ago, the personal computer networks have been uniquely suited for sharing sharply focused news and commentary. From CompuServe's forums (which, significantly, were originally called "SIGs" or "special interest groups") to the newsgroups of the Internet, cyberspace always has offered features for thousands of specific topics. Ham radio; the latest jokes; technical details of new hardware and software—subjects range from watchdogging IBM and AT&T to news and views on abortion and government spending and to the special needs of people who play saxophones. In fact, another way of viewing this whole phenomenon of Net surfing is as a digital drifting from one electronic special-interest group to another.

WHERE THIS BOOK COMES IN

"Special interests" also can refer to the online resources about the policies and the issues that fuel continuing political debate in this country. In this book, we shall approach special interests from several directions.

In the next two chapters, for instance, we'll view them from the perspective of the political parties and presidential candidates who debate them. The sites described will bring you to the front lines of the current campaign. You can read the speeches, compare the position papers, look at the polling results, study the strategy, and watch the contenders bob and weave in the digital update of our traditional quadrennial dance toward the White House.

Next, we'll approach the issues themselves. Chapter 4, the largest chapter in the book, shows you how to connect with interest groups of all political persuasions, from the National Rifle Association to PeaceNet, from Greenpeace to the World Health Organization. Together, we'll discover how to tap into any of hundreds of causes currently represented on the Net: homelessness, handicapped persons, gay rights, environmentalism, feminism, abortion, children's rights, gun control, health care, welfare.

The second part of this book moves us to yet another vantage point. We'll examine special interests, not from the heat and rumble of the campaign trail, but from the relative stability and cool quarters of day-to-day government and business. We'll learn how to use the Net to link up with specific departments of the federal government, state and local government resources, related consumer and business sites, and the news media and commentators.

THE JOURNEY AHEAD

Throughout the book, a single thread is the third part of our mission: learning how to make politics in the modem nation work for you.

You are the ultimate special-interest group. As you travel alone through cyberspace, uniting with other travelers purely through mutual interests and shared concerns, there ought to be ways to use this technology to improve your life, to raise your civic voice, to extend your political reach. There are, and we'll find them together.

Understanding Web Addresses

In the next chapter, we begin to list addresses for pages displayable on the Internet's World Wide Web. Here is an example:

http://bobbynet.edu/resume/Accomplishments.html

To access an address, simply type it in the appropriate field of the web browser program you use on the Net, and press the Enter key. Web browsers usually have a field, in the top half of the screen, labeled "Document URL" (URL stands for Uniform Resource Locator). This is the standard way to refer to sites or pages, also known as "resources," on the Web. However, some more recent Web browser programs are doing away with references to URL. The latest versions of the popular Netscape program, for instance, label that field as merely "Netsite."

The syntax for a URL is:

scheme://host.domain[:port]/path/filename

These days, the "scheme:" portion is usually "http:," an indication that a file exists on the World Wide Web. The letters stand for "hypertext transport protocol," a techie way of saying "the address to which you want to *go*" (be transported). "Hypertext" is the computer technology that holds the World Wide Web together, enabling visitors to move about by simply clicking their mouse pointers on highlighted or underlined "hyperlinks." The "scheme:" element can also refer to some of the older, pre-Web Internet sites, such as "gopher:" (to reach a file on a Gopher server), "telnet:" (to connect to a Telnet-based service), "news:" (for a Usenet newsgroup), "WAIS:" (for a file on a WAIS server), or "file:" for a file on your local Internet service provider's computers or on an anonymous FTP site.

The "host.domain" portion ("bobbynet.edu" in the example) is the address of the computer system on which the file resides.

The ":port" can generally be omitted; unless someone tells you otherwise, leave it out. The default HTTP (http://) network port is 80. If the HTTP server in our example resided on a different network port (say, port 1234), the address would read:

http://bobbynet.edu:1234/resume/Accomplishments.html

The "path/filename" unit spells out the pathway on the directory of the host computer (the "resume/" portion of our example) and then the actual file name ("Accomplishments.html") and the file we are to see. Be careful to type in all addresses *exactly* as they appear in the book. Internet is notoriously persnickety about upper- and lowercase letters; the "Accomplishments" portion of

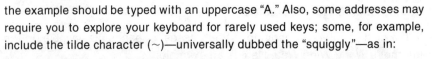

the example should be typed with an uppercase "A." Also, some addresses may require you to explore your keyboard for rarely used keys; some, for example, include the tilde character (~)—universally dubbed the "squiggly"—as in:

(http://www.cs.dartmouth.edu/~crow/whitewater/scandal.html)

The tilde appears on different keys, depending on keyboards' design.

If you visit a new website for the first time, like what you see, and think you'll want to revisit it in the future, save the address via your web browser's "bookmark" or "hot list" feature, which allows you to build your own collection of favorite places. Once a site address is saved in your hot list section, you don't have to manually enter the lengthy URL address before each visit. Instead, you can simply call up the hot line and click on the name of the site you want to visit.

As a nation, we are starting a fascinating voyage. Politics and government will never be the same. No one yet knows what will be the privileges and responsibilities of citizens in a modem nation, a modem world. Many of the tools that will empower us in this new environment haven't even been created yet. But among all the unknowns is one truth: We have come to a time and place where new knowledge begins.

Chapter 2

Plugged-In Politicians

In nature, a web is the home of a predator, a combatant—a fitting reminder for those of us visiting the contentious political reaches of the
Internet's World Wide Web during its first presidential election year.

But then, confrontation *always* has been native to the Net. In
fact, netheads have their own word for it: flame. It's a verb as well as a
noun in cyberspace. To flame or to send a flame is to skewer someone
or something in an electronic message, either in front of everyone on
one of the tens of thousands of public bulletin boards or in the privacy
of one's own electronic mailbox.

How the Net came by its love of the flame is not apparent. Perhaps we all feel especially feisty as we sit cloistered at our keyboards,
communicating on a medium that appears for all the world to be performing solely for our own amusement. One thing is sure: Targets are
infinite. People flame each other over everything from favorite football teams to the pros and cons of sunscreen lotions.

When this uniquely cyberian energy source touches politics, the
fireworks really get going. Where else but on the Internet's World Wide
Web could you find a Countdown on the Clinton Presidency, updated
daily with lines like "Day 869 for Excuses, Whining and Avoidance"?
Or another called What's Newt? with its "Top Ten Signs that Newt Has
Gone Mad with Power"? The same Net that supports a rather gentle
site devoted entirely to remembering the Ronald Reagan presidency,

17

complete with charts and graphs comparing the Gipper's economic and social performance with predecessors and successors, also invites you to the Anti-Rush Limbaugh Page and "some refutations of the Fat Man's lies and his 70 more-than-questionable 'truths.'" The webscape hosts a war of words, and the last word is nowhere in sight.

But the messages aren't *all* flame-throwing and name-calling. Beyond the hyperbole and hijinks are features with some real substance. Better political sites on the Web, like those covered in this book, can help you become a more active political animal. For instance, if you've always wanted to be part of a big political campaign, this chapter will show you how your computer can plug you into the process, using features like:

▶ E-mail, phone, and fax contacts. Want to tell a candidate, or the office-seeker's staff, what's on your mind? Got an idea for the campaign? Want to request some personal attention for your problem or question? Candidates have lots of ways to hear from you these days, and we'll give you the necessary contact points.

▶ Directories. The global Web is also a super utility for finding *local* resources. Many political sites have lists of regional campaign organizations, so you can find the group nearest you. Also look for lists of local and regional events, including campaign stops, speeches, and programs.

▶ Volunteer offers. Some sites have online forms you can fill out if you want to work the phones in the local campaign office or help with mailings.

▶ Contribution connections. You can make donations via modem to some of the campaign organizations, charging the amount on a credit card.

▶ Research aids. If Uncle Edgar is getting the best of you in those post-Sunday-dinner verbal donnybrooks, perhaps you need to do a little homework on your candidate (and Uncle Edgar's). For the truly wired, this means hitting the databases. Archives of candidates' speeches and position papers abound, along with databases of relevant newspaper and magazine reports on the campaign. We'll show you where to find them; next Sunday, the dinner table won't know what hit it!

CLINTON: THE FIRST ONLINE PRESIDENCY IS ON THE LINE

Bill Clinton is proof that the Modemocracy is going to be a hard constituency to court.

He and Al Gore came to office as the first Administration to sing the praises of the Information Age. Their 1992 campaign was backed by a substantially larger assembly of computer industry executives than George Bush had managed to attract. The new kids in town immediately demonstrated their Networthiness by setting up e-mail addresses for about half of official Washington and staking out a claim on a site of the Web. Gore continued to beat the drum for their campaign promise to create a door-to-door information network to link every home, business, lab, classroom, and library by the year 2015.

However, before Clinton's first year was logged, grumbling was coming from some computing corners. By the spring of 1994, the grumbling had grown into such a full-fledged revolutionary chorus that influential *Wired* magazine, under the headline "Save the Bill of Rights!" trumpeted: "The national security state, with the backing of the Clinton–Gore administration, is attempting a stealth strike on our rights. If they succeed, we could shortly find ourselves under a government with the automated ability to log the time, origin, and recipient of every call and e-mail message, to monitor our most private communications, to track our physical whereabouts continuously, and to keep better account of our financial transactions than we do."

At the heart of the harangue was Clipper, an encryption computer chip the National Security Agency and the FBI wanted someday to have installed in all telephones and computers. The chip would scramble communications, the agencies said, making the data unintelligible to all but the intended recipients. Well, almost all: the government would hold the "key" for descrambling, in case agents ever want to tap that particular phone/data line. The Clipper proposal died months later, after privacy advocates loudly accused the government of trying to spy on users of the new technology. However, as *The Wall Street Journal* noted, in early 1996, "the idea of leaving a back door open for government agents has remained alive." For instance, the *Journal* observed, under reportedly intense government pressure and in exchange for leeway on export restrictions, IBM agreed to include a special "key" that will help government investigators tap into data messages in IBM's Lotus Notes software. Reportedly, other companies were negotiating similar compromises in return for export privileges on encryption products.

This finagling has left some of Cyberia so soured on the Clinton team that, by October 1994, president Mark Stahlman of New Media Associates in New York was grousing, in *Wired:* "Haven't we learned anything? The job of career politicians is to get re-elected—not to shrink government. Replacing Big Steel with Big Silicon doesn't change anything—it's still the same political system. . . . In our zeal to make our technologies and our digital culture mainstream, we've fallen into a trap—a very old trap. We've become co-opted. We've forgotten why we mistrusted government in the first place. We've fooled ourselves into thinking that we've won and that the 'good guys' are fondling the levers of power now. We've become cyberdupes."

Curiously, though, technological issues like high-tech snooping are generally *not* what gets Clinton creamed in the computer 'hood. Just drop by David Sussman's Clinton Exposé Web (http://www .en.com/users/bthomas/expose.htm) and you'll see that the Net's anti-Clinton ranks seem warmed by the same flames—Whitewater, health care, draft records—that keep the home fires burning on conservative radio talk shows.

Sussman, a computer staffer with the Oakland University School of Business Administration, has made it part of his online mission to preserve the records of charges and rumors that Clinton has accumulated, from his student digs to the Arkansas governor's mansion and to 1600 Pennsylvania Avenue. The website has assembled files on: Whitewater (the people and corporations involved, and the status of various investigations of the Arkansas-based financial controversy); alleged drug usage during Clinton's college days; questionable commodity and stock dealings; Clinton's Vietnam War draft board issues; and various alleged broken promises over the years. Carrying on work started in 1995 by Dartmouth College student Preston Crow, Sussman also has a feature called "What Really Happened to Vince Foster?" which examines assorted theories about the 1993 gunshot death of the White House lawyer/Clinton pal. The official ruling of suicide is disputed by Clinton foes. The site even links to other "conspiracy theory pages" around the Web, including those on the Waco Branch Davidian tragedy and the Oklahoma federal building bombing case.

Most of David Sussman's Clinton Exposé Web (http://www.en.com/users /bthomas/expose.htm) concentrates on preserving the details of Clinton Administration problems, but it saves some room for humor, as in these bumper stickers:

Inhale to the Chief

Hope ain't in Arkansas . . . it's in 1996

You voted for change, that's all you'll have left

Voting Republican means never having to say you're sorry

Hillary Happens

At least Gennifer got kissed

> **Bashing Bill: Other Net Clinton-Clobberers**

He also tips his hat to other Clinton-clobberers around the system:

▶ In His Own Words, Broken Promises from the President (http://www .umr.edu:80/~umrcr/lies.html), alleged quotes from Clinton on various topics, and the dates they were spoken. Subjects include the middle-class tax cut, the tax burden, eliminating the deficit, welfare reform, corporate tax rates, Haiti, Bosnia, Somalia, social security, the drug war, the line-item veto, crime, and the purchase of more national park land. Each is accompanied by what is put forth as evidence of a broken promise.

▶ Clinton Watch (gopher://dolphin.gulf.net:3000/hh). Backed by *The Washington Week,* a conservative political magazine published exclusively on the Internet, Clinton Watch offers regular updates on Whitewater and other Clinton-oriented issues. Incidentally, don't miss its "What's New in Politics," which lists political features newly added to the Web.

▶ Countdown on the Clinton Presidency (http://www.acs.ncsu.edu/~nsyslaw /scripts/rawdeal-nsyslaw). Started by Lou Williams, a computer programmer at North Carolina State University, just days after Clinton's election, this site is based on Rush Limbaugh's "Raw Deal Countdown." "Like FDR's New Deal," says the page, "the Clinton Presidency gives us the Raw Deal." It is updated daily.

Finally, if you've always wanted your own copy of that perennial favorite among Bill bashers in Clinton campaigns—young Clinton's 1969 letter to the University of Arkansas ROTC program, stating his views on the draft and the Vietnam War—aim your browser at http://www.winternet.com/~ssarazin /clinton.draft.html, where the letter to Lt. Col. Eugene Holmes has been preserved in its entirety.

Most of Clinton, Yes! (http://www.av.qnet.com/~yes/) is passionately partisan, but tucked away in one corner of the site is a feature that will be useful to visitors of all political stripes. "How to Be Your Own Lobbyist" is Tarja Black's growing collection of Congress-watch pages, various Congress rating organizations, and e-mail/fax addresses for all the senators and representatives.

How to Be Your Own Lobbyist

If you're a new surfer in political waters, this is a good place to get your feet wet. For instance, suppose you need to find out how your senators and representatives voted on a particular piece of legislation. The page can link you to at least two different resources, Project Vote Smart, which provides Congress members' voting records, biographical information, campaign financial data, and evaluations (more about Project Vote Smart later in this chapter), and The First 100 Days, which assembles the environmental record of Congress.

Do you need to find out how to e-mail your federal representatives? The same page has links to several databases containing that information.

The site even tells how to send a message in the old-fashioned ways. For instance, you can reach the offices of your Senators and Representatives by calling 202/224-3121 or by writing: Senator [name], U.S. Senate, Washington, DC 20510; or Representative [name], U.S. House of Representatives, Washington, DC, 20415.

But Sussman concentrates mainly on Clinton and his associates. Want to refresh your memory on the 1993 controversy over the White House travel office? How about digging up the dirt on the Clintons' alleged ties with Tyson Foods, or other affiliations? Those are just some of the flames the page continues to fan. Sussman invites others to contribute material by sending him e-mail at djsussma@oakland.edu.

The Clinton camp will be happier if you spend your online time with Tarja Black instead. A veteran grassroots activist from Clinton's 1992 California campaign, Black has made her Clinton, Yes! page (http://www.av.qnet.com/~yes/) a never-ending pep rally by modem. Intended for those who are unabashedly pro-Clinton, the page features details on what the Administration claims as accomplishments, and liberally slams the GOP in a posting titled, "How the Republicans' 'Contract on America' Is Hurting People in Your State." If you're looking for

Usenet: Internet's Bulletin Boards

Usenet newsgroups are Internet's bulletin boards, where computer users from around the world post messages on virtually any conceivable topic. Currently, there are more than 15,000 newsgroups, most of them "unmoderated," meaning the tone and the choice of wording are entirely up to the participants. The not-so-fine art of flaming reaches new limits in the newsgroups when the topic is politics or social issues.

Newsgroup names are *hierarchical,* and elements of the names are separated by periods. For instance, "alt.politics" might discuss general political topics, "alt.politics.democrats" is a different newsgroup intended specifically for Democratic Party topics, and "alt.politics.democrats.clinton" focuses on the Clinton Administration. Think of these hierarchies as a kind of outline: the categories have subcategories, then subsubcategories. From left to right, the listing goes from general to specific. The first part of the group's name is the major hierarchy to which that newsgroup belongs. Here is a list of the major groups:

alt	alternative newsgroups; many different topics
biz	business, marketing, ads
comp	computer topics
k12	kindergarten through high school; education topics
news	about Usenet itself
rec	recreation, hobbies, the arts
sci	science of all types
soc	social issues

Anyone can join or "subscribe" to a newsgroup (usually without any fees). Subscribers can read and contribute to the messages. Notes that make up the newsgroups are received and made available on Internet-linked computers and computer bulletin board systems around the world. How you go about actually reading newsgroups depends on the software or online service you're using. Online services like CompuServe and America Online have "Newsgroup Reader" options, and many of the Internet service providers offer newsgroups among their features. Most of the software/services direct you to "subscribe" to newsgroups of interest and provide some facilities for searching newsgroups of interest.

a little ammunition for your watercooler arguments, she invites you to examine her links to the "clickable despicables," a collection of put-downs and put-ons of Clinton foes, from Gingrich and Limbaugh to Phil Gramm, Bob Dornan, and others. This is a proudly partisan site; the last time we surfed through, she even offered an article on how physicist Edward Witten, "arguably the smartest person in the world," is a liberal Democrat.

There's a decidedly fan-magazine quality about the Clinton, Yes! page. You can find out what Bill Clinton reads for inspiration (*Mere Christianity* by C.S. Lewis) and what he quoted at the 1995 White House Correspondents' Association dinner (W.H. Auden: "In the deserts of the heart/Let the healing fountain start,/In the prison of his days/Teach the free man how to praise.") The site also can give you on-line and "real world" contacts with Democratic Party organizations across the nation. Tarja Black is always on the lookout for more research material. If you want to chat with her, send e-mail to yes@qnet.com.

If you need to collect the Clinton camp's spin on your specific part of the country, don't miss Accomplishments of the Clinton Administration (http://whitehouse.gov/Accomplishments.html), a state-by-state display of what the Administration says it achieved in its first years in office. An on-screen U.S. map invites you to click any state for specifics. (Click on Indiana, for instance, and learn that the state had 20,300 new manufacturing jobs in 23 months, after 10,500 jobs had been lost during the previous four years; that the unemployment rate dropped from 5.9 percent to 4.3 percent; and that home sales increased 20 percent.)

NEWT GINGRICH, THE NET'S NEW GUY

"Net Newtonians"—that's what a boisterous segment of the computer literati drawn to House Speaker Newt Gingrich are beginning to call themselves. They like Gingrich's unique mixing of progressive technology with conservative economic and social ideas. And some have been attracted by the way the Georgia Republican talks. When he speaks of the modem world, he doesn't call it "The Information Superhighway," a label that sounds contrived to many who actually travel these digital byways. Instead, Gingrich uses simple terms that ring true and suggest Newt himself really has been on the Net.

The Net Newtonians will also tell you their man has remained loyal to his networking roots when the chips are down. In the summer of 1995, for instance, he surprised conservative colleagues by coming out *against* the efforts of Senator James Exon (D-Nebraska) to regulate pornography on the Net. Exon's amendment to the Senate's Telecommunications Competition and Deregulation Act of 1995, which passed in the Senate 81–18, called for fines of up to $100,000 and prison terms of up to two years for people who distribute sexually explicit material over networks. The proposal was widely condemned online as overkill, an unenforceable shotgun approach and a threat to the free flow of information.

During the TV taping of his Progress and Freedom Foundation's weekly "Progress Report" show, Gingrich was asked by a caller for his views on the debate. He turned some heads when he said the proposed Exon measure "is clearly a violation of free speech and it's a violation of the right of adults to communicate with each other." Following the online world's party line—not shared by all conservative Republicans— he added, "I don't think [the debate on the Exon proposal] is a serious way to discuss a serious issue, which is: How do you maintain the right of free speech for adults while also protecting children in a medium which is available to both?"

But, just as Bill Clinton has learned that being the first Information Age president doesn't automatically bring Web-wide support, so Gingrich has found that he makes a very attractive online punching bag.

Consider Matt Dorsey's NewtWatch (http://www.cais.com /newtwatch). This pugnacious electronic watchdog has the Right Wing smarting ("Third-Wave slime," Gingrich spokesman Tony Blankley characterizes it) and the Left Wing smirking ("Hypertext . . . is absolutely an essential medium if anyone is going to understand Newt's complex web of hidden financing," says White House techie David Lytel). NewtWatch sets its tone by opening with provocative graphics, such as an enhanced picture of Gingrich seeming to greet a space alien while Bob Dole looks on. Then the introductory text asks, "Interested about what's behind those ethics complaints you've heard about? Wondering who in your zip code contributed to Newt? How much honoraria he earned before the practice was banned? How about Newt's cosponsored 'commemorative' bills before those were banned? It's all here—and more—with more to come." Dorsey serves up the full text of ethics complaints that have been filed against the Speaker and gives

Writer/researcher Aaron Delwiche produces a Propaganda Analysis Home Page (http://carmen.artsci.washington.edu/propaganda/home.htm) that focuses on the key ways "propaganda shapes public opinion." Imitating the Institute for Propaganda Analysis, created in 1937, Delwiche starts by identifying some familiar "propaganda devices," such as Glittering Generalities (charged concepts like "love" and "freedom" used in a vaguely positive way) and the Testimonial (unqualified persons giving judgments, like "I'm not a doctor, but I play one on TV").

Knocking Newt: Elements of NewtSpeak

Delwiche then goes on to show instances of Newt Gingrich's use of "glittering generalities" and "name-calling words."

Notes Delwiche: "Four years before 'Contract With America' became a household phrase, Newt Gingrich's political action committee (GOPAC) mailed a pamphlet entitled *Language, A Key Mechanism of Control* to Republicans across the country. The booklet offered rhetorical advice to Republican candidates who wanted to 'speak like Newt.' It was awarded a Doublespeak Award by the National Conference of Teachers of English in 1990."

The booklet contained two lists of words, which Gingrich advised candidates to use according to the circumstances and the topic. Delwiche calls them:

▶ "Positive, governing words" (to be used when speaking about themselves or their policies):

active(ly)	confident	freedom
activist	conflict	hard work
building	control	help
candid(ly)	courage	humane
care(ing)	crusade	incentive
challenge	debate	initiative
change	dream	lead
children	duty	learn
choice/choose	eliminate good-time in	legacy
citizen	prison	liberty
commitment	empower(ment)	light
common sense	fair	listen
compete	family	mobilize

Knocking Newt: (continued)

moral	pristine	strength
movement	pro-(issue, e.g., flag,	success
opportunity	children, environment)	tough
passionate	prosperity	truth
peace	protect	unique
pioneer	proud/pride	vision
precious	provide	we/us/our
premise	reform	workfare
preserve	rights	
principle(d)	share	

▶ "Name-calling words" (to be used when speaking about opponents):

anti-(issue, e.g., flag,	endanger	radical
family, child, jobs)	failure	self-serving
betray	greed	sensationalists
coercion	hypocrisy	shallow
collapse	ideological	sick
consequences	impose	they/them
corruption	incompetent	threaten
crisis	insecure	traitors
decay	liberal	unionized bureaucracy
deeper	lie	urgent
destroy	limit(s)	waste
destructive	pathetic	
devour	permissive attitude	

For other Newt-knocking on the Net, check out What's Newt: Keeping Track of Newt Gingrich (http://www.wolfenet.com/~danfs/newt.html), a regularly updated collection of news items, as well as links to items such as "Newt Gags and Goodies," and the *Mother Jones* Supplement on Newt Gingrich (http://www.mojones.com/mojo_magazine.html), which contains the text of reports by writers David Osborne (1984) and David Beers (1989).

the details of Gingrich's voting records, back to 1981 and to the 97th Congress, on such issues as reproductive rights, gun control, and congressional reform, with links to "affiliate special-interest contributors."

NewtWatch calls itself "the Web's first virtual PAC" (political action committee). It seeks reader contributions for expanded online coverage. Promised additions include: vote analysis, contributors prior to 1979, staff and office expenditures for the Speaker's office, further House Ethics Committee complaints, and biographical research.

On the other side of the aisle is the Newt Gingrich WWW Fan Club (http://www.clark.net/pub/jeffd/mr_newt.html). Carried on The Right Side of the Web, a major conservative gathering spot, the Fan Club is considered by many to be the center of Gingrich's Net popularity. Of particular interest are links to the text of Gingrich's speeches. Also, the Progress and Freedom Foundation, a focal point for Gingrich's "Renewing American Civilization" course, has a major Web presence (http://www.pff.org/). The Foundation is a private, nonprofit center established in 1993 "to create a positive vision of America's future founded on our nation's historic principles." Projects include "Center for Political Renewal," "Renewing American Civilization," "Medical Innovation Project," "Center for Effective Compassion," "American Civilization," "National City Project" and "The Progress Report." Gingrich's own Web page (http://www.house.gov/mbr_dir/GA06.html) lists basic office information and his e-mail address (georgia6@hr.house.gov), as well as his legislative history and the bills he sponsored and cosponsored.

If you're researching Gingrich's rise to power and his role in the recent changes in Washington, you probably want to study his speeches. Contact *Washington Weekly*, which stores in an archive (http://dolphin.gulf.net/Gingrich.html) the Speaker's speeches back to the November 11, 1994, address to the Washington Research Group, which was his first speech after the Republican sweep of the 1994 Congress. You'll be offered the option of having transcripts of future speeches e-mailed to you.

HOW GOP FRONT-RUNNERS FOUND THEIR CYBER STANCE

To some degree, we're all slaves to fashion, but politicians are dedicated to wanting us to think they're tuned into the same trends and spins that we are. Remember how they ditched their suits a few years ago and started showing up in their TV ads in plaid flannel shirts with the sleeves rolled up? Just "reg'lar guys." Well, now they want to be reg'lar guys with 28.8K-bps modems and home pages on the Web.

Some camps have been setting up interesting experiments in electronic campaigning. They're cranked up to use the new technology for zapping out statements and responses at light-speed, for interacting in real time with voters and campaign workers across the country, for providing instant transcripts of speeches and position papers to the press and the public, and for plugging their own sound bites (or—can we be the first to say it?—"sound bytes"). Others are claiming a corner of the Web so as not to appear to be indifferent to the race for cyberspace.

Most pols are somewhere between those poles. Loath to overlook a potent new politicking powertool, they nonetheless have been somewhat sobered by the stats. With only about one in ten potential voters currently surfing the Net at all, and with reportedly more than 4 million Web pages to surf through, the odds that a receptive citizen will actually modem in to their particular sites are remote enough to make even a dark horse pale. On the other hand, the Internet is cheap and fast. The setup is not as expensive as establishing a Real World campaign headquarters in, say, New York or L.A. Scant original data are required because most of the material already has been prepared in a computer for printing and/or faxing and can be duplicated online with a minimum of recoding. In addition, once up and running, a cyber site can be kept going with little effort. It's no wonder that so many hopefuls, vying for the opportunity to take on Bill Clinton, have discovered the wonders of the Web.

Robert Dole

Going into the 1996 campaign, Bob Dole, the Senate majority leader, had none of the Net presence of Gingrich or Gore. For that reason, the Kansan surprised some observers late in 1995, when he suddenly weighed into one of the hotter online issues of the day—the controversial launch of the Microsoft Network online service.

Microsoft's competitors viewed the software giant's entry into the online arena as unfair competition by one of computerdom's royal families. Dole, however, characterized a related investigation by the

Antitrust Division of the U.S. Department of Justice as "overzealous," adding, "A company develops a new product—a product consumers want. But now the government steps in and is, in effect, attempting to dictate the terms on which that product can be marketed and sold. Pinch me, but I thought we were still in America."

Dole also used the case to highlight a broader issue. Some members of Congress wanted to give the Justice Department what he thought was too much power to enforce telecommunications laws under a new bill to reform the telephone and cable industries. "Antitrust standards are not only sufficient," Dole said, "but it seems to me that the current Department of Justice is overzealous in its use of these statutes." On the Microsoft Network issue, he backed the winning horse, it turned out, because the Justice Department ended up retreating by summer's end. The Redmond, Washington, software publisher was allowed to press ahead with its campaign to start its new online unit.

Early in 1996, the Official Bob Dole for President site (http://www.dole96.com) rolled out. Campaign loyalists found it worth the wait. If you want to know virtually anything about the Dole campaign, this should be your first stop. There is biographical material—"From his childhood in the fields of Kansas," says an online statement, "through his heroism on the field of battle to his ongoing leadership in Congress . . ."—as well as a library of press releases, speech transcripts, and audio and video files. If you want to know what groups and organizations are supporting Dole, click on the Coalitions option.

To check the progress of the campaign across the country, visit the "Dole Coast to Coast" feature, where an interactive map provides state wrap-ups, details on local political leaders who have come on board, dates for state primaries and caucuses, and specifics on how you can take a more active role in the campaign on a local level. If you'd like even more information, the "Electronic Mailing List" option enables you to subscribe to the campaign's official newsletter and status reports, which will be delivered to your e-mail address.

The Dole camp also has been using the Web to sign up help. If you want to make a campaign contribution, the whole transaction can be handled through the page's "Donations" option. If you want to work at the local campaign headquarters in your area, click on "Volunteers" and file the on-screen form, which will ask how the Dole troops can reach you and what kinds of things you would be interested in doing

When Republican presidential candidate Bob Dole's campaign bus first rolled onto the Information Highway, it hit a pothole.

The first Web page devoted to Dole appeared in early 1995, shortly after the senator announced his candidacy for the Republican presidential nod. The page was undoubtedly launched by a Dole detractor. Beneath the words "This page is dedicated to Robert Dole and all the things he's done," the entire site was blank. The dirty trickster offered no links to any other Internet locations. The page was a complete digital dead end.

The Dole Campaign's Rocky Start on the Web

By midsummer, fellow Kansan Andrew Apple had stepped in to rectify the situation by creating the Unofficial Bob Dole Home Page (http://www.seas.upenn.edu/~lapple/bobdole.html), which shared articles, answered frequently asked questions about the candidate, and generally held the fort until the real campaign could find ways to get wired. In early 1996, the Official Bob Dole for President site (http://www.dole96.com) was launched.

(make phone calls, host an event in your home, help with mailings, work on a primary election day, attend rallies or meetings, recruit local volunteers, or place a sign in your yard). Once filed online, your application will get you a staff contact by either phone or e-mail.

THE CROWDED RING: EARLY GOP CHALLENGERS

What are the most effective ways for a political hopeful to use the Web? No one can give a definitive answer yet. The current election year is the laboratory, the best test to date of the medium's political potency.

Early in 1996, with arguably the most to gain, all the GOP challengers—particularly those with the most ground to try to make up between themselves and front-runner Bob Dole—got their home pages hooked up fast. As everyone expected, the ring did not remain crowded all the way to the summer GOP convention. In fact, by spring, Kansan Bob Dole had clinched the nomination. But the also-rans at least made some history by trotting out some of the more imaginative electronic experimentation of the campaign. Headed toward the first primary elections, the various staff computer wizards and online aides-de-camp tried out assorted ideas.

After the November 1996 general election, cyberspheric sages surely will sit down with the political pundits and figure out just what worked on the Web and what washed out. We'll let them worry about that. For now, let's just review the show.

Tennessean Lamar Alexander did not jump to an early lead in his bid for the GOP nomination, but he does claims a bit of Net history for himself: he was the first presidential candidate to announce his candidacy *simultaneously* in cyberspace and in the Real World. Press releases referred frequently to Alexander's announcement on America Online. Alexander's band also claimed the establishment of the first presidential website where he immediately launched into some ardent courting of the Net vote. "As America accelerates into a new era of technology and communications," he said in an online statement, "we cannot afford to have a president who uses a rear view mirror as his road map into the 21st century. I think it's important that he understand how deeply this new age of information technology affects us all. This technology will shape the next century as much as this president will." One unusual idea in the Alexander camp was the site's "VCR Alert" feature which told the faithful when and where to set the timers on their videocassette recorders in order to catch their man's next TV appearances. Also online were biographies of the top Alexander staff members as well as a "Back to the States" option: where the campaign stood in state primaries.

The Patrick Buchanan for President site, headlined "Welcome 1996, The Year of Our Second American Revolution," received early praise from Time Magazine as the "most information-packed site" for a candidate in the early going of the primary fight. Indeed, a "Newsroom" feature offered *daily* updates on breaking stories, and the site manager placed dates beside items to show how current the updates were. They frequently were accompanied by analyses and statements from the political-commentator-turned-candidate. The site was used by the volunteers (the "Buchanan Brigade") to send out alerts, often with a quite personal tone that was uncommon on the sometimes-cool Web. For instance, during the weeks before the important Iowa

Caucus, one campaigner addressed the site's online visitors this way: "If you are here in Iowa or have friends or family in Iowa, PLEASE CALL ME!!! We must get as many Caucus goers as possible and Pat needs your help. I'm in the Des Moines office, but I can get you in touch with other Brigadiers across Iowa who will join with you to present a united force. . . . If you have never been to a Caucus before we can give you the information on how it all works. I have a gun show this Saturday and Sunday but I'll be in the office on Monday or you can just leave a message. . . ."

One of the more innovative ideas of the primary season also arose from the Buchanan camp: a "Web Sticker," that is a graphic miniature of a political bumper sticker. Recognizing that an ever-growing number of Web surfers now also have their *own* home pages on the Web, the Buchanan Brigade invited visitors to its site to download the Web Sticker (a red, white and blue "Buchanan for President" sign) and then incorporate it on their own home pages as a sign of support.

Magazine publisher Steve Forbes, a late entrant in the race for the GOP nomination, tried to use his website in his rapid move to the front of the pack. Reaching out to cyberspace's well-documented conservative, pocketbook vote, the Forbes campaign seemed to share the Net's love of numbers and to communicate its appreciation of the word-count feature in most word processing software. This was the online incarnation of Forbes's call for tax code revision: "We can start by scrapping the monstrous tax code. . . . The Declaration of Independence is only 1,300 words long. The Holy Bible—the Word of God—is only 773,000 words long. But the tax code—the words of the politicians in Washington—is a whopping 7 million words—and still growing." Also in an attempt to humanize the Forbes campaign and warm up the sometimes cool Web world, the site had a "Forbes Family Album." Visitors could click in to see pictures of the candidate and his wife of 24 years, along with their five daughters. Family vacation shots, wedding pictures and photos from Forbes's own childhood, growing up as the firstborn of *Forbes Magazine* founder Malcolm Forbes were in the album.

Texas Senator Phil Gramm hit cyberspace at a sprint. An official cyberspace site maintained and funded by Phil Gramm for President Inc. was up and running on the Web by the summer of '95, a full 18 months before the 1996 general election and a half a year before most of his major opponents. And as a further indication of the conservative mode of much of the modem community, three *unofficial* Phil Gramm pages quickly joined it on the Web. Unique among the candidates' pages was a "Quote of the Day" option, not necessarily from the candidate himself, but often from others speaking about Gramm. For instance, visitors were sometimes greeted by a remark by columnist George Will: "A successful candidacy requires money, ideas and luck. Gramm probably will be the best financed and most conservative candidate in the Republican race. If luck really is the residue of design, Gramm is poised for a run of luck."

Former United Nations ambassador Alan Keyes topped his website with this word-banner: "America does not have *money* problems—it has *moral* problems." Elsewhere, the site featured articles with titles like, "Reasons Why Conservative Christians Should Support Alan Keyes." The site served up text of Keyes speeches, as well as transcripts of his appearances on TV's Larry King Live show, his cover interview in *World* magazine, and his online interview on CompuServe. He also made the site a vehicle for distributing assorted campaign asides, such as t-shirts, bumper stickers, and video and audio tapes. Material on his book, *Masters of the Dream: The Strength and Betrayal of Black America,* was also available.

The Richard Lugar for President Home Page was opened by volunteer/supporter Doug Miller in the spring of 1995, providing campaign news and information about the Indiana hopeful. Lugar also used the site for some random polling. A "Pulse of America" option sought visitors' opinions on issues such as the national sales tax, the Balanced Budget Amendment, prayer in public schools and the determination of school curriculum, abortion, etc. Results of the polling were posted biweekly. An innovation the Lugar camp added to the field of online campaigning: a call for visitors to the site to use electronic mail to write letters to the media on behalf of the candidate. Tips and e-mail addresses for major print and broad-cast resources were provided. Among them were *Newsweek* (letters@newsweek.com), *TIME Magazine* (timeletter@aol.com), *USA Today* (usatoday@clark.net), *US News & World Report* (71154.1006@compuserve.com), NBC Dateline (tdmned@cityview.com), NBC Nightly News (newsroom@cmonitor.com), and *The New York Times* (webmster@nytimes.com).

Using the Web's Search Engines

We may call the programs "web browsers," but with more than 4 million pages on the World Wide Web and more being added every day and with the addresses of existing pages regularly being changed, *browsing* is hardly the most effective way to find information on the Internet. To slice and dice these data—and more importantly, to stay up-to-date on those daily additions—you need a "search engine," one of the free search-and-retrieve tools that work as electronic directories.

Connect to them as you would any other website. Type in the address in the field your browser reserves for URLs. Then, in a resulting query box on the screen, enter a keyword or phrase that describes what you are looking for—say, CALIFORNIA POLITICS, or REPUBLICANS, or PRIMARY ELECTIONS—and let the search engine do its stuff. In a few seconds, the search engine returns a list of "hits," that is, sites around the Web that match your query. The list includes some lines that are highlighted (underlined or printed in a different color), indicating that they are hyperlinked. To visit one of the sites, simply click on its highlighted name. Popular search engines, each with its own URL, include Alta Vista (http://www.altavista.digital.com), Yahoo (http://www.yahoo.com) and Lycos (http://query2.lycos.cs.cmu.edu).

Or you can do what some of the smartest Web wanderers are doing these days: use a search engine of search engines. In March 1996, Cnet: the computer network, a San Francisco company that produces a cable TV computer news show and related material on the Web, launched a new site that organizes hundreds of general and specialized search engines around the Net. From a single site (http://www.search.com), you use any of some 250 of the Web's more popular resources for finding information on the Net. Background material provides details on the usually subtle differences between them. Cnet hopes to makes its site a first stop by Web regulars. The site provides query boxes for all the major engines such as Alta Vista, Yahoo and Lycos as well as lesser-known ones like Magellan, Infoseek Guide and WebCrawler. It also has 20 categories of specialized Web search utilities that keep track of arts, business, sports, entertainment, government, health, legal issues, science, travel and other topics. The page even enables you to create your own Web page with the search services you prefer.

You also can use search engines to keep track of changing addresses on the Web. A fact of life in the pioneer days of the Web is that URLs change frequently. If the information provider's host computer system reorganizes its file structure, it may mean a minor change in the address. Or if the information provider moves to a new Internet service, it could mean a completely new address. Often the information provider will leave a message at the old address hyperlinked to the new pages. But when no such handy forwarding address is provided online, try using your favorite search engine. Just enter the name of the feature in the search query box; often the resulting list will include the new site.

If the partisanship of most of the sites described in this chapter gets to you, there are some Web pages you can visit for a nonpartisan take on the current election.

Vote Smart Offers Nonpartisan Data

Project Vote Smart (http://www.vote-smart.org) is the major program of The Center for National Independence in Politics, a national organization formed to provide citizens/voters with information about the political system, issues, candidates, and elected officials. The group aims to provide factual, relevant, independent information about the candidates (that is, data not generated by the campaign staffs) and material on the issues, in an effort it calls a "Voter's Self-Defense System." The founding board of the Center is headed by former presidents Jimmy Carter and Gerald Ford.

The group seeks to maintain a careful balance of viewpoints, does not lobby, and does not support or oppose any candidate, issue, or cause. To retain its independence, the organization accepts no government or corporate contributions. It survives on individual memberships and grants from the Carnegie, Markle, Ford, Joyce, Schumann, and Columbia foundations, among others.

Project Vote Smart is a year-round system. During off-election years, the focus changes to offering citizens a way to monitor those they have elected, using a hotline and online computer access to follow voting records, performance evaluations, campaign finances, and key legislation. A new service, "CongressTrack," allows citizens to follow the progress of the Contract with America and other legislation on a daily hotline: 1-800-622-SMAR.

Meanwhile, individuals on the Web are providing noteworthy jumping-off places for nonpartisan election contacts. Michael Gonzalez has a passion for politics from which we all can benefit. His bright, colorful Election '96 page (http://dodo.crown.net/~mpg/election/96.html) has been following the current presidential hunt for almost a year now. Offered as a clearinghouse for dozens of election-related resources around the Net, it provides clickable links to home pages of all the major candidates, parties, issues, and news. Because it is regularly updated, this is an ideal resource for political surfers.

Pat Paulsen: Carrying the Campaign to the Computer

Comedian Pat Paulsen is still running. Is this an ongoing joke? Or are the times getting so strange that Paulsen's perennial bid for the presidency has begun to sound serious? You can decide for yourself. On his website (http://www.amdest.com/Pat/pat.html), Paulsen says he's gone high-tech, promising to be the first aspirant to the Oval Office to run his campaign entirely via the Internet. Here is his platform on various issues:

Names on the Net

Pro Choice: Yes and no.

Foreign Aid: We don't want any.

Health Care: I don't think we need to care for healthy people.

Crime in the Streets: Take it off the streets and put it back in the home where it started.

The Future: Worrying about the future is a thing of the past. I don't think about it.

Gun Control: I can't control my car, let alone my gun.

National Debt: Let the kids pay it; they still owe us rent and gas money.

Social Security: Why should old people get it? They just sit around all day doing nothing.

Ross Perot: What can you say about him that hasn't already been said about The Lollipop Kids?

Bill Clinton: Wrong or wrong, he is still our president.

Finally, you may wonder who was the first presidential candidate to have a site on the World Wide Web. Ask two Republican hopefuls—Alexander and Gramm—and you'll get different answers. As Dan Balz wrote in May 1995 in *The Washington Post*, "Lest anyone think the rules of play are more genteel in cyberspace, there is already a fight between Alexander and Gramm over who got there first. Alexander's staff swears their man hit the Net before Gramm, but the Texas senator has never been one to claim second best in any contest . . . . That may not seem like much—for much of the electorate it may have no meaning—but in the world of presidential primary politics, every propeller-head counts."

PRESIDENTS AND CANDIDATES, PAST TENSE

The Internet may be the political stumping ground of the future, but it also has resources for those interested in fighting again the battles of the past. Websites are coming along for those who want to study specific campaigns and presidents of earlier years and to examine the political material of presidential libraries.

Ronald Reagan

Brett Kottmann says his Ronald Reagan Home Page (http://www .dnaco.net/~bkottman/reagan.html) is "dedicated to the greatest peace-time expansion in U.S. history" and to preserving the memory of Ronald Reagan's legacy. Sections are set aside for Reagan's words and deeds on tax cuts, the deficit, the budget, social spending, jobs, living standards, and more. Kottmann links to U.S. Census Data and other government information to let visitors examine rates of inflation, jobs, "the misery index," and other items, and compare the Reagan years with other administrations. The page even has sound bites. Anti-Reaganites might be surprised to find among them the infamous "sound check" gaff (when Reagan tested a microphone by saying, "Ladies and gentlemen, I'm pleased to tell you I've signed legislation today that will outlaw Russia forever. We begin bombing in five minutes."). Others are more in keeping with the program ("Government is not the solution to our problem; government IS our problem.").

But the Gipper gets no grace period on the Net. Kottmann's arch rival, known on the Web only as "The Stilt Man," operates The Debunking of the Ronald Reagan Home Page (http://www .teleport.com/~stiltman/Politics/debunk.html), which advises Reagan fans it "assumes no liability, either express or implied, for any urge you may have to put an axe through your monitor in fury." It seeks to challenge Kottmann's claims, offering its own tables and charts on Reagan and the national debt, taxes, expansion, the concentration of wealth, congressional spending, and the like.

Also of interest to Reagan students is the text of his "A Time for Choosing" speech, presented at a Barry Goldwater fund-raiser in the 1964 presidential race, which is available online (http://www.asc .oakland.edu/~djsussma/stuff/reagan.html).

Barry Goldwater

At the point where politics meets nostalgia, you'll find The Goldwater Page (http://www3.dive.com/GoldWeb/GoldwaterHome.html), perhaps the only website dedicated to presidential politics of more than three decades ago. Opening with a picture of Arizona Senator Barry Goldwater and his most famous quote ("Extremism in defense of liberty is no vice . . . moderation in the pursuit of justice is no virtue"), it is something of a shrine among the Web's considerable conservative coalition.

But aside from its frequent political pronouncements in the form of Goldwater quotes ("The conservative movement is founded on the simple tenet that people have the right to live life as they please, as long as they don't hurt anyone else in the process"), the site is of interest to political history buffs for its rare graphics and text files. Come here to find out the ins and outs of the Goldwater Draft movement, which the page calls "the first successful bona fide presidential nomination draft in the history of the United States." Come here for the text of Goldwater's speech, delivered to the 1964 GOP convention. Come here for pictures and memorabilia from Goldwater's presidential race against Lyndon Johnson—campaign buttons, letterhead, posters, and snapshots, as well as a flyer advertising a rally that featured The Goldwaters, a folk music group from the Young Americans for Freedom.

Jerry Brown

On the other side of the Web—waaaaaay over on the other side—is the We the People Home Page (http://www.hia.com/hia/wtp), dedicated to liberal Californian Jerry Brown and the activists who ran the former governor's 1992 bid for the Democratic nomination. Maintained by Peter B. Kaplan, the page outlines the organization's platform ("that an increasingly pervasive corporate structure has destroyed democracy; jobs, media and national elections are under the financial influence or control of a small minority"). Working out of Oakland, California,

Jefferson Lives On on the Net

Not all the presidents on the Net are of our century. Thomas Jefferson, a renowned defender of free speech and an advocate of science and technology, is an icon in the information world. A technology that Jefferson couldn't have imagined honors him today worldwide.

Names on the Net

Ask Thomas Jefferson (http://www.mit.edu:8001 /activities/libertarians/ask-thomas-jefferson/jefferson .html) compiles some of the third president's most quoted comments on politics and many other issues. You can browse randomly or by topic (politics, history, religion, literature, human nature, and society.) Jefferson enthusiasts can also access an online folder of his work (gopher://gopher.vt.edu:10010/11/106).

the group uses the page to provide recent position papers, upcoming events, notes on Brown radio programs, and more.

Presidential Libraries

The official papers and records of many presidents are cataloged online through the National Archives and Records Administration in Washington, but are, at this writing, in text-only format. Some universities and other institutions have begun creating more graphic World Wide Web sites for some of the libraries. Here are the key addresses for the sequence of presidents from the 1930s to the 1980s:

Franklin D. Roosevelt Library
(http://gopher.nara.gov:70/1/inform/library/fdr)

Dwight D. Eisenhower Library
(http://gopher.nara.gov:70/1/inform/library/eisen)

John F. Kennedy Library
(http://gopher.nara.gov:70/1/inform/library/kennedy)

Lyndon B. Johnson Library
(gopher//ffp.cc.utexas.edu:3003/11/pub/lbj-library)
(http://gopher.nara.gov:70/1/inform/library/johnson)

On the theory that nobody can nail you like your own neighbors, Nando. Net, the electronic extension of the *Charlotte News and Observer,* offers The World According to Helms (http://www.nando.net/sproject/jesse/helms.html), a home-state hammering of Senator Jesse Helms (R-North Carolina).

"We guess that the rest of the world has finally figured out what most of us in the Tar Heel state have known for a long time," says the introduction. "Our senior senator occasionally talks out of school. Frankly, we're used to it but apparently the rest of the world isn't. So here is a sampler of Jesse quotes and other good-ies we have collected over the years."

Hooting at Jesse Helms

The site has a fair selection of photos and local political cartoons by Duane Powell, but is at its best with quotes ("Mr. Clinton better watch out if he comes down here. He'd better have a bodyguard."). The text of the original byline story by James Rosen, which started a national flap with that quote, the text of Helms's response, and a commentary by the paper's editor, Frank Daniels III, make interesting reading.

The *News and Observer* offers more in its printed book, *Jesse Helms Quoted,* which "like the senator . . . opens from the right."

Richard M. Nixon Library and Birthplace
(http://www.chapman.edu/nixon)
(http://gopher.nara.gov:70/1/inform/library/nixon)

Gerald R. Ford Presidential Library and Museum
(http://www2.sils.umich.edu/FordLibrary)
(http://gopher.nara.gov:70/1/inform/library/ford)

Jimmy Carter Library
(http://gopher.nara.gov:70/1/inform/library/carter)

Ronald Reagan Library
(http://gopher.nara.gov:70/1/inform/library/reagan)

Chapter 3

Delivering the Party Line Online

There is no tradition of a two-party system online. From its earliest days, American cyberspace has attracted alternative politics, from Socialists to Libertarians to Ross Perot's United We Stand. Each has seen in cyberspace an opportunity for a public hearing that cannot always be expected on the evening news. Actually, the newcomers on the Net are the Big Guys—the national headquarters of the Democratic and Republican parties. In this current politicking season, both camps finally recognized the enormous potential for getting their message out electronically to their increasingly plugged-in partisans.

The fact that this brave new cyberworld is willing, eager, and able to listen to every political voice does not mean it is itself indifferent or without its own philosophical feuds. On the contrary, controversy is a fact of online computing life, and new arrivals quickly learn that labels they may have thought they left behind in the old unplugged world are just as common in the cybersphere. The Net may not have a top and a bottom, a front and a back, an inside and an outside, or a beginning and an end, but it *does* have a Left and a Right. Whether you're an idealistic liberal, a pragmatic conservative, or some breed of political animal that defies conventional designation, you can count on the Internet to connect you with at least some kindred spirits.

In this chapter, you'll see how to use your Net connections to:

▶ Join national and local political organizations, or compare parties by examining their current and past platforms and positions on issues.

▶ Be added to mailing lists for party newsletters and bulletins that can arrive via e-mail or the U.S. Postal Service.

▶ Become a mover and shaker in the party of your choice by getting in on the ground floor of new projects, fresh campaigns, and political drives.

▶ Receive expert advice, via online bulletin boards and through e-mail, on strategies, fund-raising efforts, and similar realities you may face in your own political quest, whether for public office or a school board, town, or club election.

▶ Sign up for workshops and political training sessions hosted by party pros.

▶ Prepare for debates by researching issues and positions of your candidates and their opponents through the parties' own online data reservoirs.

▶ Contact people around the world who share your special point of view.

Politics is not new to the Net, but political organizing is. Come along; we've all got a great seat for the show.

THE DEMOCRATS GET DIGITAL

Someday, when the story of the cybersphere is told in some future medium, one page will note the irony of Bill Clinton's being the first president on the Web at the same time his own party seemed to drop out of the political drag race that was starting on the information superhighway. By the time of the midterm elections in 1994, it was generally acknowledged that House Speaker Newt Gingrich was gunning the GOP machine into the lead.

However, in mid-1995, the Dems came roaring back into the pack, driving a new Web entry of their own. With a commitment of $200,000 and three staffers to maintain the online material, the Democrats

Listserv Brings Internet to You

A true Nethead never gets tired of going to the Net, but even the most die-hard digital dude occasionally likes to be a Net recipient. Electronic mailing lists, which are online newsletters, bulletins, and message collections, allow people to exchange ideas on numerous topics. In Net speak, the concept is known as "listserv," borrowing the name of the software that manages the mailing lists on the Internet.

Tech Tip

In your online exploration, you will see opportunities to subscribe to mailing lists through listserv. Many of these invitations are fully automated through your web browser software; others will invite you to subscribe "manually." To do that, send an e-mail letter to the cited listserv address, with this as the text of the message:

subscribe [listname] [yourname]

The *listname* variable is the name of the mailing list you want, and *your name* is your first and last name with a space between them. For example, if something called "Belief-L" is an online mailing list on various issues that you want to follow, you could write in this text on your e-mail:

subscribe belief-l john doe

and post it to the cited e-mail address. When the authors of Belief-L prepare and mail the next issue, it will be sent automatically to your electronic mailbox, because listserv automatically takes addresses from any messages sent with the "subscribe" instruction.

Especially large mailing lists use a system called "majordomo." It works the same basic way, except that no name or address is necessary with lists that use majordomo. If the mailing list you're interested in has majordomo in its address, the text of your message to subscribe should read:

subscribe listname

To *stop* receiving these automatic mailings, you need to "unsubscribe." Send e-mail to the source and, in the body of the message, write:

unsubscribe [listname] [your name]

or, in our example,

unsubscribe belief-l john doe

launched their own home page (http:/www.democrats.org) to provide publications, press releases, audio and video clips, and links to other Democratic Internet destinations, and to invite the faithful to contribute to party fund-raisers by charging their donations to their credit cards.

If you're looking for ways to get involved in Democratic politics on the local, state, or national level, don't miss this page, especially its "Organizations" section. You'll find links to Democratic regional units (listed by state), and the data on state party chairpersons include how to reach them both off the Net (by phone, fax, and U.S. Mail) and on the Net (through e-mail and Web pages). At this writing, more than a dozen state Democratic organizations, from Maine to California, have their own websites, as does a group called Democrats Abroad, the official party organization for some 3 million Americans living outside the United States. The site also has browseable articles on the activities of college-based Democrat groups and of Democratic organizations devoted to issues of interest to women, Latinos, Asian Americans, and African Americans.

A "What's Hot" option connects with the latest party news: current White House press releases, daily Democratic National Committee (DNC) briefings and "talking points" (the 1990s "in" word meaning "debatable issues"), updates from Democratic House and Senate leaders, key speeches by Bill Clinton, and Administration briefings.

The "Connecting with America" section of the site explains how you can get more involved with the party, from how to become a delegate to the national convention to how to contribute to the DNC online. Click on this section if, for instance, you're a civics student and want to see the official charter and bylaws of the Democratic Party, along with the party's most recent platform.

From here, you can link to information about how you can attend the Democrats' "Campaign Training Academies" and learn politicking strategies. If you're eager to hit the campaign trail, an online form enables you to sign up as a campaign volunteer worker on whatever level you prefer (presidential, state, or local). College students can use the same form to apply for party internships. Additional selections connect to other sites of interest, including humor, details of future Democratic Party events, and audio and video highlights of the 1992 Democratic national convention.

In early 1996, the Democratic National Committee (DNC) launched its "Online News Service," a collection of electronic mailing lists that allow subscribers to stay up-to-date on party activities. To sign up for any of these services, send electronic mail to:

majordomo@democrats.org

How to Have the Democrats Coming to You

In the body of the message, write one line to indicate each mailing list you want to be on. Here are the key lines for the available lists:

subscribe news	Democratic News gives you the DNC briefings, press releases, party publications, and information about candidates, events, and issues, as well as news of additions to the DNC website. As a subscriber, you'll probably receive several e-mails a week.
subscribe news-digest	News-Digest, a streamlined version of the Democratic News mailing, provides a single weekly e-mail, with highlights and reports on events and issues.
subscribe events	Democratic Events shows the latest calendar of DNC events. Occasionally updates about special activities, such as televised presidential addresses, are issued.

Other Democrat Digs

Nationwide, the Democratic Party is mainly concerned with winning elections and keeping the electorate happy. Other partisan sites on the Web focus on Democrats already working at elected or appointed jobs. If your main interest is the current officeholders and what they've been doing, you ought to have a list of regular stops on the Web.

To tap into current congressional action, Representative Richard Gephardt's (D-Missouri) House Democratic Leadership Home Page (http://www.house.gov/democrats) updates the latest legislation through a daily "Whip Wind-Up" bulletin. It also shares floor statements from party members, news from the Democratic Caucus, and general Senate press releases. A "Hot Topics" area gives the Democrats' spin on the budget, crime, education, the environment, foreign affairs, national security, the minimum wage, tax policy, and welfare reform.

For the corresponding party perspective in the U.S. Senate, try Senator J. Robert ("Bob") Kerrey's (D-Nebraska) Democratic Senatorial Campaign Committee Home Page (http://www.dscc.org/d/dscc.html). This site, which serves up the "Daily Senate Talking Points" bulletin, can be feisty. During our last fly-by, these headlines were typical: "Senator Gramm: Call Home," "Arkansans to Huckabee: 'Take a Hike, Mike'," "Majority of South Carolinians Want Strom Thurmond to Retire."

If you're a computing Democrat, the mere fact that you're online qualifies you to sign up with at least one group. The Digital Democrats, through their Democratic Party Activists Home Page (http://www.digitals.org/digitals), seek to build an online organization of 100,000 Democratic Party activists before the general presidential election in

Robert F. Kennedy Remembered

An assassin ended the life of Senator Robert F. Kennedy in 1968, at the height of his presidential aspirations, but gunfire did not end the dream of his followers. RFK's legacy has new life on the Web.

Names on the Net

The Robert F. Kennedy Progressive Democrats Page (http://www.webcom.com/~albany/rfk.html) is operated by the RFK Democratic Club of New York. The page is intended, the group says in an online statement, as a rallying point for progressive Democrats "to coalesce and to speak out against the rising tide of conservative ideology and reactionary extremism."

Anyone who lived through the turbulent 1960s will be interested to see how new technology showcases audio of RFK speeches and eulogies, Kennedy family photographs, and text of memorable quotations.

November 1996. Describing themselves as "committed to revitalizing the Democratic Party through the use of online technology," the group wants your ideas on just how the modem nation can be mobilized for political action. The site also serves as a reference desk for scores of links to other Democratic Party resources around the Net, and it facilitates quick e-mail connections for reaching the party leadership.

REPUBLICANS REWIRE THE WEB

The Republicans have not only settled in cyberspace, they've set up an entire virtual town. Called "Main Street," the Republican National Committee (RNC) site (http://www.rnc.org) is organized around a map of a make-believe community. Visitors click on graphic representations of stores and buildings, such as a schoolhouse, a café, a newsstand, a post office, and a gift shop, to retrieve information about official GOP-emblazoned gifts, e-mail connections, partisan news and statements, schedules, and fund-raising pledges, as well as forms that volunteers can fill out to request work assignments in campaigns.

Want to find out how to get involved with your local Republican organization? Click on the building labeled "RNC Headquarters" and you'll be shown text about party members, whom to contact in your state, and what other regional GOP organizations are open to you. Here's where you'll also find the history and rules of the Republican Party, and biographies of the current party leadership.

Do you need information on the 1996 Republican Convention? Click on the "Convention Center" building and a countdown display will tell you how many days are left until the GOP kickoff, the latest cumulative presidential primary results, and the delegate allocation information.

If you're thinking of running for office yourself—or if you want background on a particular political topic in the current campaign—click on the "School" building. You'll get the facts on the RNC's latest training programs and on online "classrooms" on issues. During our recent visit, discussions were offered on "Interest Rates Since Clinton's Election," "The Value of the $500-Per-Child Tax Credit," and "Whose Income Tax Is Eliminated by the $500-Per-Child Tax Credit?" Other backgrounders covered foreign policy, national defense, and the economy.

If you're looking for news and comment from the Republican perspective—fodder for that next political discussion around the office watercooler—visit the "Newsstand." *Rising Tide,* the party's bimonthly magazine, is free for the asking here, as are "Monday Briefing," an eight-page weekly political digest distributed to GOP leaders in Washington and around the country, and "Net Works," a biweekly column focusing on politics and the Internet. You can also sift through the latest press releases and statements.

Visit Main Street's "Café" if you'd like to chat with Republicans from around the world. The site is an Internet Relay Chat (IRC) server that enables you to "talk" in real time with other visitors. You simply type your thoughts on your keyboard, then read replies as they come

"A well-informed public is our strongest ally." With that pronouncement, Republican National Committee Chairman Haley Barbour launched a series of electronic mailing lists for subscribers who want to stay up-to-date on party activities. To sign up for any of these lists, send electronic mail to:

How to Have the Republicans Coming to You

majordomo@rnc.org

In the body of the message itself, enter one line for each of the lists you want. Here are the key lines for the mailing lists available at this writing:

subscribe presslist — Press List gives all the RNC press releases, talking points, backgrounders, issue briefs, and memos to GOP leaders.

subscribe briefinglist — Briefing List gets you delivery of the RNC "Monday Briefing," the eight-page weekly digest of political news, strategy, and survey data.

subscribe goptvlist — The GOP-TV List offers programming information for the hour-long televised "Rising Tide" broadcasts, including data on features and guest appearances.

As the person listed in the "From:" field of the e-mail, you automatically will begin receiving future mailings.

across your screen from others who are online at that moment. If you don't feel especially chatty, you can post a public message on the Café's bulletin board.

Elsewhere in the RNC's virtual town are video and audio clips taken from the party's televised "Rising Tide" broadcasts (the "GOP-TV" building), e-mail addresses of House and Senate members ("Post Office"), catalogs of GOP gifts ("Gift Shop"), connections to other Republican sites ("Travel Agency"), and downloadable software utilities for using video and audio clips found on Main Street and elsewhere on the Net ("Hardware Store").

Other Republican Connections

Five years before the Republican National Committee discovered the Internet, Dr. Adrian Scott had created a GOP outpost on the Cyberian frontier. Launched in 1991, his Cyber-Republicans site (http://www.rpi.edu/~scotta/republican.html) was intended to lead other Republican organizations into cyberspace through the Internet, commercial online services, and "other future approximations of cyberspace." Said Scott, "Our virtual organization will have a spunky, fuzzy character as it moves at a fast-forward pace to help the world!"

Today, Scott's site links to all the official GOP resources—House and Senate Republican venues, and RNC press releases, for example—but also serves up some home-grown features, such as a newsletter and his popular In His Own Words, Broken Promises from the President, an anti-Clinton feature. Scott also advises visitors of upcoming events and speeches through his Conservative Calendar. If you're an online Republican, Scott is seeking your thoughts and suggestions. He hopes his page ultimately will help the GOP develop a "cyberspace strategy playbook" and training programs for using the Net in future campaigns.

Meanwhile, just as Democratic members of Congress have Net resources, the GOP's federal officeholders have staked their own claims on the Web:

▶ Senate Republican Conference (ftp://ftp.senate.gov/committee /repub-conf/general/src.html) is the Internet extension of the organization that traditionally has assisted Republican senators with media services. It offers links to general government resources and GOP-specific Net pages.

▶ U.S. Senate Republican Policy Committee (ftp://ftp.senate.gov /committee/repub-policy/general/rpc.html), with position papers and members' profiles, links to Republican publications, specific home pages for GOP senators, and politically conservative home pages.

▶ House Republican Conference (http://www.house.gov/gop /HRCHome.html) carries press releases and statements. Of particular interest to GOP partisans, and to political science students who want to know the party's perspective, is "Republican Plan for America's Future," a 38K essay on "creating a safe and prosperous future for our generation and our children."

CompuServe Forums Serve Democrats and Republicans

For years now, CompuServe has operated forums with political ties, including those for the Democratic and Republican parties.

Off the Web

The Democratic Party Forum, which is overseen by the Democratic National Committee, maintains a hotline for national political updates. The forum's libraries contain the party platform, press releases, lists of candidates, speeches, and the like.

The forum administrators are all with the Democratic National Committee in Washington. Reach the forum by entering GO DEMOCRATS anywhere on CompuServe.

The Republican Forum (GO REPUBLICAN) is a clearinghouse for GOP news and information. Besides press releases and talking points, the Forum provides in its libraries *Rising Tide* (the Republican National Committee's new bimonthly magazine), the RNC's "Monday Briefing" (a weekly briefing for party leaders and activists), reports from Capitol Hill, and more. Its administrators work at the Republican National Committee's Publications and Electronic Communications Department.

For general political discussions on CompuServe, see the Political Debate Forum (GO POLITICS), which is intended as a platform for all political parties. Its message sections focus on topics of interest, including health care, the economy, defense, and the environment. Other sections are devoted to Libertarians and to Empower America, a nonpartisan political advocacy committee whose codirectors are William Bennett, Jack Kemp, and Jeane J. Kirkpatrick.

How to Become a Community Activist

Writing for the Republican National Committee (RNC) "Main Street" site (http://www.rnc.org), Co-Chair Evelyn W. McPhail noted: "The strength of American democracy can be traced to the involvement of its citizens. Our country's political system requires the actions of its citizens as active participants, not only as voters, but also as volunteers and financial supporters."

Names on the Net

Meant to rally the Republican faithful, the essay actually provides advice for people of *all* political persuasions who want to become community activists:

▶ Call the local office of the party of your choice. Websites may go deep enough to show the grassroots, but the numbers probably are listed in your phone book too. State party organizations usually have a headquarters in the state capital.

▶ Join an affiliated unit of your chosen party. Expect to find groups for women, college students, and minorities, each with its own governing board. Contact your state party headquarters for details.

▶ Call the White House Comment Line at 202/456-1111 and give your opinion. A recorded message will guide you through an automated survey of issues.

▶ Subscribe to your chosen party's online and offline publications.

▶ Write a letter to the editor of your local newspaper. The talking points and press releases found in websites should give you plenty of ammunition.

▶ Call, write, or e-mail your senators and representatives when important votes are pending in Congress, and let them know where you stand.

▶ Organize a neighborhood get-together to coincide with a televised debate, party broadcast, news conference, or speech.

▶ Make sure your opinion is heard on talk radio and TV call-in programs, and shows up on the bulletin boards and in the chat rooms on the Internet and other computer online services.

▶ Use your position in community and civic organizations to spread the party message. For instance, establish contact with your alumni organization and speak out on issues. If you're a senior, set the record straight on Medicare.

▶ Above all, talk to your friends and neighbors. "You are the party's most credible spokesperson among your peers," says McPhail in her essay. "This is a historic time in America—enjoy the role you're playing in it."

LIBERTARIANS LINK WITH THE WEB

Wanting little from their government except protection of the freedom to come together and communicate, some of the Web's new breed of wired individualists, having rejected traditional Democrat or Republican politics, are attracted to the nation's other major political party.

The Libertarian Party was born just 25 years ago, so perhaps it is natural that this group, only a few years older than the personal computer itself, is so at home on the Net. Active for nearly a decade on online bulletin boards and in chat rooms, the Libertarians were quick to expand their influence in the early 1990s, when the developing World Wide Web offered new opportunities for colorful, hyperlinked home pages.

These days, Libertarian politics—which emphasize personal freedom and civil liberties and endorse a generally conservative stance on economic and foreign policy issues—seem to have a far-reaching echo on the Web, even when a philosophy is not identified strictly as "Libertarian." Regularly, across cyberspace, come calls for stands that Libertarians have taken for years: opposition to laws that limit personal behavior (including those regulating prostitution, gambling, and sexual preferences), support for a free-market economy with a minimum of government aid and regulation, and advocacy of a neutral foreign policy and the withdrawal of the United States from the United Nations.

The Libertarian Party's history seems faintly reminiscent of high-tech culture and the way many computer companies came into being. Launched in the living room of a Colorado home in December 1971, the party has grown from a small group of activists to the third largest political party in the United States. In 1976, the party's single candidate (presidential nominee Roger MacBride) received only 170,000 votes in the general election. In 1992, the 700 Libertarian candidates on ballots in state and federal races garnered more than 3.7 million votes; the 23 Libertarian candidates for the U.S. Senate received more than a million votes, the highest total for a nationally organized third party since Teddy Roosevelt's Bull Moose Party was on the roster in 1914.

The Libertarian Party Headquarters Page (http://access.digex .net/~lphq/) has everything you need to learn about this movement. The site highlights current and past party platforms and position papers on issues. An "LP Directories" feature can give you lists and contacts for state and local party chapters, chairpersons, and LP members now in office. The site also offers details on affiliated student clubs across the country, many of which have their own home pages on the Web. If you want more information, send e-mail to lphq@digex.net. If you're ready to become a dues-paying member, you can fill out an online membership form. It will ask your name and address, voice phone numbers, e-mail address, occupation, and employer. It also asks for a $25 membership payment, for which you'll receive 12 issues of the *LP News* and a copy of a booklet called "Libertarianism in One Lesson." The Libertarian Party Documents site (http://lydia.bradley.edu /campusorg/libertarian/lpdocs/index.html) provides text of official party statements and pamphlets.

The Libertarian Web (http://w3.ag.uiuc.edu/liberty/libweb .html), produced by Scott Banister at the University of Illinois Urbana–Champaign campus, is a clearinghouse of Libertarian-related links around the Net. Come here for tips on LP student organizations, publications, and answers to frequently asked questions about the party.

A group called the Advocates for Self Government has created The World's Smallest Political Quiz (http://lydia.bradley.edu/campusorg /libertarian/wspform.html) to help visitors determine whether they might be Libertarians at heart.

Consisting of only ten multiple-choice questions—such as: "Military service should be voluntary. No draft or compulsory registration. (Agree. Unsure. Disagree)"—the site quizzes you on personal and economic issues, then

How to Place Yourself on the Political Spectrum

scores the results automatically on its graphic "Self-Government Compass." This on-screen diagram purports to place you somewhere on the political spectrum, based on your answers.

After you take the quiz, the Compass will label you as a Liberal, Centrist, Conservative, Authoritarian, or Libertarian, or some mixture of several categories. You might quibble over whether you can be so specifically categorized after fewer than a dozen questions, but lighten up—it's a fun exercise.

If you're a newcomer to Libertarianism, you'll especially want to check out the site's link to the text of writer Joseph Knight's article, "Understanding the Libertarian Philosophy."

The Libertarian Pages (http://www.libertarian.com/wwlp) points the way to the Web's newest Libertarian sites. Libertarian-owned businesses, organizations, periodicals, clubs, and mailing lists operate the sites. Site manager Mike Linksvayer says he hopes Pages also will be "a resource for the mainstream media," adding, "I believe that the Internet will prove a powerful weapon for ideological warfare, and no political demographic grouping is more 'wired' than Libertarians."

UNITED WE STAND

Single-handedly, billionaire Ross Perot started the United We Stand America (UWSA) organization to back his 1992 third-party presidential bid. Perot, with a high-tech background (he started Electronic Data Systems, a Texas computer company), was the first national candidate to speak of the need for national electronic town-hall meetings, so it's not surprising that his supporters quickly gravitated toward the Internet. Four years later, United We Stand America is still a Net presence.

The UWSA Headquarters (http://www.uwsa.org) has reports on the group's national activities; connections to local chapters around the country; positions on issues, legislation, and candidates; and links to related sites elsewhere. Of particular interest is a Web-size version of a slide presentation Perot's group uses in national tours to describe its efforts toward economic reform and cutting government waste.

Beyond the Headquarters page, the group's stand on current events can be researched in the latest issue of the monthly UWSA Newsletter (http://www.telusys.com/uwsa.html). At the time we were passing through, NAFTA (the North American Free Trade Agreement) was a hot topic and the newsletter detailed the party's opposition to the treaty on grounds that it would cost U.S. jobs ("the great sucking sound of jobs going south," Perot called it).

To find out more about UWSA positions, look into The Grass Roots (http://www.uwsa.com:8972/uwsa), a database of position papers, reports from state UWSA chapters, and transcripts of speeches and talks. The same resource can help you find the nearest UWSA organization.

SOCIALISTS

The increasingly capitalistic Web, where business and advertising have become the next wave, is a world that seems concerned about the rights and opportunities of the individual rather than the masses. However, some observers who have a long view of technology think the Information Age actually could be the second wind that American socialism has been waiting for during nearly a century of decline.

Telecommuting—working from home via computer and modem— has been praised as an employment equalizer for invalids, homebound mothers, senior citizens, and others who cannot do daily labor in an office or factory but can manage a computer. New technology enables millions of Americans to do all or at least part of their work remotely, creating their own schedules and working at their own pace. However, some observers see the same technology as a worker nightmare in the making: a new age of digital sweatshops. They fear that some employers, anxious to discontinue the costs of running plants and office buildings, will ultimately offer *only* homebound work. In the next century, they say, American could become a nation of "wired" piecework employees who are slaving away at all hours in cramped quarters, afraid of the economic consequences if they leave their keyboards, toiling out of sight of anyone who could fight for their health and safety and improve their quality of life.

That dark vision could mean a 21st-century renaissance for socialists. The American Socialist Party, under the leadership of presidential contender Eugene V. Debs, came into *this* century fighting for reforms to improve workers' lot. No new Debs has stepped forward to mobilize the digital masses, but the Web is a ready medium for that kind of revolt. If you're interested in researching socialist topics online, you can visit two organizations online.

▶ The Democratic Socialists of America Home Page (http:// ccme-mac4.bsd.uchicago.edu/DSA.html) uses a banner describing democracy as "not simply one of our political values, but our means of restructuring society." The Democratic Socialists of America (DSA), backers say, is the largest socialist organization in the United States and is the principal U.S. affiliate of the Socialist International. The page offers party publications, and it helps visitors find local chapters, commissions, and committees. A large collection of "Left Resources" for issues, history, and activism topics is available. If you're new to all this, check out the "Brief Guide to DSA" option, which details the structure of the organization. For contacts in your part of the country, see the "Commissions and Locals" option. Links to socialist documents, such as

On a political platform that goes beyond taxes and term limitations, the Natural Law Party (NLP) is dedicated to blending the concepts of the Transcendental Meditation (TM) relaxation technique with the running of the government.

Natural Law Party Seeks "Conflict-Free Politics"

In Fairfield, Iowa, the site of Maharishi University, TM has become a hometown industry since the late 1960s, when meditation expert Maharishi Mahesh Yogi captured worldwide attention as the guru for The Beatles, Mia Farrow, Carly Simon, and other celebrities. On the Web, the Natural Law Party Home Page (http://www.fairfield.com/nlpusa) connects visitors with the party's positions and newsletters, a schedule of appearances by its candidates, and excerpts from recent relevant speeches.

Under the headline "Promoting Conflict-Free Politics for a Problem-Free Nation," the page especially highlights activities of the NLP's 41-year-old presidential candidate, Dr. John Hagelin, a Harvard-trained quantum physicist. The last time we were in the NLP's digital neighborhood, the page featured excerpts from a *Washington Post* story about how Hagelin supported President Clinton's decision to send ground troops to Bosnia, but believes the key to the mission is a reduction of "stress and tension in the region" through TM and other "coherence creating" activities. Medicare cost could be curbed and the deficit cut, says Hagelin, by "bringing national life in harmony with natural law."

Post reporter Ruth Marcus noted that party handouts were heavily footnoted with references to journal articles that found beneficial effects from TM and stressed preventive health care, renewable energy (solar and wind power), sustainable organic agriculture, and education programs to "develop the inner creative genius of the students."

The Web page has a history of the party (it was created in April 1992, in Fairfield) and details on how newcomers can get involved. An online form is available for contributors and volunteers. The e-mail address for information is info@natural-law.org.

"Toward a New Foreign Policy," by DSA Vice-Chair Tom Del-
lums, are easy to locate.

▶ The Socialist Party USA Cybercenter (http://sunsite.unc.edu/spc
/index.html) is operated by the Socialist Party USA, the latest incarnation of the original Socialist Party founded in 1901 on the
political platform of Eugene Debs and inherited in the mid-1920s
by socialist leader Norman Thomas. At this site, you'll find information about the party's present leadership, purpose statements,
membership, and history. For the party's own view of its past, see
the online document called "The Socialist Party: Who We Are";
for political positions, see "Socialism as Radical Democracy: The
SP Statement of Principles." Other options can put you in touch
with local contacts for the party, the Young People's Socialist
League, the Socialist Institute, and the subscription process for
The Socialist magazine.

LINKING UP THE LIBERALS

If you're proudly liberal (or a sly conservative who wants to slip into
the liberals' tent and see what they're saying about your guys), sooner
or later you'll come across Mike Silverman. His colorful, contentious
Turn Left page (http://www.cjnetworks.com/~cubsfan/liberal.html)
has become the flag around which the Net's outnumbered liberals
have rallied.

He links visitors with scores of progressive organizations, such as
the American Civil Liberties Union, PeaceNet, and Amnesty International. Native American resources, groups devoted to pro-choice issues,
topics for gay and lesbian Net surfers, information for the handicapped,
and campaigns for fighting censorship are standard fare. Also connected here are what Silverman calls "resources for countering the radical right," from Brian Wright's "Militia Watch" to the home page of
Hard Response, a humor magazine with liberal leanings.

Silverman says that liberals and Democrats are not necessarily
the same breed, but he acknowledges that, historically, the Democrats
have been a liberal force in American politics and therefore his site is
correct in providing links to key Democratic venues about the Net.

Mike Silverman's Turn Left (http://www.cjnetworks.com/~cubsfan/liberal.html) is in its element when it is circulating lists and making charges. These are borrowed from its "Myths and Facts" section:

Turn Left—An Offering of "Myth and Facts"

Myth: The 1980s were a great decade.

Fact: Well, the music was good, but not much else. Most Americans got poorer, real wages fell, the deficit ballooned (thanks, Ronny), the ruinous war on drugs was begun, and more!

Myth: Liberals control the media.

Fact: Rush Limbaugh. G. Gordon Liddy. Pat Buchanan. *National Review. American Spectator.* Cal Thomas. George Will.

Myth: We need to cut social programs because they cost too much and are responsible for the deficit.

Fact: The cost of a couple of unneeded B-2 bombers would pay for all the social programs for years. But if you have to cut, why not cut wasteful subsidies to rich ranchers and corporations instead of poor mothers?

Conservatives, he says, have a penchant for making "enemies lists." Silverman counters with his own list of unfavorite sons: "The Bad Guys," from Oliver North ("such a disgrace that even Reagan recently disavowed him!") to G. Gordon Liddy ("makes Rush look like a bleeding-heart").

Silverman draws his line in the sand in his "Fight the Right" section, where liberals can find data to drive conservative friends and relatives nuts—or learn some rather classy name-calling. A quote from 19th-century English philosopher John Stuart Mill delivers one of the nastier barbs: "Although it is not true that all conservatives are stupid people . . . it is true that most stupid people are conservative."

The Left Side of the Web

Brian Wright's wild and woolly Left Side of the Web page (http://paul.spu.edu/~sinnfein/progressive.html) is a kind of digital pack rat of left-wing politics. Featured in Wright's eclectic array of progressive pages and files are: the text of a 1963 Alex Haley interview with Malcolm X; details on a home page for the Zapatistas in the Mexican state of Chiapas; directions to an archive of material from Noam Chomsky ("probably *the* critic of U.S. domestic and foreign policy"); and information on East Timor ("site of the worst genocide since the Holocaust"). Wright also will point the way to "McLibel" (information on the libel suit against Greenpeace UK by McDonald's), Bob Dornan ("probably the closest thing to a fascist in the U.S. Congress"), and "Love and Rage, the Revolutionary Anarchy Page."

If you grew up reading *Ramparts* magazine in the 1960s (or found the back issues in some aging street warrior's yard sale in the 1980s), you are going to love Brian Wright's links.

Spamily's Politics Page

Emily Way introduces her Spamily's Politics Page (http://www.io.org /~spamily/SocPolEnv.html) with this statement: "I know a lot of women who are afraid to call themselves feminists for fear of being lumped in with the shrill 'all sex in a patriarchal society is rape' crackpots. It's very easy to make off-the-wall arguments like that if you're willing to redefine your terms. I'm not. I believe in respecting people for their individuality, being aware of privileges gained unfairly and working to establish them for everyone, and being responsible for oneself and one's society. The following collection of links points to sites maintained by people who seem to see things similarly to the way I do."

The things she sees are often more personal and more social than the links of other largely issue-oriented sites. Many are for women, such as links to reproductive rights home pages and information for and on women in science and engineering. "I'm in neither," she says, "but I thought others might find it helpful." Her "Queer Resources Directory" is the Net's largest repository of information for gay men, lesbians, bisexuals, and their friends. "Fathers' Rights and Equality Exchange" is "dedicated to calling attention to the importance of fathers in children's lives, and to ending discrimination against fathers in custodial battles after divorces."

With a refreshingly personal perspective and advice from her own Net-surfing experience, Way points to pages devoted to censorship

("The File Room, a collection of documents describing at least 200 incidents of cultural censorship"), free expression ("The Secular Web—
not for the timid"), and environmental resources ("What would it be
like if there were one less car on the highway?").

The Stilt Man

We know only what he tells us about himself (in the third-person singu-
lar). He wants to be called The Stilt Man. The alias, taken in his sopho-
more year of college, is retained because he is "a very cautious person
about letting his real name get out." His tall and skinny build "often has
folks preparing to tie him down and force-feed him back to health."
He's trained in computer science, reads and writes science fiction, en-
joys watching professional wrestling (even though "I do not believe it is
real"), and plays strategy games like Warlords II, Master of Magic,
Stratego, and Robo War. Wrapped in that mysterious packaging is the
latest online tweaker of conservative noses.

Like many voters who follow current events on the Net, The Stilt
Man argues politics as a hobby and as a thinking exercise. "My core
philosophy," he says, "is that of skepticism: I believe that since all
human beings are fallible, we have no way of perfectly perceiving the
truths of society and the world around us. We can only pursue them
through observation, logic, and careful consideration."

The Stilt Man first drew smiles from the Net's liberals with his Debunking of the Ronald Reagan Home Page (http://www.teleport.com
/~stiltman/Politics/debunk.html), on which he went head-to-head with
Gipper goombah Brett Kottmann (http://www.erinet.com/bkottman
/reagan.html). Now, on a site called Truth Fears No Questions (http://
www.teleport.com/~stiltman/Politics), The Stilt Man presents a variety
of other political observations, including:

▶ "Propaganda and Politics," a nine-point examination of the nature
  of effective propaganda, and examples of how it is used by Rush
  Limbaugh and many other politicians today.

▶ "The Seeming Failure of Health Reform," a detailed explanation of
  how the President's health care proposals met with stonewalling,
  how that resistance succeeded, and the possibly dire consequences
  it has for the future of democracy in this country.

He's at his best perhaps in "Legalize Slavery NOW!" a sarcastic appeal to decriminalize slavery as a part of the tide of deregulation— "thus potentially saving trillions of dollars every year in expenses to honest, hard-working business owners."

Zines—or, if you must, "E-Zines"—are electronic magazines, publications that exist only in the cybersphere and are circulated not on paper but on your screen. Some are no more than website wanna-bes; others are new journals with ambitions to grow up and be full-fledged, self-sustaining publications. Pour in a little politics and you may have the Net's next hot number.

Liberal Zines

For now, most zines are free because they are seeking to build up a following. But look for the more successful ones to begin exploring subscription fees and/or advertising. Like any other Net site discussed in this book, a zine can be reached by plugging the address into your Web browser.

Mike Silverman's Turn Left home page (http://www.cjnetworks.com /~cubsfan/liberal.html) lists these among his favorite liberal zines:

▶ *The Ethical Spectacle* (http://www.spectacle.org), a collection of "thought pieces" on ethical issues, including some particularly strong antigun arguments.

▶ *Perspectives* (http://hcs.harvard.edu/~perspy), a Harvard/Radcliffe left-of-center students' magazine.

▶ *Meanderings* (http://www.webcom.com:80/~sppg/meanderings/me.html), an African American journal of politics, art, and culture.

▶ *Modern Times* (http://www.columbia.edu/cu/mt/mt.html), Columbia University's left-leaning periodical.

▶ *Bad Subjects* (http://english.hss.cmu.edu/BS/BadSubjects.html), a journal of traditional and nontraditional liberal thought on many subjects in everyday life. A "must see," Silverman says.

▶ *The Progressive Review* (http://www.princeton.edu/~progrev), live from Princeton U.

▶ *Hard Response* (http://turnpike.net/emporium/H/HR/index.htm), a humor mag for leftists.

Tech Tip

Web Pages and Browsers: What's Cool to You Is Cold to Me

Those of us in the Television Generation are used to receiving on a screen information that looks pretty much the same to everyone. The screen size or the quality of the color may vary, but "Wheel of Fortune" is basically the same on all viewers' sets. That's *not* the case in the wonderful world of the World Wide Web.

All Web documents are written in something called HyperText Mark-up Language (HTML), an evolving computer coding language. Every Web browser program displays the documents a little differently—some, *a lot* differently. For instance, some browsers, like the popular Netscape and a few others, support newer HTML elements (tables, transparent images, backgrounds, and various other layout elements). Others don't. If your browser does not support newer HTML formats, you may see only text representations of tables, and simple icons in place of graphic elements.

The millions and millions of pages that make up the Web are created by enterprising individuals like you and me. Some are more adroit with their HTML creations than others. The cleverer page creators have tried to write everything so that their pages "work" no matter what browser a visitor is using. Nonetheless, it's possible that your browser will not properly display all the documents at some website. If you run into that a lot, ask your Internet service provider for advice on alternate browsers. New versions of Netscape and other browsers are frequently released.

The major commercial online services—CompuServe, America Online, and Prodigy—now provide connections to the Web, although not all have kept up with the most recent enhancements to the HTML formats. If you are accessing the Web through a commercial service and frequently have problems trying to view favorite pages, make a note of the error messages the system is displaying and relay them to the customer service department of your online service. A technical representative may be able to suggest alternatives, or will take the error messages received from you as a signal that the system needs a software upgrade.

Other Liberal Log-Ins

Elsewhere on the Web, during recent explorations, we found these other liberal-minded sites:

▶ Steve Tollefson's Left On (http://www.winternet.com/~tulley /left.html), recognizes that liberal causes historically have some of their strongest supporters on college campuses. The site provides connections and directions to like-minded links at Amherst, Brown University, Indiana University, and University of Texas/Austin; various other colleges and universities; and state Democratic Party organizations around the nation.

▶ Activist Toolkit (gopher://gopher.well.sf.ca.us:70/11s/Politics /activist.tools/how .to.win/), a collection of articles entitled "How to Win: A Practical Guide for Defeating the Radical Right in Your Community," with sections on "Ten Things to Do When the Right Comes to Town," "How to Form a Mainstream Coalition in Your State," and "Organizing Against the Far Right on College Campuses." Written by a self-styled "Radical Right Task Force," the material touches on elections, religion, education, censorship, gay and lesbian rights, reproductive choice, the environment, and related issues.

▶ Progressive Pages (ftp://ftp.crl.com/users/ro/grossman/progress .html), Mike Grossman's links to resources dealing with progressive, liberal, or alternative topics: animal rights, civil liberties, computers and communications, crime and punishment, the environment, ethnic minorities, gay, lesbian, and bisexual topics,

Gophers Go for the Goods

Before there was the Web, the hottest technology for finding your way around the Internet was the "gopher," an online tool for locating Internet sites such as databases and collections of articles and software. It was named, incidentally, after the Golden Gopher mascot of the University of Minnesota, where the utility was created, but it's a convenient pun on "go for" (whatever you're hunting on the Net).

Tech Tip

Gophers are rapidly being replaced by snazzier-looking Web pages, but the technology is still in use around the Net. When you encounter a gopher address (several appear in this book), such as (gopher://cdcnac.aspensys.com:72/11), enter it in your Web browser software in the field where you ordinarily would enter an "http://" URL address. Your browser then will take you to the gopher, and you will see a text menu-driven system. For instance, if the gopher site is a collection of documents, each file will be listed with a number beside it. You need only enter the number of the item you wish to view.

When you are ready to leave the gopher and go elsewhere, enter a different address in the URL field of your Web browser program.

government, health issues, international affairs, labor, literature, media, music, partisan and electoral politics, peace and justice, personalities, poetry, religion, reproductive rights, and women's issues.

▶ Justin's Infobahn Political Page (http://www.cs.cmu.edu/~jab /politics.html), the political section of Justin Boyan's popular Links

---

Tom Tomorrow: Spoofing the Modern World

Names on the Net

Known to millions as "Tom Tomorrow," Dan Perkins and his "This Modern World" cartoon strip are the modem nation's hometown sensation. His funny, politically astute strip is self-syndicated in 70 print newspapers across the country, but, arguably, his biggest fans are online.

First published in the late 1980s in *Processed World,* a magazine about the Information Age from the point of view of office workers, the strip has gradually shifted from a focus on consumerism to the media and politics, with a liberal dose of gleeful computer bashing.

Working out of The Well, San Francisco's trendy modem milieu, Perkins manages his own website (http://www.well.com/Community/comic) and offers the original panels on a delayed basis. The print newspaper customers get first crack at them because they are paying the freight.

Perkins doesn't cut any slack on his commentary. Journalist Steve Rhodes relates how Perkins introduced a new character in the strip in the early 1990s. "Sparky, The Wonder Penguin made his debut in the *San Francisco Examiner* (a paper owned by Bush supporter William Hearst) by proclaiming, 'George Bush is a wanker and should be impeached' at a time when Bush was still soaring high in public opinion surveys." And when Sparky first appeared in *Image,* the *Examiner's* magazine, the pugnacious penguin opined that so many "progressives" didn't bother to vote, "the Mayor of San Francisco was chosen by the kind of people who enjoy *Parade* magazine!" *Parade* had just been picked up by the Sunday paper, and Perkins told Rhodes, "I wanted to let them know what they were getting into."

Perkins also offers his Net fans a semiregular newsletter. To be put on the e-mail subscribers' list, send a message to: tomorrow@well.com.

from the Underground (http://www.links.net), which reports on weird and wonderful websites. In addition to the predictable liberal links to Greenpeace and the ACLU, Boyan offers some rarities, such as articles titled "Christian Soldiers: the Radical Religious Right in America," "The Environmental Case for Campaign Reform," and "Republicans and the Politics of Destruction."

CONSERVATIVE CONNECTIONS

Jeff Donels's home page on the World Wide Web includes a snapshot of himself standing beside one of his heros. "That's me," says the accompanying text, "on the RIGHT of Rush Limbaugh!"

Donels's hugely popular Right Side of the Web page (http://www.clark.net/pub/jeffd), easily the most comprehensive right-wing site on the Web, has given him a Rush-like celebrity among the Net's digerati. Linked from sites all around the Internet, Right Side has become the first stop for many of the cybersphere's conservative contingent. Paying tribute to Ronald Reagan—the page often is topped with a color photo of the grinning Gipper—the site also boasts an "antitribute" to Bill Clinton, with a message inviting visitors to contribute comments to an online "Monument to the Clinton Presidency." Right Side provides links to virtually every right-wing site known to earthlings. Its connections are grouped as "Culture and Society," "Economics," and "Foreign Policy," for easy surfing.

Unlike some other political pagers, Donels isn't at all shy about taking an editorial stand, even if at odds with other conservatives. The last time we modemmed through the Donels domain, in the summer of 1995, the page was proclaiming the candidates it wanted and didn't want on the GOP presidential ticket for 1996—and why.

Pat Buchanan: "you know where the guy stands."

Pete Dupont: "solid conservative whose fiscal libertarianism is very appealing."

John Engler: "very good on education and welfare reform."

Steve Forbes: "a Kemp conservative on economic growth who seems to be good on the issues as far as we know."

Alan Keyes: "a Lincoln Republican—not a 'big tent' Republican—who knows why the Republican Party was formed in the first place."

Tommy Thompson: "a very solid record on welfare reform."

Malcolm Wallop: "strong conservative."

Getting only a tentative nod as "people who MIGHT find their way back onto the list" were Bob Dornan ("his attacks on the draft record of Phil Gramm are inexcusable") and Phil Gramm ("lack of backbone on social issues").

On its feistier no-way list in the summer of 1995 were:

Bob Dole: "a 'moderate' who is always called by the media a 'conservative' for some reason."

Barry Goldwater: "endorses Democrats over real Republicans and supports Arlen Specter for President."

Richard Lugar: "BORING; makes Al Gore look exciting."

Lynn Martin: "another 'moderate.'"

Colin Powell: "Is the guy a conservative? . . . If he is, then why is he so afraid to speak out and admit it?"

Dan Quayle: "'Standing Firm' . . . not really."

Arlen Specter: "whole presidential platform is based on getting rid of the vast majority—'Religious Right'—of Republicans."

William Weld: "would drive the Reagan Democrats right back to Clinton."

Christine Todd Whitman: "no real experience."

Pete Wilson: "has not done a very good job of even managing California."

On his might-find-their-way-back list, Donels included Lamar Alexander ("why does he think he can pull off posing as an 'outsider?'"), Newt Gingrich ("we love him . . . but it may be disruptive of the agenda in Congress for him to run"), and George Bush ("we know HE'LL never have 'jack-booted Nazis' breaking into his home. Don't any politicians ever pay attention to these horror stories of the BATF and FBI before they go off and make dumb statements?").

The Right Side of the Web has amused itself by inviting its visitors to contribute to A Monument to the Clinton Presidency (http://www.clark.net/pub/jeffd /cgi-bin/dodger.cg:.html): "We thought it would be only appropriate to have slogans that change by the minute on the inscription, to match Clinton's indeci- siveness on every issue." Among the suggested inscriptions:

Right Side's Tribute to the Clinton Presidency

The buck never got here.

"Veni, vidi, eravi" (translated from the Latin: "I came, I saw, I goofed").

Listen to your pollsters, not your conscience.

A product of firing George Bush was a reminder of why we had him in the first place.

The president between Bush and Dole.

He felt our pain . . . at the ballot box.

Commander-in-brief.

Proof that anyone can become president of the U.S. of A.

Man, I never thought ANYBODY could make Jimmy Carter look like a good president.

This space for rent.

He loved not wisely, but too often!

If I was the answer, it must have been a stupid question . . . .

It is not amazing that he shot himself in the foot, but it is truly amazing how quickly he could reload.

The Conservative Link

Jeff Williams said that he started The Conservative Link (http:// www.portcom.com/BMDesign/CICG/c:cghome.html), in May 1995, primarily for his own purpose of keeping track of conservative political information around the Internet, but "the word got out and now hun- dreds of people are using this forum every day for similar purposes." Who's welcome? Williams says his followers, "sick of being categorized as mind-numbed dittohead robots," are generally "people who want to back up political beliefs with facts."

Williams provides clickable on-screen buttons to reach other like-minded sites, publications, gopher/FTP sites, e-mail links, conservative entertainers, 1996 election information, liberal websites, and related destinations.

He can be testy, too. A "Listing of Liberal Lies," credited "Author Unknown," invites e-mailed additions from readers. Here are some of the juicier red-meat items:

> Rush Limbaugh is more dangerous than Louis Farrakhan.
>
> Only the rich benefited during the Reagan years.
>
> Abortion is a God-given right; therefore, it should be subsidized and encouraged whenever possible.
>
> If government pays for a program, then it is free.
>
> Conservative talk-radio programs were directly responsible for the Oklahoma City bombing incident.
>
> When the Christian Coalition advocates a return to the morals that founded this nation and made us great, they are religious extremists. However, when an entertainment company such as Disney rewrites the history of Pocahontas (to make it pro-"Native American") and injects pagan rituals into *The Lion King*, they are just making a wholesome family movie.
>
> Bill Clinton didn't inhale.

Conservative Generation X

Think only liberals are hip? Don't tell Paul Colligan and Ehren Filippello, who edit Conservative Generation X (http://www.cgx .com), which says up front: "We've got a radio, a Bible, a politician, a news anchor, an old college textbook, and our hearts all telling us different things. We're not complaining. We're just trying to sort it all out." They add, "We're conservative. This has very little to do with Rush, Reagan, or Newt. They are nothing more than the result of a majority of Americans who think like we do. We like the whole basis behind conservative thought and will probably stay with it for some time."

Among its unique features are "The Wall Beta" (for public messages from passersby), "GETAJOB!!" ("our response to the complaint that Xers are willing to do anything else. We offer you one of the most comprehensive employment-related pages anywhere"), and "Interactive Democracy" (tips on e-mailing influential people and groups).

The Christian Coalition

Pat Robertson's Christian Coalition offers a website (http://www .cc.org/) that is a main rallying point for politically active religious

---

Russ Lay and Steve Miller call their DeMOCKracy (http://www.clark.net/pub /theme/demockracy/) a cartoon strip that "turns spin doctors into whirling dervishes as it ridicules the pompous pisspots of the White House." Its cast of characters include:

DeMOCKracy Mocks Dems

▶ Rick: "a conservative Young Republican type, who likes *Star Trek,* athletics, and high-tech gadgets. In college, he once organized a Young Republicans protest against Clinton visiting campus, but had to ask Will for advice on whether a chardonnay or zinfandel would be appropriate for a daytime protest."

▶ Ben: "a Libertarian banker with unruly hair and a love of baseball hats. 'nuff said."

▶ Will: "a bumbling liberal weenie who is periodically drafted by the White House to help out in various hot spots using his unique abilities. In Haiti, this meant driving a school bus. In college, he was caught listening to Amy Grant."

▶ Dagny: "a reporter who once shocked Ben and Will by dating Rick."

▶ Milton: "a rascally dog who managed to get a cushy White House job because he saw Socks fooling around. As a latter-day Fawn Hall, ate crucial Whitewater documents when he confused them with hamburgers."

▶ Digger: "comes from a long line of moles living underneath the White House. He is the official White House 'mole' and has VERY sensitive hearing!"

conservatives. It provides contact addresses for local representatives, details on opinion polls, press releases, a "congressional scorecard" (for tracking issues of interest to regulars), voters' guides, and speeches and position papers.

A centerpiece is Robertson's "Contract with the American Family," which is subtitled "A Bold Plan to Strengthen the Family and Restore Common-Sense Values." The site has welcoming messages from Robertson and from Director Ralph Reed, and information on how to become a member.

If you want to study the Christian Coalition's strategy for upcoming elections, start with the online edition of its *Christian American* newsletter. Articles describe legislation the group is backing, a perspective on candidates, and a congressional "scorecard" for tracking votes on key issues. You then might want to progress to the Christian Coalition's

---

A number of free online electronic magazines ("Zines") are intended for politically conservative readers. Here is a sampling:

Conservative Zines

▶ *The Harvard Salient* (http://www.salient.org/Salient) is a 15-year-old biweekly political journal "naturally conservative but free from political allegiances," says an online statement. The publication was founded "by students who sought to provide a journalistic alternative to a predominantly liberal campus press."

▶ *Keep Right* (http://www.crl.com/www/users/jm/jmcraven), edited by J. M. Craven, calls itself "the online window to conservative philosophy." It features columnist Cory T. Echols and others.

▶ *ABCDEFG* (A Basic Citizen's Definitive Electronic Freedom Guide) (http://www.dakota.net/~pwinn/abcdefg), Phillip Winn's Christian Libertarian zine, promises to be "one-sided, arbitrary, and completely biased—in short, like all of us." Issues typically covered include gun control, Christianity's conflict with censorship, and militias.

▶ *Drudge Report* (http://www.lainet.com:80/~drudge), published by Matt Drudge, covers media, Hollywood, and politics. Its "White House Inner Circle Talk" focuses on Clintonites, especially those in the film and television industries.

voter guide for religious conservatives, which includes advice for reaching organizations in your region. Tips on contacting Congress members, details of upcoming seminars, opinion polls in which visitors can participate, texts of speeches, and position papers are also provided.

Other Conservative Quarters

Other conservative connections on the Web include:

▶ Americans for Tax Reform (ATR) (http://www.Emerald.Net /ATR) is Grover G. Norquist's organization. According to its purpose statement, it opposes all tax increases "as a matter of principle. . . . We believe in a tax system that is simpler, fairer, flatter, more visible, and lower than today's. The way to tax reform is through spending restraint, eliminating or downsizing government programs in order to eliminate specific taxes beginning with those that are most damaging to the economy and invasive of personal privacy." Norquist adds, elsewhere on the site: "The

---

CompuServe Hosts Conservative Town Hall

Town Hall is a private CompuServe forum for conservatives who wish to share ideas and opinions, conduct research, and develop strategies leading to what a printed statement says backers hope will be a "political and cultural revolution" in America.

Off the Web

A joint venture by *National Review* magazine and the Heritage Foundation think tank, the forum offers daily bulletins and updates, live panel discussions, articles from *National Review* (available before they appear in print), and daily press releases from the White House, Congress, and assorted conservative organizations.

On CompuServe, users can enter GO TOWNHALL details. At this writing, unlimited access to the forum is offered for a flat rate of $16 a month. For offline information, call 800/441-4142. Town Hall president Timothy Butler says, "If Thomas Paine were alive today, he'd still be a rabble-rouser. He'd still be fighting for the cause of freedom and giving the government fits." But, says Butler, he wouldn't be passing out pamphlets; he'd be online.

government's power to control one's life derives entirely from its power to tax. We believe it should be minimized." The ATR says it seeks to lead the way in creating a coalition of conservative sites on the Web. "Ambitious plans focus on uniting activists across the country, providing information and a common meeting place to exchange initiative referendum and ideas."

▶ The Cato Institute (http://www.cato.org/main/home.html) is operated by the 20-year-old nonpartisan Washington (DC) public policy research foundation. ("Cato's Letters" were libertarian pamphlets that helped lay the philosophical foundation for the American Revolution.) The Institute seeks to guide public debate toward issues of limited government, individual liberty, and peace. "Toward that goal," says an online statement, "the Institute strives to achieve greater involvement of the intelligent, concerned lay public in questions of policy and the proper role of government." Featured on the site is "The Liberty Manifesto." P. J. O'Rourke, the commentator, is a Cato Institute Mencken research fellow.

▶ The John Birch Society (http://www.primenet.com/~tevans /jbs.html), perhaps the oldest, best known conservative organization in the country, is in charge of this site. It provides answers to frequently asked questions about the group's principles and beliefs. Visitors can get electronic versions of its *New American* magazine, and a recommended reading list.

Chapter 4

Taking Issue on the Internet

In politics, one year's prime candidate can be reduced to a historical footnote by the next election. But some of the *issues* that fired a campaign may continue to be debated for years afterward.

In a national election year, incumbents and challengers dash around the country like cavaliers galloping from one fiery skirmish to another. In New Hampshire, the sore point may be NAFTA and international trade treaties in general. In Iowa, they may duel verbally over farm subsidies. In any university town, the focus may be student aid or the future of lucrative research grants. The headline issues, especially in a national election, are set by newspaper and magazine columnists and broadcast media commentators and analysts. Success comes to the candidate who can thrust satisfactorily toward the headline issues and parry with genuine interest on the concerns of the current audience. Topics can be as diverse as the economy, flag-burning, and reform of election financing laws. As the campaign continues, the candidates' websites reflect the urgent need for agility, aggressiveness, and a firm stance.

In contrast to the raid-and-rumble mentality of the campaign, the issue-oriented sites in cyberspace routinely dig in for the long siege. Trench warfare is the strategy of the venues devoted to debates over abortion, gun control, or gay rights. Regulars behind the opposing barricades have been lobbing verbal volleys at one another for so long that few have any realistic expectations of completely routing the other side. Victory in this theater of political combat usually is measured in small successes: converts won among the uncommitted onlookers; a few inches of rhetorical territory gained through the exploitation of newfound weaknesses in the opposition's arguments; demoralization of opponents through news of reinforcements arriving in the form of support from new candidates; case verdicts or court rulings; or crusading commentators.

As in all bunkers, the bitterness can run deep and the invective is infectious. However, because these battles have been raging much longer than the duration of a single campaign, some good can come of all this growling and grumbling: many of these sites have built up impressive arsenals of facts, documents, and arguments. Their quickly accessed and detailed data can provide Net travelers with valuable insights and education. For instance, do you want to be brought up to speed quickly on a specific environmental issue? A civil liberties question? A workplace safety proposal? An hour or so of tiptoeing through some of the philosophical minefields described in this chapter could be the equivalent of days' worth of panel discussions.

In these parts, as everywhere in the Net, it's wise to be skeptical. These are patently partisan "news" sites. Most of them feel absolutely no obligation to try to provide balanced coverage or even to *acknowledge* another side of the argument. Furthermore, as in most political debates, some enthusiastic advocates can get so carried away with their causes that they bombard the rest of us with details while providing no real perspective or analysis. The result: too many facts and too little information. Cyberspace, with its virtually unlimited storage capacity, threatens to only exacerbate the data deluge from television, radio, and print media.

This chapter will help you avoid online babble and zero in on the valuable substantive information that some of the better issue-oriented sites offer. Rather than list every conceivable website on issues, we've focused on the best, the ones that can get you started on your own online exploration. We've concentrated on a *variety* of subjects and on *balanced information*. The sites we report represent different points of view on the same question. For instance, in the section on the abortion debate, discussions of pro-choice and pro-life sites are placed back-to-back. This

Discerning the Net's "True Names"

More than a decade ago, science-fiction writer Vernor Vinge wove an imaginative novel called *True Names* around the challenge of trying to figure out the real identities of people conversing on computer networks, most of whom, in the book, were using pseudonyms like "DON.MAC" and "Mister Slippery." The novel's protagonist discovers what many of today's datanauts have learned: people online "are" only who they *say* they are. In other words, cyberspace affords each of its citizens the opportunity to create an online persona that reveals only as much "real-world" data as he or she wants to share.

So far on our journey together, identity hasn't been much of an issue. Most of the websites in the preceding chapters have originated from established organizations. Many have U.S. mailing addresses and voice phone numbers to call if you want to confirm their true connection with the online site. And some sites in this chapter share complete resumes of the people involved in the pages—their names, ages, addresses, occupations, and qualifications for providing the data.

By contrast, many of the issue-related Net pages we will meet in this chapter are created by ordinary private citizens, some of whom are adamant about maintaining a *private* status. Most Web pages print at least the names of their authors; others list no name, or perhaps only a first name, or hide behind an obvious pseudonym or an e-mail address.

Either way, the important thing to remember is that Net wanderers can do little to verify what page producers say about themselves, whether they give merely a name or a full-blown curriculum vitae. In producing this book and reporting on websites, we have had to take background information at face value and pass along whatever personal data and credentials we could glean from the online pages. When you surf the Internet, anonymity is a fact of life—but we can suggest a strategy for dealing with it.

First, don't assume that the reasons people opt to keep their identity to themselves are necessarily sinister. Some Netheads frankly are a little overwhelmed by the global nature of the Web and a bit reluctant to hang out a shingle on such busy traffic lanes. Second, if one of your favorite Web pages is produced anonymously but lists an e-mail address:

- ▶ Write to it.
- ▶ Introduce yourself. Share some facts about yourself and your reasons for interest in the page.
- ▶ Let the originator know what you think of the site, and feel free to ask questions and make suggestions.

> Don't be shy about volunteering your services if you have something to share.

You might be surprised at the results. On many of these sites, the authors' only compensation is the feedback they receive from readers. You're far more likely to get a personal reply from one of these pages than from, say, the site of a busy campaign. And if you share a little information about yourself, your e-mail's recipient is far more likely to open up to you.

approach increases your likelihood of finding pages that match your particular attitudes on key issues, and gives you resources for knowing what the people on the other side are saying and for gauging how they will respond.

In this chapter, you also learn about:

> Electronic petitions. New technology has inspired new ways to get your voice heard; among them is the automated petition drive. A click of your mouse button adds your "signature." Organizers later handle printouts and delivery of the document to the petitioned lawmakers or targeted authority.

> Online letter-writing campaigns. Electronic mail is reviving the American passion for letter writing. Sites you meet in this chapter can train you as an "e-mail activist," increasing the effectiveness of your issue-oriented e-mail by showing you when and to whom to write.

> Reaching the lobbyists. Through your computer, you can communicate with national and regional organizations that are trying to persuade lawmakers on the hot issues of the day. Electronically, you can contribute your dollars and your ideas to their efforts.

> Opening incoming lines of information. Through electronic and printed bulletins and journals sent to your e-mail address, you can keep up-to-date on the issues that matter most to you.

Finally, you can begin creating your *own* online contacts. The Net can be a lonely place, but once you start visiting sites like those described in this chapter, you may find you no longer have to surf alone. As you discover sites you particularly like, drop a line to the pages' authors. (E-mail addresses often are listed at the top or bottom of home pages that invite correspondence.) Do your favorite pages have hypertext links to still other sites you might like? Exploring these recommended added attractions can provide you with even more opportunities to reach out by e-mail to kindred spirits.

ABORTION

The abortion issue is argued from perspectives ranging from civil liberties to religion to sexual freedom to the role of government in our lives. Among the arguers no one wants to appear to be "anti" anything. On one side are the pro-choice advocates, who defend the laws permitting abortion; on the other are the pro-life forces, who seek to end the nation's policy of abortion on demand.

Pro-Choice Sites

"In the 'war' over abortion rights, only one side is using guns," says Adam Guasch-Melendez on his Abortion Rights Activist Home Page (http://www.cais.com/agm/index.html). Intended as a primary Web resource for "information about the struggle to preserve abortion rights," the page includes breaking news, reports and statistics on violence at abortion clinics, contacts for clinic defense and escort groups, and links to other Internet resources on both sides of the argument. Guasch-Melendez also offers connections to data from the National Abortion Federation (NAF).

If you're new to this debate, you might have a special interest in the site's link to the NAF's Community Action Guide, called "This Door Stays Open." Click on this option for lists of ways to get involved in guaranteeing access to abortion.

Kathleen Watkins, a long-time Net surfer who now creates Web pages for businesses and teaches classes in Internet-related topics, has been a primary information provider for the Net's pro-choice advocates. Her wide-ranging California Abortion Rights Action League (CARAL) page (http://www.caral.org) was created for the 17-year-old San Francisco-based nonprofit organization of the same name. The site's "Email Activism" option includes a form for anyone who wants to volunteer to write letters and e-mail messages, send faxes, call legislators, organize committees, distribute literature, or, in northern California, work in CARAL's real-world office. The form also invites visitors to indicate issues of greatest interest (selections include clinic violence, minors' access to abortions, abortion funding for poor families, contraception, sex education, waiting periods for abortions, welfare reform, elections, and/or California and federal legislation). The "Issues" option gives the latest pro-choice news flashes and "action alerts" (a bulletin on a proposed ban of late-term abortions was headlined "Contact the President and Urge Him to Veto This Bill!"), as well as items such as "CARAL Factsheet on Clinic Violence, Intimidation and Terrorism." The site also gives background on CARAL's own initiatives, for example, a legal brief filed in a California parental consent abortion case, and letters to the editors of California newspapers on sex education and other matters.

Elsewhere around the Web are two other major pro-choice sites:

▶ Campus for Choice Homepage (http://ux5.cso.uiuc.edu/~hindin /choice) is operated by a student-run organization at East-Central Illinois State University, as a project of the Public Affairs department of Planned Parenthood. Through online bulletins and its Internet newsgroup (uiuc.org.choice), the organization says it seeks to increase community awareness about reproductive rights. If you're a college student near the Illinois campus, the page's meeting information and news of other activities may be of particular interest.

▶ NOW and Abortion Rights/Reproductive Issues (http://now.org:80 /issues/abortion/abortion.html), operated by the National Organization for Women, offers the history of the abortion rights movement in this country, and news of recent activities, such as a transcript of NOW President Patricia Ireland's remarks before the Senate Labor and Human Resources Committee hearings on the nomination of Dr. Henry Foster for Surgeon General. NOW spells out actions you can take if you want to join its pro-choice activities. During our most recent visit, the site was calling on its readers to send e-mail to the president to urge him to veto the bill to ban late-term abortions. This is also a source for status reports on NOW's abortion-oriented agenda, current court cases, workshops on clinic violence, and plans for national marches and demonstrations.

Pro-Life

Tens of thousands of words about the anti-abortion movement—its history, published reference resources, and philosophical positions on everything from contraception to sex education and religious teachings—have been brought online in a massive reference work called *The Pro-Life Encyclopedia* (http://hebron.ee.gannon.edu/~frezza/plae /contents.html).

Written by Brian Clowes and published by the American Life League (ALL) of Stafford, Virginia, this 140-chapter work should be your first online stop for any information about this side of the abortion argument. Some sections cover pro-life organizations; magazines, journals, key books, and pamphlets; and pro-life activities for newcomers to get involved in. Others are more subjective: they suggest tactics for winning pro-life debates, and discuss various church positions on abortion. Other portions of the text, especially later chapters, range rather far afield of a strictly pro-life/pro-choice argument (Chapter 93, "Communism: An Inherently Anti-Life System"; Chapter 114, "Homeschooling: The Alternative for Caring Christian Families"; Chapter 121, "Homosexual Groups: Organized Sex Perverts on the March"; and Chapter 130, "The 'New Age' Movement: Highway to Hell"). Still, for a synthesis of the pro-life movement's positions on the key issue and many related topics (euthanasia, fetal tissue research, adoption, rape, incest, and overpopulation), this is a comprehensive guide.

The home page of the encyclopedia's publisher, the American Life League (http://www.ahoynet.com/~all/index.html), also has

Document: Roe v. Wade

Seldom has a single document become so central to a national controversy as the 1973 U.S. Supreme Court decision in *Roe v. Wade.* Through the Cornell University Law School, your Internet connection (http://www.law.cornell .edu/supct/classics/410us113.ovr.html) can provide you with a copy of this landmark ruling, with links to the majority opinion, dissenting opinions, and related material.

Kathleen Watkins: Showing the Way to Online Activism

Californian Kathleen Watkins has created a rarity in the world of online politics: a feature that is boosted by liberals and conservatives alike. Her TAO—The Activist's Oasis (http://www.matisse.net/~kathy/activist)—is routinely included as an alternative resource on pages serving the left and the right sides of the Web. Visitors who click in find a huge collection of links to dozens of causes and issues, research centers, women's rights, student organizations, mailing lists, newsletters, and more.

Names on the Net

She has the Net equivalent of bipartisan support, but Watkins has never hidden her own political agenda. As the former administrative director for the California Abortion and Reproductive Action League North, she is ardently pro-choice and has created *Choice Net Report,* a weekly newsletter distributed only on the Internet (gopher://gopher.well.sf.ca.us/11s/Politics/Abortion).

Working now as a consultant on teaching people how to get connected to the Internet and use its tools, Watkins is particularly interested in getting more activists online. To that end, she has compiled some of her ideas in a breezy, tightly composed online pamphlet called "An Activist's Strategic Guide to the Internet." Here are some of her points:

▶ Know who's on your side. "When you find like-minded people online, treasure them, keep track of them, share information with them. Never forget that online communication is still person-to-person communication."

▶ Find out who else is out there. "You can learn what organizations are doing, their strategy and their spin, by reading the materials they make available online."

▶ Determine who's listening. "Use online access to the media to tell your side of the story. Be sure to respond promptly when your issue is in the news. Pay attention to how your opposition uses online media."

▶ Stay focused. "Cyberspace contains the most amazing and complex set of distractions ever created by humans. You can literally spend hours saying, 'Wow, this is so cool.' There's nothing wrong with that, of course, but get something done first, OK?"

▶ Log your exploration. "Keep track of your search results. Start a list of your search 'keywords' . . . so you remember what you've already done . . . ."

Kathleen Watkins (continued)

When you do this, you create your own information ecosphere, a place where you're soaking in information that matters to you."

Names on the Net

▸ Make yourself at home. "We all need a place where we can be comfortable being ourselves. It may be a mailing list that makes you smile every morning when you open your e-mail box. It may be a small BBS, or you may be more comfortable as an anonymous ID number on a huge system. Pay attention to the 'feel' of a place, and look for an online home. You'll be more productive and a better person for it."

Watkins thinks the cybersphere is changing the way politics works. "Grassroots activism is facilitated by tools like the Internet," she recently told moderator Kevin Pursglove and an online audience during a real-time conference sponsored by the Internet Roundtable Society. "One person with a good idea can spread that idea quickly, and if it truly is a good idea, a lot of people will join . . . in trying to make that activity or event happen. And the truth is, I think a lot of national groups are very concerned about the Internet because they're afraid of losing the kind of influence and control of information that they currently have."

become a major homebase for the pro-life faithful, because of its comprehensive reference-desk links to other sites around the Web. The ALL page connects to the LifeGuard computer bulletin board system, where you can share your thoughts with others passing through. Back issues of ALL's *Celebrate Life* magazine and text of all its pamphlets and brochures are retrievable.

Among other pro-life sites that offer a different slant on the debate are:

▸ The Stop F.T.R. Home Page (http://www.mcs.com/~dougp /stopftr.html) is an electronic petition drive operated by a McHenry, Illinois, organization dedicated to reversing federal legislation legalizing human fetal tissue research (FTR) and transplantation, and human embryo research. The petition is the site's main activity, but the page has other original material. One option invites you to "read the emotional story of baby Taylor as written by his mother. Baby Taylor was born alive at 20 weeks gestation." Another is entitled, "My Hardest Night: A Gut-Wrenching Story from a Registered Nurse." Beside the human-interest stories, the page provides a "Get Involved" section for details on sending e-mail to the president and Congress and to media outlets, and researching how Congress members voted on key abortion issues. An extensive list of local and national pro-life organizations, online and offline, is available.

▶ Steve Frezza's The Pro-Life News (http://hebron.ee.gannon.edu/~frezza/AboutPLN.html) has become a gathering site for opponents of pro-choice. Frezza provides a bimonthly electronic journal with news and comment on pro-life issues. The free monthly, begun in January 1991, contains readers' contributions of news and personal experiences, and regular features such as "On the National Front," "What Works?," "Reader Questions," "Across the Pond," and "Quote of the Month." The site also facilitates searching of the publication's indexes.

▶ LifeLinks (http://www.nebula.net\~maeve\lifelink.html) has become a popular additional Net location for right-to-life advocates because of its connections to data from "Feminists For Life," quotes from Mother Teresa, reference material for postabortion problems, medical data on fetal development, and a feature called "What Does the Bible Say?" There are even connections to men's rights and gay/lesbian rights groups that oppose abortion.

AIDS (ACQUIRED IMMUNE DEFICIENCY SYNDROME)

Jaison Laird created the AIDS and Related Topics Home Page (http://www.actwin.com/aids/vl.html) as a virtual library page that deals with the social, political, and medical aspects of AIDS, HIV, and related issues. This is an excellent central resource for links to relevant material around the Net: obscure medical databases that might not be found by the casual Net surfer, and AIDS information in languages other than English.

Laird's page provides major articles and studies about AIDS, and answers to frequently asked questions on prevention, confidentiality, treatment options, and similar issues. Newsletters and resources include a document database developed by the Global Programme on AIDS, which contains the full text of World Health Organization publications on the disease. The National Library of Medicine's online information service, which offers free access to the MEDLARS (the Medical Literature Analysis and Retrieval System) databases relating to AIDS, is described in detail. (MEDLAR access is by application only, and is limited to the United States. An online form that can be printed, and then faxed or mailed to the management, asks applicants to indicate their profession and describe why they are interested in the data. Name, regular-mail address, and phone number must be supplied.)

Three other AIDS-related Net sites provide information from medical, scientific, and educational perspectives:

◗ National AIDS Clearinghouse of the Centers for Disease Control (gopher://cdcnac.aspensys.com:72/11): regular bulletins and announcements from researchers.

◗ AIDS Patents Project (http://patents.cnidr.org): information from the U.S. Patent Office about new developments in the war against AIDS. A "What's New" section has the latest input, and a database provides details on older patents related to AIDS research.

◗ Just Say Yes (http://www.actwin.com/aids/jsIndex.html): an irreverent and unabashed sex education pamphlet for teens. It covers AIDS issues, birth control, pregnancy, and abortion. Sex is discussed in everyday language; directions for using condoms and having safe sex are explicit.

ANIMAL RIGHTS

On separate paths, Ben Leamy and Donald Graft came to the Web with the idea of establishing international information resources for the defense of animals, whether domestic or in the wild. Mutual admiration for each other's work inevitably drew them to seek each other out, and they now have combined their efforts.

Their Animal Rights Resource Site (ARRS) (http://envirolink .org/arrs/index.html) is a massive repository of information and encouragement. Animal-related topics are diverse: wildlife preservation and endangered species, vegetarianism and the meat industry, hunting, furs and the clothing/fashion industry, fishing and sea life, and the entertainment industry's use of animals in movies and on television. ARRS features news, essays, guides, pictures, and links to related sites elsewhere. Data contributions from its regular visitors, such as tips on local news and activities that might be of interest to the site's global audience, are invited.

One of ARRS's earliest advocates was Stephen Ronan, who also operates his own site, Animal Health, Well Being and Rights (http:// www.tiac.net/users/sbr/animals.html). The page links to general animal-related sites and to those devoted to endangered species. Come here for references to specialized sites that have health-related information on bats, birds, cats, cows, dogs, dolphins, ferrets, fish, foxes, frogs, guinea pigs, hamsters, horses, manatees, primates, rabbits, raccoons, reptiles, turtles, wolves, and wombats.

CHILDREN'S RIGHTS

The murder of 12-year-old Polly Klaas, following her knife-point abduction from a slumber party at her Petaluma, California, home in October 1993, prompted a national outcry for changes in legislation and for stronger measures to prevent crimes against children. Within a year, the Klaas Foundation for Children was formed by Polly's father, Marc Klaas, to promote parental awareness of child safety measures, to urge communities to take steps to create safer neighborhoods, and to fight for establishment of uniform laws to punish and monitor criminals who target children.

In early 1996, the Klaas Foundation came to the Web. Its KlaasKids site (http://klaaskids.inter.net/klaaskids) had a unique *dual* function: (1) share the foundation's safety resources internationally and invite new members and donors, and (2) shine an unrelenting light on the judicial system. To accomplish the latter goal, the page published daily updates and commentary on the trial of Polly's accused killer, Richard Allen Davis.

The National Child Rights Alliance (NCRA) shares with its online visitors its Youth Bill of Rights (http://www.ai.mit.edu/people/ellens/NCRA/rights.html), intended to illustrate the group's belief that "civil rights apply to all people, including children and youth." Adopted at an NCRA convention in 1989, the Youth Bill of Rights advocates:

Youth Bill of Rights

▶ The Right to Liberty: No children shall be forced to live in any household against their will. This includes biologic as well as foster and adoptive households. No children shall be forced into marriage. No children shall be institutionalized against their will without due process rights.

▶ The Right to Safety: All children shall have the right to safe haven on request, without fear of criminal charges. NCRA supports Sanctuary for Children, and is establishing a fund in defense of this right.

▶ The Right to Survival: All children have the right to adequate food, shelter, medical care, and a healthy environment. NCRA supports a free national health care system for children which is not dependent on parental income nor parental permission; living wage rights for workers; and a guaranteed income for those unable to work, so that families need not be torn apart by poverty.

▶ The Right to Education: All children shall have the right to a free education—including college and technical schools—at public expense. Programs must be free of cultural, racial, or gender bias in all respects.

▶ The Right of Free Speech: All children shall have the right of free speech. This includes . . . personal expression and . . . school-based and public media.

▶ The Right of Nondiscrimination: NCRA supports all efforts to end curtailment of a child's potential and self-esteem based on age, race, gender, language, country of origin, the economic or marital status of parents, religious or sexual preference, and physical or mental limitations or differences.

▶ The Right of Free Choice: No child shall be either forced or forbidden to choose a religious or political affiliation, philosophy, or creed.

▶ The Right to an Attorney: All children shall have the right to legal representation whereby the attorneys act as an attorney for—not guardian of—their clients.

"This will become an effective tool to help involve and empower concerned parents and trial spectators," said Mike Angiletta, president of Silicon Media, which assisted in creating the website. "Now, they have one place where they can go to share their thoughts and concerns, learn how to support and affect local efforts related to children's safety, and receive timely updates on the trial proceedings."

Besides the trial coverage, the KlaasKids site provides a guide to Net resources on children's issues, advice on how to keep children safe, and an invitation to send legislators, via e-mail, comments on pending bills affecting children.

KlaasKids is the latest indication that the uncensored and contentious Net, which some fear is potentially harmful to and exploitative of children, can support sites devoted exclusively to protection of the young. A 10-year-old Durham, North Carolina, group, formed by six survivors of child abuse and neglect, was one of the first in cyberspace to spread the word on the issue. The home page of the National Child Rights Alliance (NCRA) (http://www.ai.mit.edu/people /ellens/NCRA/ncra.html) continues to encourage challenges to economic, social, legal, medical, cultural, and parental practices that harm youth. Managed by acting NCRA Chairman Jim Senter, the page carries an extensive collection of relevant articles ("Are Children Property?" "The Time for Sanctuary Has Come," "When a Child Wants a Divorce"). Details on how to become a member are given.

For more on children's rights, see the Children Now page (http:// www.dnai.com/~children), produced by the nonprofit group of the same name. Its agenda ranges from fighting abuse and neglect to arguing against children's exposure to violence on TV. The page's "Sites" option has links to dozens of little-known pages dedicated to children's safety and health, family economic security, parenting resources, federal government action resources, and education.

CHRISTIAN POLITICS

The Christian Coalition, the organization that verbalizes the positions of the fundamentalist political base created by its founder, Reverend Pat Robertson, has established an active website (http://cc.org) to spread its word in Cyberia. Its hottest option, "Scorecard," gives details of voting records of legislators, by state, regarding issues on which the coalition has taken a stand. Press releases, electronic copies of Christian American newsletters, voter guides to fundamentalist issues and legislative affairs, opinion polls, and a "Religious Rights Watch," as well as speeches and position papers from Robertson, are standard offerings. A feature called "Contract with the American Family" is characterized as "a bold plan to strengthen the family and restore common-sense values."

On the same wavelength is the home page of Robertson's Christian Broadcasting Network (CBN) (http://the700club.org), which promulgates press releases, viewer guides to the CBN-TV 700 Club, details of local stations carrying CBN broadcasts, and articles on current issues.

For different spins on the merging of religion and politics, the following sites are devoted respectively to the issue of "creationism" and to Christianity and Libertarianism:

▶ Center for the Advancement of Paleo Orthodoxy (http://www
   .usit.net/public/CAPO/capohomne.html) is devoted to creationism and bringing "ancient biblical light to modern issues," according to an online statement from the Oak Ridge, Tennessee,

Some happy heretics who call themselves The Internet Infidels have made it their mission to provide an electronic alternative to religious fundamentalism and biblical literalists online.

The group's Secular Web (http://freethought.tamu.edu) sends out information and directives to sites that are devoted to atheism, agnosticism, free thought, humanism, general skepticism, and related topics. Secular Web

The Secular Web: Tweaking the Nose of Convention

also links to information on secular bookstores, publishers, periodicals and organizations.

The Freethought Web (http://freethought.tamu.edu/freethought/) offers an exhaustive collection of secular texts, including classics by Clarence Darrow, Charles Darwin, Thomas Hobbes, David Hume, John Locke, Thomas Paine, Percy Shelley, and Voltaire.

Topics such as "Why Come Out as an Atheist?" "Why the Resurrection Is Not a Well-Documented Historical Event," "Why I Believe in Fair Taxation of Church Property" are calculated to make traditionalists squirm.

group. Following its motto, "Looking for wisdom as ancient as the scriptures," the group says it believes the views of "earlier thinkers," including biblical writers, ought to be included in modern discussions about the origins of life on Earth. Also available at this site is *Premise,* the center's electronic monthly journal.

▶ The Christlib Home Page, (http://www.teleport.com/~bruceab /xlib.html) explores connections between Christianity and libertarianism. Says page manager Bruce Baugh, "By Christianity, we mean the teachings of Jesus and the traditions of the Christian Churches (groups of people who live their lives based on the teachings of Jesus); by libertarianism, we mean the idea that self-government is the best government, that exchanges should be voluntary, that force should only be used for self-defense."

CIVIL LIBERTIES

Praised and vilified for its dogged defense of the Bill of Rights against assaults from both the Right and the Left for much of this century, the 75-year-old American Civil Liberties Union (ACLU) has proved it will be a force to reckon with in cyberspace. The ink had hardly dried on President Clinton's signature enacting a bill to overhaul the nation's telecommunications industry in early February 1996, when the ACLU was in court asking a federal judge to block the new law's provisions banning "indecent speech" online. The bill, said the ACLU, created censorship that affected even the availability of abortion data on the Net.

Arguing that online speech is akin to print media and private communication rather than to television and radio (which are regulated by federal law), the ACLU articulated the legal concerns of information providers in many corners of the Web who greeted the passage of the telecommunications law with a Netwide "black-out" to indicate what some describe as "virtual mourning." (Opponents of the law changed the background color of their Web pages to black, with white or gray text. Ordinarily, text on the World Wide Web is dark-colored on a light-colored background.) Meanwhile, the full text of the suit and a status report of the case were provided on ACLU's own Freedom Network (http://www.aclu.org).

Business-as-usual at the ACLU website is comprised of pages devoted to civil liberties issues in Congress, the courts and the schools, news flashes, and details on how to join the organization. ACLU position papers on church-and-state topics, criminal justice, cyberliberties, the death penalty, free speech, AIDS, immigrants' rights, gay and lesbian rights, national security, racial equality, reproductive rights, student rights, voting rights, women's rights, and workplace rights are accessible.

Interested in finding the nearest ACLU chapter? Check out the site's "In the States" option. Click on a portion of an on-screen map, and the system provides the latest press releases from that state's local chapter as well as the contact information for the local organization.

If you're wondering what civil liberties campaigns you can participate in, start with the ACLU's "Act Now" option. You can sign up to have one or more of the ACLU's electronic newsletters delivered by e-mail. At this writing, the group had newsletters on campus issues, legislative action, computer rights, news flashes, and what's new on the website. Use "Censorship Watch" if you want to report incidents you'd like the organization to investigate.

Often, electronic mail campaigns are under way at the ACLU site. During the opening days of the group's suit on the telecommunications law, the site called on visitors to participate in an e-mail letter-writing campaign to Attorney General Janet Reno, urging her not to enforce the measure.

Because of the nature of the ACLU's work, much of the site focuses on breaking news and current court cases, but there's also a library of backgrounders and briefing papers. You'll find in-depth reports on the group's stand on matters such as lie-detector testing, drug testing in the workplace, artistic freedom, hate speeches on campus, Affirmative Action, prayer in school, gun control, abortion clinic access, and privacy rights.

CENSORSHIP AND FREE SPEECH

Every year since 1976, a nationwide media research venture called Project Censored has sought to locate news stories about significant issues of which the public perhaps should be, but is not, aware. The primary focus is on censorship and stories that were late in coming to public attention because of interference by government, business, or various agencies. The project also examines "underreported" stories—happenings that the project's officials judge to have been ignored or underplayed by news organizations.

Created by Dr. Carl Jensen, professor of communications studies at Sonoma State University in Rohnert Park, California, the project has now brought to the Web its exploration and publication of the extent of censorship in our society. The Project Censored Home Page (http://zippy.sonoma.edu/ProjectCensored) provides examples of censored stories from previous years' research, as well as background on the research effort and its goals. Each year, a panel of media experts selects the top ten censored/underreported stories of that year from files submitted by writers and editors around the country. Most of the stories deal with government research ("Unfinished Business: Occupational Safety Agency Keeps 170,000 Exposed Workers in the Dark About Risks Incurred on Job" and "The Military's Plan to Alter the Ionosphere").

You're invited to e-mail Sonoma State University if you want to nominate a story that you feel should have received more coverage by the mass media. The story must be current for that year and of national social significance. It may have received no media attention at all, or appeared in the back pages of a newspaper or in a small circulation magazine.

On the Banned Books Site (http://www.cs.cmu.edu/Web/People /spok/banned-books.html), John Ockerbloom presents a collection of famous works that have been banned at some point in time. He provides history and background on famous censorship cases that involved, for example, James Joyce's *Ulysses,* D. H. Lawrence's *Lady Chatterley's Lover,* and John Cleland's *Fanny Hill,* as well as lesser known cases, such as the 1930 seizing of Harvard-bound copies of Voltaire's *Candide* by U.S. Customs in response to an obscenity complaint. (It was defended by two Harvard professors and was later admitted in an edition with a different translation.) The site links to the full electronic text of many of the banned works.

Ockerbloom also highlights some of the stranger cases, such as the 1989 banning of an illustrated edition of "Little Red Riding Hood" in two California school districts. "The book shows the heroine taking food and wine to her grandmother," he notes, and "the school districts cited concerns about the use of alcohol in the story." He also follows censorship issues through history, such as the 1660 order by King Louis XIV of France that Blaise Pascal's *The Provincial Letters,* a defense of the Jansenist Antoine Arnauld, be shredded and burned, and pre-revolution France's banning of other works that contained ideas considered subversive to the authority of kings.

COMPUTER RIGHTS

On behalf of all the modernized community, the Electronic Frontier Foundation (EFF) ponders some pretty sobering cyberspheric problems. A six-year-old nonprofit public-interest group, the EFF says in an online statement that it is dedicated to "finding ways to resolve these and other conflicts while ensuring that essential civil liberties are protected." Noting that the free flow of information is generally a positive thing, the EFF acknowledges that it also gives rise to many troubling questions:

How do we:

Protect children and undesiring adults from exposure to sexually explicit or potentially offensive materials?

Defend intellectual property rights?

Determine which country's laws have jurisdiction over a medium that is nowhere and everywhere at the same time?

Preserve privacy while still permitting recovery for harm?

Ensure that legislators, access providers, and network users do not stifle disagreeable speech?

Come to the EFF Home Page (http://www.eff.org) for the group's position papers and news flashes. The site solicits workers to assist with e-mail campaigns, sign electronic petitions, and call legislators on cyber-speak issues of the moment. It also operates an archives.

Computer Underground Publications is a database of *Computer Underground Digest* and other EFF electronic magazines (http://www

Philip Zimmermann: Cyberlaw's Poster Boy

Nothing unites a community—virtual or otherwise—like a common cause. On-line, in the summer of 1995, one of those causes was the Zimmermann Legal Defense Fund. At the center of the storm was Boulder, Colorado, programmer Philip Zimmermann, who became something of a cyberspheric folk hero after he was targeted in a 28-month federal investigation because of a program he wrote called "Pretty Good Privacy."

Names on the Net

Believing that computer users needed protection from government monitoring in order to communicate freely, Zimmermann in 1990 gave the telecomputing world the necessary tool. His free PGP software was an encryption program that allowed senders and receivers of e-mail to encode the text of their messages. The program uses a method called "public-key encryption": someone who wants to receive encrypted electronic mail puts a "public key" on the Internet. Anyone wanting to send a message to that person can use the public key to convert it into code. But the recipient has to have another key—a "private key"—to decode it.

After someone placed the PGP software on the Internet, it was quickly disseminated around the world, and that is when federal investigators got interested. The feds' problem with PGP was that export of high-quality encryption is illegal. In September 1993, the U.S. attorney's office in San Jose, California, notified Zimmermann that he was the target of a grand jury investigation, apparently trying to determine whether Zimmermann's work violated the U.S. export-control laws restricting shipment of cryptographic systems outside the country.

Within weeks, the world was aware of the federal government's interest in PGP. A legal defense fund for Zimmermann, who wrote *The Official PGP User's Guide* (MIT Press), was set up and managed by his lawyer, Phil DuBois. Zimmermann acknowledged that he was not the person who actually posted PGP for public use (though he was apparently the only person investigated), but that was not his defense. On the contrary, "I wanted PGP widely disseminated in the U.S.," Zimmermann told Jeff Ubois of *Internet World* magazine that fall. "I think that this raises First Amendment issues because the only way to comply with the law is to not publish it at all." Asked if he believed the First Amendment protects *encrypted* speech, Zimmermann said, "I should be able to speak to you in Navaho if I wanted, even if law enforcement can't understand Navaho. Can you imagine them breaking into a conversation and saying, 'Excuse me, we don't speak any Navaho. Could you please switch to English?'"

Philip Zimmermann (continued)

The free-speech implications of the case had the Net community talking, from the Cypherpunks home page (http://www.csua.berkeley.edu /cypherpunks/Home.html) to the Electronic Frontier Foundation (http://www .eff.org).

In early 1996, federal prosecutors suddenly dropped the investigation. In San Francisco, U.S. Attorney Michael Yamaguchi issued a statement saying his office declined to prosecute any individuals for

Names on the Net

posting the PGP program on the Net. William Keane, assistant U.S. attorney in San Jose, declined to comment on the reasons the government decided against pursuing the case, but told *The Wall Street Journal,* "This decision shouldn't be interpreted as meaning anything. I caution people against concluding the Internet is now free for export."

Reacting to the decision, attorney Shari Steele of the Electronic Frontier Foundation said, "We are so excited that the Justice Department has finally realized they don't have any facts to pursue this witch hunt."

And Curtis Karnow, a San Francisco intellectual-property lawyer who worked with Zimmermann's legal team, added, "It's very difficult to know what the government was thinking [when it dropped the case]." He said the prosecutor may have been "affected by Phil Zimmermann's folk-hero status. Thousands of people see Phil as a voice of conscience and someone who has dedicated his life to protecting people's rights."

Later, Zimmermann himself told The Associated Press, "I'm just really pleased that the sword of Damocles is not over me anymore, and I wonder why it took so long. This is not just for spies anymore. It's for the rest of us. The information age is here. The rest of us need cryptography to conduct our business."

.eff.org/pub/Publications/CuD/). Electronic editions of *EFFector,* the group's newsletter, are available at the site.

Here are three other noteworthy computer rights sites:

▶ Computer Professionals for Social Responsibility (http://cpsr.org /home), a nonprofit public-interest organization concerned with the effects of computers on society. The site links to numerous discussion groups around the Net on topics such as privacy, free

speech online, community networking, gender and minority issues, computer ethics, software piracy, hacking, and so on. It also
has a searchable archive of material.

▶ The Alliance for Public Technology (http://apt.org/apt/index
.html), a coalition of public-interest groups and individuals intent
on fostering broad access to affordable, usable information/
communication services and technology. The group believes that
new communications opportunities could improve citizens' health
care, educational opportunities, job availability, and more.

▶ Center for Democracy and Technology (http://www.cdt.org), a
Washington (DC) group that aims to develop and advocate public
policies that advance constitutional civil liberties and democratic
values in new computer and communications technologies. The
site offers links to breaking news stories and what-you-can-do-
about-it position papers.

CRIME, PUNISHMENT, VIOLENCE, AND ABUSE

Dr. Jeffrey L. Edleson, the principal investigator for the Minnesota
Higher Education Center Against Violence and Abuse, manages what is
perhaps the Web's most comprehensive clearinghouse of information
on violence and abuse.

The site (http://www.umn.edu/mincava/) points to literally thousands of gopher servers, interactive discussion groups, newsgroups, and
websites around the world. And it is a well organized series of topical
Web pages on child abuse, violence against women, sexual assault and
harassment, human rights abuses and genocide, personal stories, general reference materials, scholarly papers on violence and abuse, interactive news and discussion groups, and teaching resources.

From the Web, you can even get help in learning how to defend
yourself. For information on the general topic of violence, check out
the Assault Prevention Page (http://galaxy.einet.net/galaxy/Community
/Safety/Assault-Prevention/apin/APINindex.html). Sponsored by Personal Power Assault Prevention Training, this page can give you information on self-defense, martial arts, related topics, and recommended
reading. Of particular value are guidelines on choosing a self-defense
course, and safety tips. The site offers personal stories contributed by its

regulars, news and announcements of camps and programs, and crime statistics.

Domestic Violence and Violence Against Women

New Yorker Aliza Sherman is an ardent defender of women's rights and an expert on how to use a computer to combat domestic violence. Her SafetyNet page (http://www.cybergrrl.com/dv.html) assembles much of what she has learned so far.

On SafetyNet, you'll find a handbook on domestic violence compiled by Peace at Home (formerly, Battered Women Fighting Back) in Boston, as well as lists of important phone numbers: coalitions against violence, rape crisis centers in each state, and New York City shelters for battered women and their children. The page has recent statistics and bibliographies of books on domestic violence.

Sherman, whose personal page is called Cybergrrl! (http://www .cybergrrl.com), also has links to the Intimate Violence Internet Mailing List. The list's 400-members, across the country, range from medical professionals, counselors, and women's shelter workers to students and survivors of abuse. Discussions cover domestic violence and child abuse.

For different perspectives on the issue of domestic violence—including academic, medical, and journalistic contributions—look into these selected sites:

▶ Stop Violence Against Women (http://www.io.org/~irishg /mainpage.html), a public education campaign sponsored by the Body Shop and featuring inspirational and practical discussions on violence and prevention. Recent topics: "What Is Empowerment?" "Take Charge of Your Space," and "Don't Just Stand There. . . ."

▶ DV Resources (http://marie.az.com/~blainn/dv/index.html), Blain Nelson's collection of domestic violence resources. Includes material from *Academic Family Medicine,* and from some resources on men's issues. Personal stories from women and men involved in abusive relationships are narrated.

▶ Investigative Report on Domestic Violence (http://www.ultranet .com/newstandard/projects/DomVio/domviohome.HTML), a series

Off the Web

Prodigy Provides Home for DV Victims

Polly Johnston, who operates the "Domestic Violence" area of the Homelife Bulletin Board on the Prodigy online service, still shivers as she tells about an e-mail she got from an abused woman. "She never wrote anything on the topic," Johnston recalls, "because the Prodigy account was in her husband's name and she was afraid to write. But she read all the messages and drew strength from them, and that very day she was packing up and moving out."

The bulletin board (reached with the Prodigy jump word of HOMELIFE BB) discusses topics ranging from child-rearing to neighborhood relations. It launched the domestic violence message "folder" in 1994, shortly after the start of the highly publicized O. J. Simpson murder case. Originally, Johnston thought the online discussion would be temporary, but interest ran so high— more than 1,500 messages in just its first few months—that she made the subject a standing topic.

Regulars on the board have applauded that decision. Most abused women, they say, need something permanent, like the board, to cling to as they come to terms with their situation. Deborah Levenstein, clinical manager at the Women's Center and Shelter in Pittsburgh and a regular contributor to the BB, says the interactive, nonstop conversation of the Prodigy message board is exactly what most abuse victims need.

"We have found that support groups are usually much more helpful to victims of domestic violence than individual counseling. Part of this is the group validation of the woman's experience. A more important part . . . is to break the social isolation that is perhaps THE most basic dynamic in the process of victimization. Just as in other terroristic and hostage situations, this isolation is a powerful means of control, which is what domestic violence is all about. It is not about losing one's temper or anger management, but all about one person's attempt to control his partner."

of sixty articles on domestic violence published in *The Standard-Times* of New Bedford, Massachusetts.

▶ Boston University's Violence Site (gopher://software.bu.edu/11 /Things%20You%20Should%20Know/Safety%20Resources /Safety%20Issues/Domestic%20Violence), emphasizing violence against college women, and local Boston-area resources.

Child Abuse

More than a hundred years ago, William Thurston, president of the Bethlehem Iron Company, established an interim care facility for children in crisis in the firm's home town of Bethlehem, Pennsylvania. Later, a house and six acres of land were given by Captain James Wiley to set up a foundation that became known as "Wiley House."

Today, the same movement of support for ailing and abused children continues in cyberspace, in association with the Lee Salk Research Center, as KidsPeace: The National Center for Kids in Crisis (http://good.freedom.net/kidspeace/). The site provides information on research at the Lee Salk Center, as well as various advice to parents. The "Seven Standards for Effective Parenting," for example, are value, nurture, teach, discipline, and encourage your child; speak the truth, and never give up. The site also features "24 Ways You Can Prevent Child Abuse," "15 Ways You Can Help Your Kids Through Crisis," and "What Every Preteen Wants You to Know . . . But May Not Always Tell You."

A Kidspeace "Parenting Quiz"—with separate sections for parents of infants, toddlers, school-age youngsters, preteens, and teenagers—is intended to enable family members to learn more about each other. The quiz is designed to challenge parents' knowledge of how the needs of their children continually change as they grow. If the kids are present when the quiz is taken, the questions (e.g., How effective is fear in discipline? Where would you turn for help from outside the family in a child-rearing crisis?) might serve as what politicians call "talking points" around the dinner table.

For a variety of material from medical and educational sources, click on:

▶ Facts for Families (http://www.psych.med.umich.edu/web/aacap /factsFam), a set of nearly fifty fact sheets maintained by the American Academy of Child and Adolescent Psychiatry to provide recent material on the depressed child, teen suicide, stepfamily problems, child sexual abuse, and related issues. Available in Spanish and French as well as English, the materials give data on children and divorce, eating disorders, drug and alcohol abuse, children and grief, and autism.

Blain Nelson has collected much original material on domestic violence at his DV Resources website (http://marie.az.com/~blainn/dv/index.html). Noting that some people have difficulty determining whether they are in an abusive relationship, he offers these questions to help identify a victim:

Are you afraid of your partner?

Do you feel that you have to walk on pins and needles sometimes, to keep your partner from getting angry?

Has your partner ever hit, slapped, or pushed you?

Do you ever feel as though you deserve to be punished?

Do you ever feel that you've done something wrong but you can't figure out what it is?

Have you lost all respect or love for your partner?

Is your partner very good to you most of the time—sometimes down-right wonderful—but then, every once in a while, is very cruel or scary?

Does your partner drive you crazy or make you feel that you're going crazy?

Do you find yourself sometimes thinking of ways of killing your partner?

Have you believed that your partner would kill you?

Have you been told by your partner that he or she would kill you?

Has your partner threatened to commit suicide?

Were you abused as a child?

Have you been forced by your partner to do something you didn't want to do?

Have you lost all or most of your friends since you've been with your partner?

Do you feel isolated, as though there's nowhere to turn for help and no one would believe you anyway?

Have you lost a job because of your partner?

Do you feel that you have to say you're doing OK even when you really aren't?

Are you afraid to tell anybody about what's going on in your life because you don't want your partner to get in trouble or go to jail?

If these warning signs apply to you or someone you know, contact a domestic abuse center in your area. Numbers should be listed in your local phone book. If they're not, check with the local library's reference department, a newspaper, or the police department.

▶ National Center for Missing and Exploited Children (http://www
.scubed.com/public_service/missing.html), a database of known
information and pictures of missing children. The site is maintained around the clock and works in conjunction with the
missing children hotline, 1-800-843-5678. Visitors are asked
to view the online pictures of missing kids and, if they recognize any of them, to call the 800 number or send e-mail to
webmaster@scubed.com. The group asks that a picture of a recognized child *not* be redistributed, because of concerns for "the
feelings of parents who might have to deal with a deceased
child."

▶ Child Quest International (http://www.childquest.org), maintained by a nonprofit organization devoted to protection and
recovery of missing, abused, and exploited children. Child Quest
says it differs from other nonprofit groups in the field because
it uses new technologies: computer photo-digitizing of missing
children, age enhancement to current age, on-site scanning and
poster-making, and worldwide distribution of likenesses of missing
children and their alleged abductors. The site's Missing Children
section has these options: "Open Cases," an alphabetical listing of
all Child Quest cases; "Abductors," the names of those for whom
warrants have been issued; and "Sightings," a depository for information on any of the cases.

Sexual Assault

Chris Bartley, a computer science major at the University of Tennessee,
Knoxville, has built a substantial Sexual Assault Information Page
(http://www.cs.utk.edu/~bartley/saInfoPage.html) to provide comprehensive data for researchers, practitioners, and survivors, as well as an
electronic newsletter on the subject.

Among the topics covered on the Bartley page are: acquaintance
rape, child sexual abuse, crime victims' compensation, crisis centers, incest survivors, law, male victims, myths, offenders, prevention, references, ritual abuse, secondary victims, self-defense, sexual harassment,
and victims. The page has links to important resources such as the
Rape, Abuse and Incest National Network, which gives referrals to local
crisis centers; support groups such as SAVE (Survivors and Victims

POLITICIANS, PARTIES, AND POLICY

102

Empowered); and sites to assist in counseling, self-defense, and claims for victims' compensation in various states.

Other related sites include:

▶ University of Maryland's Sexual Harassment Resources page (http://inform.umd.edu:86/Educational_Resources /AcademicResourcesByTopic/WomensStudies/GenderIssues /SexualHarassment), which supplies information on sexual harassment, the laws related to sexual harassment, and recent examples such as the Tailhook case and the Anita Hill/Clarence Thomas testimonies.

▶ Stop Prisoner Rape (http://www.ai.mit.edu/people/ellens/SPR/spr .html), a collection of information on prisoner rape, mostly focused on male rape victims.

Prisons

The monthly Prison Legal News (PLN) (http://www.synapse.net /~arrak:s/pln/pln.html), published by prisoners, covers prison-related news and analysis from within the United States and around the world. Started in 1990 by Washington State prisoners Dan Pens and Paul Wright, the PLN concentrates on court decisions affecting prisoners and is intended for prisoners and their families. To fulfill its motto, "Working to Extend Democracy to All," the publication seeks to help prisoners and their supporters "to be a progressive force in developing a public policy debate around the issue of crime and punishment." Typical articles in recent online files were titled "Prisons Cause Crime?" "Problems Prisons Can't Solve," "Furlough Fears," "Mothers in Prison," and "US: World's Highest Rate of Incarceration."

The Prison Issues Page (http://www.igc.apc.org/prisons), which has an international slant, provides data on crime and prisons, news stories, and analysis of issues. The site, intended for both educators and activists, offers a range of breaking news stories as well as an "Urgent Action" feature that encourages e-mail, boycotts, and phone-call campaigns on specific cases around the world. The last time we were in the area, the page was calling for protest letters to Congress because disturbances at federal and state prisons in 1995 were due largely to Congress's refusal to equalize drug sentencing laws for possession/use of crack and powder cocaine. The site publishes an electronic newsletter on topics such as political prisoners, the death penalty, racism, and prison construction. To subscribe, send e-mail to majordomo@igc .apc.org and use as the text of your message: subscribe prisonact-list.

ENVIRONMENT

When French President Jacques Chirac decided in 1995 to resume nu-clear testing at Mururoa Atoll in the South Pacific, it was a shot heard 'round the world—at least via the World Wide Web.

Thousands of Australians stormed Chirac's e-mail address in Paris. (The address was supplied by AUSNet, one of Australia's biggest Internet access providers, and by local newspapers, which set up a protest page on the Web called "Your Say." AUSNet even created a form letter that Netheads could instantly send as e-mail to the French government, in either English or French.)

Within days, a company called Cyberpages International had set up, on a Web page, an ongoing straw poll to register online opinion. In the first months, about 95 percent of responses were against the re-sumption of testing. Cyberpages collated results every day and turned them into a colorful graph that represented votes per region. (The largest number of voters came from Europe—excluding France, which is in a separate category. Australia and New Zealand hosted the second largest group of voters, and North America was in third position. France was fourth, just ahead of Asia.)

In one month, three Japanese graduate students had garnered 20,000 electronic "signatures" from 79 countries on an e-mail antinu-clear petition. Yuichi Nishihara and two other Tokyo University students told signers they would submit the petition to the French Embassy in Tokyo on August 6, 1995, the fiftieth anniversary of the dropping of the atomic bomb on Hiroshima. The students said the largest number of signers—some 6,600—came from Germany; 1,500 were from the United States, and 1,300 from the Netherlands. Some 1,200 people responded from Australia and there were 1,150 responses from Japan.

The French foreign ministry, also present on the World Wide Web, obligingly provided a sample of the electronic mail it has received on the subject. "'Stick your bloody nuclear bombs up your president's xxxx,' reads one of the more colorful messages," reported the Agence France-Press International News Service.

Environmental issues have always held an important place in the hearts of the online global citizenry. Dozens of sites are maintained by international organizations such as Greenpeace, the relatively quiet Wilderness Society, and the radical Earth First movement.

Greenpeace International

It's been 25 years since Greenpeace organized in Vancouver, Canada. The original name ("The Don't Make A Wave Committee") was replaced but the goal is unchanged (to "bear witness" by "drawing attention to an abuse of the environment through their unwavering presence at the scene, whatever the risk, to non-violence and to independence"). The organization immediately grabbed international attention in its founding year when twelve members sailed a small boat into the U.S. atomic test zone off Amchitka, Alaska. They didn't stop nuclear testing, but they introduced the world to a force to be reckoned with on environmental issues.

Today, Greenpeace is an international organization with 43 national offices and 1,330 staffers in 30 countries. It runs a major website (http://www.greenpeace.org) to issue bulletins on abuse to the environment around the globe. Its current headquarters is in Amsterdam, The Netherlands.

This site has the latest news on Greenpeace's current campaigns, such as the voyage of its SV *Rainbow Warrior,* an effort to fight the contamination of fish oil by toxic chlorine chemicals, and to protest continued whaling in the Antarctic region. Photos and pamphlets, mailing lists, membership information, and extensive links to other environmental sites around the Net are available.

Econet

Greenpeace may be the best known name among the Net's environment resources, but larger by far is Econet (http://www.igc.apc.org /econet), the environmental network created by the Institute for Global Communications (IGC), the San Francisco group that also operates PeaceNet, ConflictNet, WomensNet, and LaborNet.

Econet offers original features and links to other Web resources on scores of environmental issues. Topics include: acid rain, agriculture and trade, biodiversity, climate, development, endangered species, environmental education, environmental justice and environmental racism, environmental law, forests, health, mushrooms and mycology, pesticides, population, sustainable development, toxic hazards and wastes, transportation, water (seas, oceans, and rivers), and wildlife.

The EnviroWeb

The EnviroWeb (http://envirolink.org:/start_web.html) goes beyond the usual links to *other* green Net sites by helping to develop several valuable online tools. For instance, it maintains a World Species List of plants, animal, and microbes; a Sustainable Earth Electronic Library devoted to publications that teach about preserving the earth's resources; and the Environmental Education Network, a multimedia clearinghouse for educational information, materials, and ideas.

The service, a product of the Pittsburgh-based EnviroLink Network, was created in 1991 by Josh Knauer, then a freshman at Carnegie Mellon University. From a simple mailing list of 20 student activists, it has grown to become one of the world's largest environmental information clearinghouses.

Other Environmental Sites

Various other ecological sites are more political; they concentrate specifically on wildlife preservation or seek visitors' direct participation. Here is a sampling to get you started with your own exploration:

▶ EarthWatch (http://gaia.earthwatch.org), dedicated to getting ordinary citizens involved in cultural and environmental research and to assisting scientists and scholars on projects ranging from coral reef surveys to public health studies. More than 40,000 citizens have participated since the Watertown, Massachusetts, group's creation in 1972. Its website provides a catalog of 150 scientific field research expeditions the public can participate in; they range from one week to three weeks. Destinations vary, from preserving public art in Venice to tracking timber wolves in Minnesota or

---

building solar ovens in Kenya. A search option enables you to locate expeditions by scientific discipline, time of year, geographic location, or your specific skills and interests. Reports on the findings of Earthwatch-sponsored research studies are available.

▶ Green Parties of North America (http://www.rahul.net/greens), where environmentalism gets a decidedly political spin. The site tracks environmental candidates through states and provinces in North America, letting voters know their backgrounds, position statements, platforms, and the like.

▶ Wilderness Society (http://town.hall.org/environment/wild_soc /wilderness.html), devoted primarily to public land protection and management issues. Founded in 1935, the group has these favorite topics: America's public lands, ancient forests of the Pacific Northwest, Arctic National Wildlife Refuge, California Desert, endangered species, the Everglades, forest fires and forest health, the Grand Canyon, the general mining law, grazing on public lands, National Park concessions, the National Wilderness Preservation System, the wetlands, and more.

▶ Environmental News Network (ENN) (http://www.enn.com), a regional news and information service that focuses on the environment. Since 1991, ENN has covered the Northwest and Intermountain regions in the states of Alaska, Colorado, Idaho, Montana, Nevada, Oregon, Utah, Washington, and Wyoming. The service provides hard copy and computer access, via the Internet, to national, regional, and local environmental news and information sources.

▶ Earth First! (gopher://gopher.igc.apc.org/11/orgs/ef.journal), a proudly radical environmental movement that says it is intended for those who "hate the smell of compromise" and "believe in using all the tools in the tool box, ranging from grassroots organizing and litigation to civil disobedience and monkeywrenching." The group has backed angry demonstrations and sit-ins against commercial logging, nuclear testing, and similar proposals. A few years ago, it took over the Office of Surface Mining in Columbus, Ohio, to protest what the group described as a strip mine in the nearby Wayne National Forest.

In 1986, a group of California activists started PeaceNet as a vehicle to link people and organizations working on related issues. The brainchild of several computer and nonprofit professionals in Palo Alto, California, PeaceNet sought to fill progressive organizations' need for efficient communications. The following year, the Institute for Global Communications (IGC) was formed to manage PeaceNet and the newly acquired EcoNet. IGC was dedicated to providing information and resources to individuals and organizations working in environmental fields.

IGC Brings Issues Online

Since then, IGC has added ConflictNet, an information and communication source for a network of people promoting the constructive resolution of conflict; LaborNet, to serve the trade union community; and WomensNet, to link people concerned with women's rights issues.

In the early 1990s, IGC, along with six international partners, cofounded the Association for Progressive Communications (APC), an international coalition of progressive computer networks. At this writing, it includes eighteen autonomous but affiliated members in Argentina, Australia, Brazil, Canada, Colombia, Ecuador, England, Germany, Mexico, New Zealand, Nicaragua, Russia, Slovenja, South Africa, Sweden, Ukraine, United States, and Uruguay. Additional "on demand" connections to the APC network can be made at over fifty other locations, from Austria to Zimbabwe.

IGC is a billed system (an individual account costs a one-time $15 sign-up fee plus a monthly subscription fee of $12.50 for six hours of network use; time over six hours is billed at the rate of $1 an hour). Organizers say the five networks combined link more than 11,000 members and an additional 20,000 activists and organizations via the APC membership. Local access to the IGC nets is available in more than 133 countries.

FEMINISM

Sarah Stapleton-Gray has played her strengths—a computer user, a free-lance correspondent for *TIME* Magazine, a working political activist—to popularize her favorite causes on the Net. The quality of her extensive Feminist Activist Resources on the Net, one of the first feminist sites on the Web, attracted the praise of *Boardwatch* magazine, the oldest and most respected publication focusing on telecomputing topics. Her work now has been incorporated as a page (http://www.igc.apc.org /women/feminist.html) on WomensNet, described below.

Stapleton-Gray's page can lead you to dozens of sites operated by women's organizations and established specifically as feminist resources, general activist sites, and sites intended for amusement and recreation. She and her husband, Ross, also manage the new home page of the world's best known feminist group, the National Organization for Women (NOW) (http://now.org). The NOW page offers extensive articles and position papers on abortion rights/reproductive issues, economic equity, electoral politics, global feminism, legislation, lesbian rights, racial and ethnic diversity, violence against women, and other subjects. It also links with NOW's online newspaper and points to related sites around the Net.

NOW has the more recognizable name, but a larger collection of feminist data is on WomensNet (http://www.igc.apc.org/womensnet), a site that recently joined the Institute for Global Communications (IGC). The San Francisco-based service is intended to promote the political, professional, and social concerns of women, by providing news, reports, and opportunities for discussion. The site can provide contact information on scores of women's organizations affiliated with WomensNet around the world.

The WomensNet site on the Web also has its own agenda. During the summer of 1995, for instance, the site was helping women organize for the Fourth World Conference on Women, in Beijing, China, by providing official United Nations documents and other material online, computer setup and support at preparatory events, and online planning forums. The site invites women around the world to participate in electronic conferences on health, the environment, human rights development, media, and similar issues.

Other Feminist Resources

One of the best lists of other Web resources on women's rights and feminism is compiled by Jim Mansfield, a technical officer at the Institute for Biodiagnostics, part of the National Research Council of Canada, in Winnipeg. Borrowed from Mansfield's Feminism and Women's Resources page (http://www.ibd.nrc.ca/~mansfield/feminism.html), this list shows the diversity of women's resources available on the Net. Here are its most accessed components:

▶ Virtual Sisterhood (http://www.igc.apc.org/vsister/vsister.html), Barbara Ann O'Leary's site dedicated to increasing women's access to and effective use of electronic communications. O' Leary offers advice on how to use electronic publishing tools, how to engage in online discussions, how to create an organizational presence on the Net, and how to encourage electronic volunteerism.

▶ Global Fund for Women (http://www.ai.mit.edu/people/ellen /gfw.html), the home page of an organization that is a major

Laura Doyle: Finding Fem Sci Fi

Inspired by Margaret Atwood's *The Handmaid's Tale* and Marge Piercy's *Woman on the Edge of Time,* Laura Doyle decided that what the World Wide Web needed was her Feminist Science Fiction, Fantasy & Utopia page (http://www.uic.edu/~lauramd /sf/femsf.html).

Names on the Net

"I looked around for a long time, trying to find other authors writing the same sorts of things," Doyle says. "Eventually I began reading some of the wonderful things written about feminist utopias, science fiction and fantasy. To this day I am still discovering the wealth of worlds that women (and woman-friendly men) have created" in that genre.

She adds that, although science fiction traditionally has been a male domain, the genre "offers unparalleled opportunities for feminists to explore societal configurations other than the patriarchal societies."

On her site, you can explore:

▶ Sociological thought experiments, "in which gender arrangement is a key factor in a society; societies that have been re-envisioned, such as utopias and dystopias," Doyle says.

▶ Biological thought experiments, "a gender re-envisioned from an individualistic perspective—sex changes, etc.—or biological—sex eliminated through evolution or genetic tinkering."

▶ Feminist retellings of myths, fairy tales, and folklore, "science fiction/fantasy that portrays strong women in nonconventional or nontraditional roles."

In the wake of the deadly bombing of the federal building in Oklahoma City, on April 19, 1995, the Women's Leaders Online (http://worcester.lm.com/women /women.html) launched a "Love Creates/Hate Kills" Campaign and circulated a "Civility Pledge" aimed at reducing the level of hatred and paranoia in contemporary political debate. Laurie D. T. Mann said, in an online statement, "While we recognize that legitimate political debate must permit the expression of diverse views—often with passion and strong disagreement—we must strive to find a balance between such feelings and the danger that disagreements on issues can cross a line where they become advocacy of hatred and invitations to violence. We must also find a balance between criticizing government policies and inventing conspiracy theories which feed the existing paranoia towards the government."

Group Urges "Civility Pledge"

The Civility Pledge reads:

I pledge to:

A. Refrain from using words in relation to those who disagree with me which:

—Go beyond civil disagreement on issues or criticisms of actions taken and actually encourage hatred or violence towards those who disagree with me.

—Dehumanize those who disagree with me.

—Impugn the motives of those who disagree with me without substantiating evidence.

—Conjure up vague conspiracies by those who disagree with me without substantiating evidence.

B. Discourage others of all political persuasions who advocate hatred and violence and unsubstantiated conspiracy theories by:

—Condemning these expressions when I become aware of them.

—Denying advocates of such views any forum which I control.

—Refusing to participate in forums controlled by hosts who advocate or encourage such expressions.

—Speaking out publicly against hatred, violence and political paranoia.

▶ Global Fund for Women (http://www.ai.mit.edu/people/ellen /gfw.html), the home page of an organization that is a major source of funding for a large number of women's groups.

▶ Voices of Women Home Page (http://www.voiceofwomen.com /VOWworld.html), known for *Power Tools for Visionary Women,* an electronic magazine devoted to "real women . . . telling their stories, discussing issues, sharing hard-won wisdom, and finding tools, inspiration and support." The magazine compiles lists of goods and services provided by women and urges readers to support them.

▶ Laura Mann's Women Leaders Online (http://worcester.lm.com /women/women.html), launched in early 1995 as a feminist response to the conservative "Contract With America" agenda. Within two weeks of its launch on the Net, responses came from more than 1,000 women who identified themselves as businesswomen, lawyers, doctors, nurses, ministers, teachers, scientists, computer programmers, administrative assistants, secretaries, film makers, women's advocates, union activists, social workers, and university professors, administrators, and students. The group has expanded to offer a media watch feature that reports on actions, opinions, and related resources. Laura Mann also provides Feminist Mailing List Website (http://www.lm.com /~lmann/feminist/feminist.html), which links to feminist and pro-choice sites in the abortion debate.

GAY AND LESBIAN RIGHTS

Homosexual activists have reminded us of an old lesson about hateful words: the intended targets of a pejorative can sometimes capture such a verbal bomb, turn it around, and effectively defuse it. In the online community, that is what has happened to the word "queers." Most of us grew up hearing that word as a hurtful slang synonym for gays and lesbians. But, starting in this decade, gay activists began embracing the term as their own, inviting colleagues and companions to join them in "The Queer Nation."

On the Net, where written words are the bricks and mortar (as well as the brickbats), the effort to defang this particular defamation has been particularly effective. Witness the success of the remarkable Queer Resources Directory (QRD) (http://vector.casti.com/QRD /.html/QRD-home-page.html).

Ron Buckmire founded QRD—an electronic library of news clippings, political contact information, newsletters, essays, and images of interest to the gay, lesbian, and bisexual community—in 1991 as an electronic archive for the then-new Queer Nation movement. These days, Buckmire, who holds a PhD in mathematics and works in Los Angeles, continues to audit quality control and user services, but the directory's daily administration is handled by David Casti, an information scientist in Washington (DC), and a half-dozen other volunteers.

QRD is a relatively new kind of resource on the Internet. Rather than being a single site or entity, it is an information system administered on four continents. Its communiqués range from news of upcoming events around the world to the history of the Queer Nation's "rainbow flag," which displays six stripes representing the colors of the rainbow. The flag was designed in 1978 by Gilbert Baker of San Francisco. "In 1989, the rainbow flag received nationwide attention after John Stout successfully sued his landlords in West Hollywood, when they prohibited him from displaying the flag from his apartment balcony." Covered in the directory are issues of family, coming out, youth and campus life, religion, health and sexuality (including safe sex and AIDS data), media (magazines, TV, movies), culture, history and origins ("what makes us unique, where we've been and where we come from"), news, politics, organizations, directories and newsletters, and links elsewhere on the system.

Other sites that show the diversity of gay/lesbian resources are:

▶ Michael Whitbrook's Information about the Queer Nation page (http://www.cs.cmu.edu/Web/People/mjw/Queer/MainPage .html), which points to sites devoted to gays, lesbians, and bisexuals, and to articles on politics, arts, hate crimes, scientific studies, news events, and the like. Whitbrook also provides links to *cmu-OUT*, a gay publication originating from Carnegie Mellon University, and photos and reports on recent protest marches and demonstrations.

▶ Information = Power.Queer Resource Center (http://www .actwin.com/queerindex.html), a collection of events calendars, reports for state organizations, images, AIDS data, and links to other sites. The site is especially strong in resources available in New England, with links to the Massachusetts Gay and Lesbian Political Caucus, the Harvard Gay and Lesbian Political Caucus, and Digital Queers of New England.

▶ Out.com (http://www.out.com), the electronic extension of *Out* magazine, a leading print publication of the gay/lesbian community. It features online forums inviting electronic visitors to comment on issues of the day. Also online are readers' forums for gossip and opinions, and an entertainment section for news on books, films, music, TV, and the Web.

GUN CONTROL AND THE RIGHT TO KEEP AND BEAR ARMS

Gun control is a lopsided debate on the Net. Proponents at the Center to Prevent Handgun Violence (http://bianca.com/lolla/politics/handguns/handgun.html) hold a lonely line against the National Rifle Association (NRA) (http://www.nra.org) and scores of other sites supporting firearms owners.

The Center features data from doctors, lawyers, researchers, law enforcement officers, teachers, entertainers, civic groups, and the media to make its case that gun violence is "epidemic" on many fronts. It uses the site to propose legal and educational solutions, to make proposals to the entertainment industry about lessening the glorification of violence, and to share contact addresses with electronic visitors, among other causes.

On the other side of the aisle, the NRA uses its Net presence to share an enormous collection of news reports, congressional bulletins, phone numbers, and advertisements of products (such as "the 2nd Amendment Research CD-ROM" and "transcripts of the congressional Waco hearings"). Another section includes text from NRA pamphlets (such as "How to Refuse to be a Victim"), information on state and federal firearms laws, status of federal legislation, firearm safety programs, and the like.

But, as often occurs on the Net, some of the liveliest websites are those operated by enthusiastic supporters, not the organizations themselves. Here is a sampling on gun control:

- Scott W. Ostrander, in Firearms and Liberty (http://www.cica
  .indiana.ed/hyplan/scotto/firearms/firearms.html), maintains a
  regularly updated guide to relevant Net resources—other websites, recent articles, pertinent sections of state and federal law,
  and related material.

- David M. Putzolu's Right to Keep and Bear Arms Page (http://
  sal.cs.uiuc.edu/rec.guns/rkba.html) offers some of the same links
  as Ostrander's site, plus articles on scientific studies of firearms
  in society, information about bans on firearms, philosophical arguments for and against firearms, and other pro-firearms docu-
  mentation.

- Bob   Dellicker's   Firearms   Page   (http://ramcad2.pica.army
  .mil:80/~rjd/guns) has extensive sections on firearms safety and
  sportsmanship.

- Jeff Chan's Firearms WWW (http://www.portal.com/~chan) includes tips on writing letters to editors, Congress, and others, and
  the status of legislation.

- Karl Kleinpaste's Firearms, Individual Rights, and Politics
  (http://www.cs.cmu.edu:8001/afs/cs.cmu.edu/project/nectar
  /member/karl/html/firearms/firearms.html) is especially strong
  in its assembly of magazine articles (such as "The False Promise
  of Gun Control," from *The Atlantic Monthly;* "The Value of
  Civilian Arms Possession as Deterrent to Crime or Defense
  Against Crime," from *American Journal of Criminal Law;* "The
  Second Amendment and the Ideology of Self-Protection," from
  Constitutional Commentary).

- James Bardwell, on a page called National Firearms Act and
  Other Gun Laws (http://www.cs.cmu.edu/afs/cs.cmu.edu/user
  /wbardwel/public/nfalist/index.html), maintains a huge collection
  of court rulings on firearms cases as well as graphics of various
  weapons.

- Patrick Fitzgerald's Right to Keep and Bear Arms Page (http://
  iquest.com/~fitz/politics/rkba) contains articles, essays, a picture
  gallery, and cartoons.

- Home pages for the Second Amendment Foundation (http://www
  .CCRKBA.org:80/saf.org) and the Citizens Committee for the

Right to Keep and Bear Arms (http://www.ccrkba.org) share a searchable database of articles and files relating to gun control. Among the resources are congressional phone and fax numbers, articles by *Gun Week* editor Joseph Tartaro and various pro-firearms civil rights activists, and press releases.

▶ Wayne Warf's Firearms Page (http://bronze.ucs.indiana.edu /~wwarf/firearm.html) gives the perspective of an instructor in basic firearms courses and emphasizes safety. Also offered is a thumbnail compilation of concealed-carry laws for all states and U.S. territories, texts of crime bills, and related legislation.

HEALTH MATTERS

Because there is an urgent need for specialized health information, the Internet now has literally thousands of sites devoted to general and quite specific topics of medical science. There are so many, in fact, that an entire book could be filled with links to health topics alone. For that reason, we won't even try to identify all the medical resources on the Net. Instead, we'll focus on the narrower subject of political and social issues as they relate to health, and direct you toward several major gathering points from which you can launch your own research for specific topics.

For general medical data, statistics, and situation reports from around the globe, nothing quite beats the World Health Organization Home Page (http://www.who.ch). Operating from WHO's Geneva, Switzerland, offices, the page features medical updates (such as the status of the battle against the Ebola virus, the latest travelers' health advisories, and upcoming health-related events), extensive collections of addresses and phone numbers around the world, databases of other Internet health sites, and general United Nations material.

For online connections to a specific hospital, check out the Hospital Web (http://demOnmac.mgh.harvard.edu/hospital.html). This site has an ambitious goal: to provide a simple and globally accessible way for patients, medical researchers, and physicians to get information on those facilities that have come to the Web.

For Information on drugs, visit the Pharmaceutical Information Network Home Page (http://pharminfo.com), which provides a drug

Georgia Griffith: An Online Original

Georgia Griffith teaches us much about the soul of this new medium. She's not a hardware or software guru nor does she have some magic formula for high-tech marketing. She has something more important: first-hand experience with the fundamentals of the Net: the actual data that fuel it, and the technology that can be a liberating factor in individual lives.

Names on the Net

For more than a decade, Griffith has been a mentor for tens of thousands of Net travelers on CompuServe and elsewhere, and she continues to be one of the hardest working and most admired information providers on the Net.

Griffith, a music educator by profession, came onto CompuServe in 1982. She helped out with a short-term computer experiment sponsored by a group of newspapers around the country. From that work arose the Issues Forum (GO ISSUES on CompuServe) which Georgia still manages today. The following year, Griffith launched another project that was especially important to her, the Handicapped User's Database (GO HANDICAPPED). HUD is an ever-growing collection of articles and reports that are of interest to subscribers with disabilities. Along with the HUD database, she operates IBM/Special Needs, which she coordinates with IBM.

Griffith has been the driving force behind many new CompuServe discussion forums, including the White House Forum (GO WHITEHOUSE), the National Political Debate Forum (GO POLITICS), the Religion Forum (GO RELIGION), and the Religious Issues Forum (GO RELISSUES).

Many people who communicate with her through any of these electronic enterprises never realize that Georgia Griffith has overcome her own severe obstacles to become part of this online world. Griffith has been blind since birth and she lost her hearing as a young woman. She was the first blind student at Capital University in Columbus, Ohio, and she graduated Phi Beta Kappa with a bachelor's degree in music. Since her first days on CompuServe, she has talked with the digital world through a device that alters modem data into a form of communication she can read like braille.

Griffith would be remarkable if her online work were the extent of her activities, but that's just part of her story. In 1971, through the National Braille Association, she became the Library of Congress's only proofreader of braille music. She also has worked with LINC Resources Inc., a Columbus, Ohio, nonprofit organization that assists educators in locating instructional

Georgia Griffith (continued)

materials and training resources. In 1990, Georgia Griffith was nominated as an Outstanding Woman of America, one of only 2,000 in the country, and she received a presidential citation for her work with the Library of Congress.

Names on the Net

Her friends are proud and amazed at her accomplishments, but Griffith has always taken them in stride. Not long ago, she told *CompuServe Magazine* the philosophy she has shared with online friends over the years: "Whatever your lot in life, build something on it."

information database as well as files on other pharmaceutical Net links, publications and science bulletins, reports from medical journals and conferences, and related data.

For data on issues relating to handicaps and disabilities, see Disability Resources (http://www.disability.com) from Evan Kemp Associates, a Capitol Heights, Maryland, firm that markets transportation, rehabilitation, and technical support services; sports equipment; and assorted medical supplies and products for disabled patients. Check out the "Disability Mall" (describing products and services designed for disabled persons) and the *One Step Ahead* newsletter for information and research. Features include "Washington Update," a summary of political actions; "Technology Watch," news of technical and medical developments in the field; and "Legal Briefs," interpretations of laws such as the Americans with Disabilities Act and the Individuals with Disabilities Education Act.

HOMELESSNESS

The growing number of public-access computers in libraries, community centers, and shelters is opening up the power of "home computing" even to those who don't have homes.

The Washington-based National Coalition for the Homeless (NCH) uses its home page (http://www2.ar:.net/home/nch) as a source

Few subjects stir the living as much as the dead—and how they got that way. For a growing number of people around the world, "quality of life" also has come to mean a "quality death." This view has led to open discussion of topics such as euthanasia and physician-assisted suicide, which traditionally have been unspoken terms in many parts of the world.

DeathNet Offers an Unflinching Look at the Last Days

DeathNet (http://www.IslandNet.com:80/~deathnet) is an international library specializing in all aspects of death and dying, "with a sincere respect for every point of view," says an online statement. A wide range of materials related to the legal, moral, medical, historical, and cultural aspects of human mortality are offered. Most are not readily available from any other source on or off the Internet.

Created by John Hofsess, director of The Right to Die Society of Canada, and Derek Humphry, founder of the National Hemlock Society and author of *Final Exit,* DeathNet provides the world's largest collection of "right to die" materials and services, and has gathered a wide array of information dealing with specific illnesses and severe disabilities, especially those that are life-threatening. The site provides links to medical libraries and other on-line services dealing with bereavement, care-giving, emotional support, and counseling. It offers advice on "living wills," palliative care, and various aspects of assisted suicide and euthanasia.

Transcripts of the 1995 Senate Special Committee on Euthanasia and Assisted Suicide, as well as the group's own statements to the senators, are available.

In what may be seen by some as morbid humor, the site lets you click on an icon to see the current estimated world population.

of information about homeless shelters around the country, and to raise public awareness with facts, figures, and stories from the streets. "What's it like to be homeless?" says the text accompanying one of the page's options. "Hear homeless people share their experiences. This page will feature different voices each month." Users can click on the selections to hear a homeless person telling his or her own story. NCH also provides data on current legislation and policy issues, the status of its many projects, details on new publications, directories of state and national homeless/housing advocacy organizations, upcoming events, and more.

Meanwhile, Dee Southard and Lynn Schaper have produced substantial homelessness archives (http://csf.Colorado.EDU/homeless) as part of a website operated by Communications for a Sustainable Future, a Colorado group founded on the idea "that computer networking should be used to enhance communications with the objective of working through disparate views and ideologies to secure a more promising future," according to an online statement. Started in January 1995, the Homelessness Page not only provides directions to major shelters and outreach programs around the world, but also supports the Homeless News Service (gopher://csf.Colorado.EDU:70/11/psn/homeless.HNS), called the first global news service for homeless newspapers (produced and sold by homeless and formerly homeless people). The Homeless List is an electronic mailing list on the subject to which you can subscribe by sending e-mail to listserv@csf.colorado.edu. The text of your message should read: "Sub Homeless [your first name] [your last name]" (with quotation marks, and with your name in the bracketed sections). A "Memories of Homelessness" option gives you first-hand accounts of what it is like to be without a home.

A site called 54 Ways You Can Help the Homeless, by Rabbi Charles A. Kroloff (http://ecosys.drdr.virginia.edu/ways/54.html), actually is an electronic book that can be read online. The book includes sections on volunteer organizations, how children can help, and how to get others involved.

HUMAN RIGHTS

Catherine Hampton grew up in El Paso, Texas, less than two miles from the Mexican border and Mexico's second largest city, Cuidad Juarez.

"Like most border cities," she says on her World Wide Web page, "Juarez was filled with very poor people who had left the countryside looking for a better life. They were prey to every kind of abuse, from harassment to false imprisonment to beatings to rape to politically motivated murder by authorities and others on both sides of the border with more power and influence than they had. I doubt I would

If any group is disenfranchised from cyberspace, wouldn't you think it would be the homeless? That's not necessarily so. For instance, in January 1996, 22-year-old Neal Berry was homeless, living along a highway near Novato, California, and spending his meager earnings on a portable computer and a cellular phone with modem, so he could stay online.

Homeless Man Stays Online

Berry said he'd rather sleep where he did—in a tent, on a mattress taken from a trash bin—than give up his laptop, which he used to connect to a bulletin board system, voice mail, and pager service, all paid for out of his $8-an-hour salary as a shipping and inventory clerk.

None of us might have ever heard of Berry if he hadn't gotten arrested on the charge that he stole heavy-duty industrial batteries from the state transportation agency to power his equipment. Highway workers said they found the batteries when they stumbled onto his campsite.

In a jailhouse interview, Berry told *The San Francisco Examiner* he chose to camp by the highway after failing to find an affordable apartment when he moved to the area in 1994. "In Novato," he said, "you can't even find a single room that costs less than $500 a month. If I were to have an apartment, I wouldn't have had any furniture, I'd just barely be able to eat. It would have sucked up all my income." So, instead, he spent $2,000 for a Toshiba laptop computer and $500 on a modem. Each month he spent $35 for an account with an online service that offered e-mail; $60 on his cellular phone bill; $50 for membership at a gym where he took showers; $42 for a storage shed for clothes and other possessions he was afraid to keep in the tent; and $12 for a mailbox. Online, he said, he made more friends in a month than he had all year.

He told authorities he was innocent of the theft charge. "I just found the batteries. Apparently someone else put them there a few months ago. I found them and started using them." But he wasn't fighting the charges. "I've never been to jail before, but there is a bright side: three hots and a cot at taxpayer expense."

Though sentenced to ninety days, he was released without bail after five days, and prosecutors recommended him for a program that will allow him to keep the arrest off his record as long as he stays out of trouble.

Later, he told an Associated Press reporter that as soon as his legal problems were cleared up, he would head north to Eugene, Oregon. "I'm

Homeless Man (continued)

going to move, find work, get a place and eventually save money and buy more hardware and software and books, so I can learn how to program," he said.

His online acquaintances had already taught him what career to be aiming for. "Not a programmer," he said confidently. "A network specialist. They make more money and they're more in demand."

have known such things existed from my own experience. It became part of my experience, though, and I've never since been able to take my freedom and lack of fear for granted." Those experiences also have motivated her to become the Web's best-known human rights advocate, through her Human Rights Web and her Amnesty International page.

Launching with a quote from W. H. Auden's "The Ascent of F6" ("Acts of injustice done/between the setting and the rising sun/In history lie like bones,/each one"), the Human Rights Web (http:// www.traveller.com/~hrweb/hrweb.html) offers data ranging from the basics ("What are human rights?" and "A Short History of the Human Rights Movement") to the details of what individuals can do to get involved, biographies of individual political prisoners around the world, and how concerned citizens can devote a block of time to working on behalf of specific people.

Closely allied to the Human Rights Web is Hampton's page devoted to Amnesty International (http://www.traveller.com/~hrweb /ai/ai.html), the 35-year-old group that is the grandfather of world human rights groups. Provided here are links to related sites around the Net, contacts, and much history (including a copy of the original newspaper article that inspired the formation of the group, "The Forgotten Prisoners: Appeal for Amnesty, 1961" which appeared in the *London Observer* in May 1961).

To see human rights issues from other perspectives, here are some other resources to consider:

▶ Solidariteitsgroep Politieke Gevangenen (Solidarity Group Political Prisoners) (http://www.xs4all.nl/%7Etank/english.htm), the three-year-old Amsterdam group that works globally on behalf of specific prisoners. Among its features is the Political Prisoners Page (http://www.xs4all.nl/%7Etank/prison.htm), with names and stories of people from around the world. While we were visiting the site, a major campaign called for the release of U.S. journalist Mumia Abu-Jamal, facing a death sentence in Pennsylvania in conjunction with the 1981 murder of a policeman. The page provided links to mailing lists on the protest as well as advice for writing e-mail and making phone calls in support of the accused.

▶ The Directory of Human Rights Resources (http://www.igc.apc .org/igc/hr), a ground-breaking, first-time collaborative effort by diverse human rights organizations to provide a central gathering place for news and for links to rights organizations here and abroad. For instance, when 36 socialists were arrested at a demonstration in South Korea in October 1994, the site reported on the international campaign to pressure the Korean government to release them, and gave ideas on how visitors could use e-mail to support the drive. Similar online efforts were invited later on behalf of Koigi wa Wamwere, described as an Amnesty International "prisoner of conscience," who was imprisoned in Kenya on a robbery charge that some say was politically motivated.

▶ DIANA, An International Human Rights Database (http://www .law.uc.edu/Diana). Intended primarily for scholars, the database offers connections to law school files and other information—documents of the United Nations, the Organization of African Unity, and the Organization of American States. Come here also for human rights bibliographies and lists of research guides to literature in the field of general human rights, women's rights, and international law relating to indigenous people's rights.

LABOR

When a strike by six unions representing 2,500 workers shut down the *Detroit Free Press* and the *Detroit News* in mid 1995, both sides turned to the Net to plead their case with the public.

Management attracted attention by producing an electronic version of its paper; the digital medium kept open the lines of communications with readers. But the strikers—including all those computer-savvy writers and columnists—also had a prominent seat in cyberspace. Their site used a corner of LaborNet (http://www.labornet.org/labornet) to provide regular updates and position papers from the picket lines. News from the union perspective, as well as editorials, columns, and interviews, filled the site for the strike's duration.

It's all in a day's work for LaborNet, the Institute for Global Communications' (IGC) clearinghouse for national and international trade union information. At its core is a massive collection of contact numbers (including e-mail addresses) for union organizations around the world, as well as details on publications and booklets, breaking news from union hot spots such as strikes and lockouts, a labor legislative tracking report, information on upcoming labor-oriented events and observances, and links to related sites around the globe. The network also hosts scores of ongoing electronic conferences on topics ranging from safety and health care to boycotts and women's issues.

For several years, LaborNet was cyberspace's only major resource for trade union information, prompting some to characterize official labor organizations as being computerphobic. However, in late 1995, Big Labor proved the critics wrong by embracing the Web in a big way.

Do you want to know how to form a trade union at your workplace? Or learn what companies and products the AFL-CIO currently is boycotting? Would you like to get organized labor's views on candidates in national elections, or find out how you can make your voice heard in Congress on issues ranging from workplace safety to the minimum wage? Are you interested in finding out how to train to become a union organizer yourself? These and other topics are explored on LaborWEB, the new home page of the AFL-CIO (http://www.aflcio.org).

Built around AFL-CIO News Online, the site has weekly updates on labor stories: the status of strikes across the country; contract negotiations; plant closings and layoffs; the latest labor-oriented legislation in Congress; and negotiations on job safety measures in various industries. AFL-CIO has 73 unions and 13.6 million members, from Actors Equity to the Communications Workers of America, the Steelworkers Union, and the United Mine Workers of America.

An "Organize" option gives you information from the AFL-CIO Organizing Institute, which has among its goals the recruiting and training of a new generation of union organizers. Click on here if you're interested in organizing a union where you work. You can fill out an on-line form if you are unsure of which union to contact; someone will get back to you by e-mail. Another online form enables you to apply for the institute's training program if you want to become a union organizer.

Elsewhere on the site, you can find links to specific unions on the Web, see a list of national boycotts sanctioned by the organization, and examine its press releases and policy statements on issues such as specific strikes, changes in international labor treaties, the trade deficit, and Affirmative Action.

MEN'S RIGHTS

David Throop's Men's Issues Page (http://www.vix.com/pub/men /index.html) covers topics as diverse as the male perspective on sexual harassment and the rights of fathers in divorce cases. Throop examines how the men's rights movement has run parallel with the feminist cause, and provides links to a wide variety of Net resources for legal information (custody, child support, harassment) and for social issues ("Friendships among Men," "Patriarchy and Male Dominance," "Romance and Relationships"), economic matters, veterans issues, and more.

Among other resources are:

▶ On behalf of FREE (Fathers' Rights and Equality Exchange), Brent Wellman operates a website (http://www.vix.com/pub/free /index.html) that provides information for single fathers, and campaigns, says an online statement, for fathers who "are willing and prepared to pay their fair share of child-support, and who wish only to be treated with respect, fairness, and dignity by the State, the Family Law System, and . . . society."

▶ The home page of the National Coalition of Free Men (http:// www.liii.com:80/~ncfm2), managed by Alistair Duguid and Tom Williamson, is devoted to examining "the way sex discrimination affects men." Offered are details about men who have been honored by the group for advancing its cause, suggested reading lists, and discussions of topics such as "How do those who organize university activities react to the women's movement?"

Dean Hughson: When Breaking Up Is Hard to Do . . .

A SUPPORT CENTER FOR THE DIVORCED, THE NEVER MARRIED BUT HURTING FROM A FAILED LOVE, AND THE SEPARATED. So reads the electronic shingle that hangs in front of Dean Hughson's online offices. But, to its many visitors, The Divorce Page (http://www.primenet.com/~dean) is simply the wayside website that hopes to "reduce the suffering and organize the help" that is available online. And to bring a few smiles, Hughson says. Beside one clickable icon, Hughson writes, "If you think that dreams alone will take care of your problems and you have a sound card, here is the theme from 'The Love Boat.'"

Names on the Net

"For those just joining the divorce crowd," he writes in another portion of the page, "may I be the first to welcome you to the back of the bus. It is terribly painful for many people when they first realize that they have entered this weird zone. You have paid your taxes, taken care of your families, worked your jobs, and been good citizens all of your life. When the gavel goes down, you all of a sudden become a 'second class citizen.'"

Hughson provides his own tips for those recovering from divorce:

Sleep.

Eat healthy.

Don't talk about it all the time.

Don't use alcohol and drugs to escape.

Get involved helping others in divorce.

Laugh.

Play with your kids.

He also suggests neat links around the system to help with some of these goals, especially laughter when "Dumping Your Lover Electronically." For those darkest-before-the-dawn moments, Hughson provides links and phone numbers for hot lines, advice resources, and other outlets to blow off steam.

▶ Fathers' Resource Center (http://www.parentsplace.com
/readroom/frc/index.html), operated by a nonprofit family service
agency in Minneapolis, says it takes a "moderate stance which is
pro-father but . . . not at the expense of women." Among its features
are the *Father Time* newsletter and links to other Net facilities.

▶ FatherNet (gopher://tinman.mes.umn.edu:80/11/FatherNet) is an
"electronic continuation" of "Family Re-Union III: The Role of
Men in Children's Lives," a 1994 national conference on family
policy moderated by Vice President Al Gore and cosponsored by
the Children, Youth and Family Consortium and the Tennessee
Department of Human Services. The resource includes transcripts of the conference proceedings; policy and opinion documents to inform users about the myriad of social, economic, and
policy factors that support and hinder men's involvement in the
lives of children; and related research.

MILITIAS

Soon after the bombing of the federal building in Oklahoma City, in
April 1995, many on the Net began turning to Brian Wright's
new Militia Watch (http://paul.spu.edu/~sinnfein/progressive.html)
for articles that explored possible connection to various extreme
right-wing paramilitary groups. Drawing material from such diverse
sources as the Anti-Defamation League, *Covert Action Quarterly*,
and Political Research Associates, the site seeks to trace the history
and background of the militias. That the material has a decidedly liberal slant (it is, after all, part of Wright's Left Side of the Web) is illustrated by titles such as "Armed Militias, Right Wing Populism and
Scapegoating," "Nazis, Militias, and the Abuse of History," and "Is
Idaho a State of Hate or Just Confused?"

On the other side of the philosophical fence is the Counter Revolution Resources Page (http://nyx10.cs.du.edu:8001/~nmonagha/arc
.html), which contains lists of books, journals, and videotapes that are of
interest to those in the militia movement, and information on shops and
mail-order outlets where they can be obtained. The site provides links to
discussion groups, background on "American Paleoconservatism," the
European "New Right," "Ethnic Nationalism," "Integrism," and what it

describes as "Counter Revolutionary Texts" (Confucius's "Analects," Plato's "Republic," Aristotle's "Nicomachean Ethics" and "Politics," Edmund Burke's "Reflections on the Revolution in France," G. K. Chesterton's "Orthodoxy," and José Ortega y Gassett's "The Revolt of the Masses").

PEACE AND CONFLICT RESOLUTION

PeaceNet (http://www.peacenet.apc.org/peacenet) is a source for information on issues ranging from disarmament to human rights; news and analysis on Middle East events; and actions in Bosnia, Nicaragua and El Salvador, and other global hot spots. As another strong link in the Institute for Global Communications (IGC) clearinghouse of Internet sites, the page is a repository for current information on economic justice, immigrant rights, the prison system, and indigenous peoples. It also shows the way to related sites that are devoted to military spending, accuracy in news reporting, hunger programs, and assorted liberal causes. Among the dozens of international organizations participating in the site are Amnesty International, the America-Israel Council for Israeli-Palestinian Peace, the Committee to Protect Journalists, Computer Professionals for Social Responsibility, the Electronic Frontier Foundation, the Latin America Data Base, the Middle East Children's Alliance, the Native American Women's Health Education Resource Center, the North America Congress on Latin America, the Washington Office on Africa, and the Worldwide Watch Institute.

The Institute for Global Communications ConflictNet (http://www.conflictnet.apc.org/conflictnet) takes a broader view of the struggle for peace. Its efforts are dedicated to promoting the constructive resolution of conflict at both individual and international levels. Working on a more scholarly basis than other resources, ConflictNet hosts discussions on critical issues in the field and current legislation, and conference and training activity. The site has links to The Carter Center (http://www.emory.edu/CARTER_CENTER), the Council of Better Business Bureaus (http://www.bbb.org/bbb), and the Institute on Global Conflict and Cooperation (http://irpsbbs.ucsd.edu/igcc/igccmenu.html).

CompuServe Covers the Crises

If you had met Don Watkins in early 1989, you would have thought he knew all there was to know about the potential of CompuServe. By then, he had not only been a subscriber for six years, but had also managed CompuServe's massive PC Users Network, a group of online discussion forums with active message boards and data libraries. Every day, he had a front-row seat to observe the power of this medium for solving problems. Forums, as electronic "clubhouses" that never close, bring together, from all over the world, people with common interests. Having spent a half-dozen years at the helm of some of the system's more active forums, Watkins thought he had a pretty good idea of the capabilities of online communications.

Off the Web

And then, late on Tuesday afternoon, October 17, 1989, the ground moved, bringing San Francisco its worst earthquake since the beginning of the century. Watkins, who lives in nearby Santa Rosa, California, will always remember that day.

"I was frustrated being so close to the earthquake, being unaffected and really unable to do anything to help without getting in the way of the professionals."

But, within hours, Watkins and others around CompuServe discovered there *was* something they could do to help—a job that was uniquely suited for the online community.

Much of San Francisco's telephone equipment had survived the quake, but phone service was stymied by a very human problem: the overworking of the long-distance facilities. At one point, as many as a million long-distance calls a minute were coming into the area, making it nearly impossible to get a call through. People in the quake area could make local calls, but could not make long-distance calls. Because CompuServe's local nodes had survived the quake in a lot better shape than the general Bay Area phone system, people online suddenly found themselves in an ideal position to serve the quake victims as a communications link to the outside world.

Soon after the quake, CompuServe subscribers in other parts of the country started posting public messages in various forums, offering to help quake victims in contacting relatives. California CompuServe subscribers who were unable to dial out directly on the overburdened long-distance lines could make a local call to the system. They were urged to leave notes for the volunteers, who then relayed any "Don't worry, I'm OK" messages to friends and families around the country.

CompuServe (continued)

Watkins, as a long-time manager of forums, saw the need for something more. Following some harried discussions with his contacts at CompuServe headquarters in Columbus, Ohio, on the morning after the quake, he helped to open a special Earthquake Assistance Forum and had it operating by noon that same day. The entire system was used to spread the word that this unique forum had opened as a central point for news reports, information on relief efforts, help in locating people, and details of transportation availability. For weeks to come, forum administrators stayed in contact with San Francisco area agencies and offered up-to-the-minute information on road closings, tips on getting emergency assistance, and so on. Eyewitness accounts of the damage and injuries were filed in the forum.

Off the Web

The Earthquake Forum also was a place for action. One forum visitor left a message saying he desperately needed to get to a particularly hard-hit area, but had found that roads were impassable. Seeing the plea, another forum visitor volunteered his own private plane and flew his fellow subscriber in, along with needed medical supplies and food.

The special forum's success surprised even the people at CompuServe. (Months after the disaster, noting that people in meetings were still talking about it, one in-house wag reportedly printed up lapel buttons that read: "The Earthquake Forum was *my* idea.")

Sharon Baker was a product manager at CompuServe at the time of the quake. "We learned a lot," she said later, "about providing service to members during a disaster. It was amazing how everyone pulled together."

And that lesson is the Earthquake Forum's legacy. The special forum stayed online only a few weeks (it was taken down after things started getting back to normal in the Bay Area), but the idea lives on. CompuServe still routinely establishes special forums and news features in times of emergency (the Persian Gulf War in 1990–1991, the breakup of the Soviet Union in 1991, and the Los Angeles riots in the spring of 1992 all prompted the temporary establishment of special forums to help share the information). It has also created a more permanent Global Crisis Forum (GO CRISIS) devoted to discussion of the world's trouble spots and disasters. (Sadly, it never seems to go begging for material.) The administrator is Atlanta writer/software designer Shel Hall, a veteran online personality. He learned the ropes in the Earthquake Forum, the Persian Gulf Crisis Forum, the Soviet Union Crisis Forum. . . .

Other resources with similar purposes are:

▶ DiploNet (http://www.clark.net/pub/diplonet/DiploNet.html), a network that focuses on the needs of diplomats in the post-Cold War period. Topics include conflict management and resolution, peacemaking, and multilateral diplomacy.

▶ Non-Violence International (http://www.igc.apc.org/ni), devoted to assisting individuals, organizations, and governments "striving to utilize nonviolent methods to bring about changes reflecting the values of justice and human development on personal, social, economic, and political levels." The group maintains a databank and publishes a directory of nonviolent action trainers. The trainers have provided strategic and tactical assistance for nonviolent campaigns and movements around the world.

RACE RELATIONS AND ETHNIC MINORITIES

The Net is rich in paradox. The epitome of anonymity, it can also be a remarkably intense personal experience. (Who doesn't drive these digital highways without eventually thinking that he or she owns the road?) The Net is at once homogeneous and the ultimate modern expression of diversity. Is it a computerized *universe* ("all" becoming "one") or some emerging "multiverse" ("all" becoming, well, still more)? Also paradoxical is the fact that, in the Net's uni/multiverse of bits, race is often a nonissue (online prejudice is more likely centered on computer know-how, hardware selection, and pro- and anti-Microsoft issues); yet, the Net is especially ripe with race-related pages. One website is intended as a celebration of multiculturalism. The Diversity Page (http://latino.sscnet.ucla.edu/diversity1.html) is one-stop shopping for finding links to resources serving African Americans, Asian Americans, Latinos, and Native Americans. Other major starting points are detailed in the following sections.

African Americans

Two years ago, members of the Black Graduate Students Association at the Georgia Institute of Technology found it very difficult to locate

Internet resources about and for African Americans. What was needed was a central gathering place where people around the world could obtain information and contact others who had similar interests and concerns. The students decided to fill the void themselves.

The result, the Universal Black Pages (UBP) (http://www.gatech.edu/cgi-bin/ubp-find), is among the Net's most extensive resources for topics related to the African diaspora. Subsequent links have reached diverse sites relating to Abayudaya Jews in Uganda, Africans in Nova Scotia, the Brazilian cities of Bahia and Salvador, Caribbean towns, Grenada, Guyana, Kenya, the Netherlands, the Virgin Islands, and Bermuda. Topics covered include schools and student organizations, professional organizations, fraternities, sororities, and living conditions. Groups are dedicated to engineering, science and technology, educational opportunities/activities, businesses, written and spoken word, music, art, history, entertainment, and the like. The UBP, seeking to help educate its visitors on how to navigate the Net, urges them to report back with any new discoveries that ought to be added to the pages.

For a more personal approach to black culture on the Net, check out Tamara Pearson's African American Haven (http://www.auc.edu/~tpearson/haven.html). A student at Spelman College in Atlanta, Pearson offers details on resources for business and culture. But she also shares a picture of her Jetta ("Isn't my car beautiful?!") and lists her descriptions of various places she's lived, including Boca Raton, Florida, and Greenwich, Connecticut. Many other sites emphasize news and politics; her pages include links to resources on African American history and art.

For other academic, journalistic, and international perspectives, here is a cross-section of other sites:

▶ African American Interest (http://www.earthlink.net/~anthony/african.html), featuring an extensive links collection, many on-line entertainment resources, college-related material, and graphics arts data.

▶ Afro-American (http://www.afroam.org/afroam/), the electronic edition of Baltimore's famed newspaper, which has been serving the black community for more than a century. Chairman/publisher John J. Oliver Jr. says he hopes to use the site to share digitally some of the paper's extensive black history data.

ONE began life as an oversized bimonthly tabloid print publication distributed in the Washington (DC) area. Intended for a young adult black audience (or as a "generational response" to existing black-oriented newspapers and magazines, according to an introductory statement), ONE promised to be a forum for black arts, politics, news, and culture—a publication primarily for a younger generation of African Americans.

ONE: Up from Print

The last print issue of the journal appeared in June 1994, before ONE was reborn online. It now is available only on the Net (http://www.clark.net/pub/conquest/one/home.html). "We did it for several reasons," says editor/publisher Eric Easter. "The rising cost of paper; a desire to expand the audience; and many others. Most of all, we were disturbed at the relatively low numbers of African Americans and other minorities who are taking full advantage of the opportunities which this technology offers. One of the reasons is the lack of information targeted specifically to the audience."

Issues typically include "think pieces" ("Afrocentricity: What it is/What it ain't . . ."), commentary ("The ACLU's South Carolina chief gives his view on the Oklahoma bombings"), and arts reporting ("Designing in Color: Black architects want to leave their own mark"), as well as links to other Net sites of interest.

"It was quite a leap of faith for us to cease printing the magazine and focus on this format exclusively," publisher Easter says, "but we think it was worth it." He notes that one obvious impact of the relocation to the Net has been the increasingly *international* flavor of the content. For instance, a "One World" section has been added to contain a "Letters from . . . " feature, inviting writers from throughout the African diaspora to discuss issues. In the January 1996 issue, for example, Regina Helen Boone, a black teacher in Japan, wrote a letter from Osaka about the mission to challenge racial stereotypes, and Olive Vassell, a Briton living in America, wrote her observations on the relationship between black Americans and black foreigners.

▶ Black/African Related Resources (http://www.african.upenn.edu /African_Studies/Home_Page/mcgee.html), Arthur R. McGee's site assemblage, with special attention to scholarly interests. Among the highlighted resources are those relating to ethnic/ intercultural relations, international development, global networking, and social/progressive activism. Many of the technical resources will be of interest particularly to students and researchers.

▶ News Briefings from the ANC (http://minerva.cis.yale.edu /~jadwat/anc), maintained by New Yorker Omar C. Jadwat, a recent Yale University economics graduate who, at the time of this writing, was in Johannesburg looking for a job. His site provides material from South Africa's African National Congress by headline, sorted by date or by article length. The data, compiled from South African press agencies, range from reports on an accident at a gold mine in Klerksdorp to an address by President Nelson Mandela to an inter-faith commission, coverage of an ongoing trial of suspects in a bombing incident, and actions of the country's National Assembly.

Latin Culture

Chicano/LatinoNet (CLNET) (http://latino.sscnet.ucla.edu) was begun at the University of California merely to bring together Chicano/Latino educational research for a linguistic minority. CLNET has evolved into a general Latino-focused Internet site serving all segments of the community. At its heart is a library of information on the leading Latino research collections, archives, and specific reference resources. It also serves as a gateway to the online catalogs of major collections that contain Latino resources, information on Latino publishers and bookstores, and related electronic publications.

Features are the CLNET "Museum," which contains various exhibits on art, murals, music, cultural customs, and other artifacts, and the "Community Center," offering directory information on community and national Latino organizations, demographics on major Latino urban areas, and information about services and resources for education, environment, housing and community development, transportation, insurance, labor resources, social services, cultural customs, and legal services. Employment opportunities and academic position openings also are listed.

The University of Texas at Austin offers the Latin American Network Information Center (http://info.lanic.utexas.edu). The site, managed by the Institute of Latin American Studies, provides links to international sites in Argentina, Barbados, Belize, Bolivia, Brazil, Chile, Colombia, Costa Rica, Cuba, Dominican Republic, Ecuador,

El Salvador, Guatemala, Guyana, Haiti, Honduras, Jamaica, Mexico, Nicaragua, Panama, Paraguay, Peru, Suriname, Uruguay, and Venezuela.

Native Americans

Marc Becker, at the University of Kansas, launched Native Web (http://kuhttp.cc.ukans.edu/~marc/native_main.html) to connect America's native people to a growing number of Net resources. Data are organized in terms of nations and peoples, geographic regions, and subject categories. In addition, the site has material on native literature, language, newsletters and journals, organizations, and the like. Other resources are dedicated to art, music, families, communities, youth, elders, women, the environment, culture, history, education, and health.

Native Web provides information and online links to a number of tribes, councils, and organizations: the Affiliated Tribes of Northwest Indians, and American Indian and Alaskan Native Network Information Systems. Other links connect with data about the Anasazi, United Keetoowah Band of Cherokee Indians in Oklahoma, Costanoan-Ohlone Indian Canyon Resource, Lakota Wowapi Oti Kin, Mashpee, Mapuche, Maya, Mohawk Nation, Navajo and Hopi issues, The Oneida Indian Nation of New York, Shoshone, and Zapatistas.

Other resources include:

▶ Electronic Pathways, Native American Internet Information (http://hanksville.phast.umass.edu/defs/independent/ElecPath /elecpath.html), Karen M. Strom's effort to create an Indian infrastructure on the Net. It provides details on councils, related links, contacts, and "mentors."

▶ Center for World Indigenous Studies Information (http://www .halcyon.com/FWDP/cwisinfo.html), the Web page of a nonprofit research and education organization "dedicated to wider understanding and appreciation of the ideas and knowledge of indigenous peoples." The group operates The Fourth World Document Project to archive the papers and documents of tribal governments and research organizations' work on the social, political, strategic, economic, and human rights situations faced by indigenous people. Thousands of historical documents from tribal and intertribal groups reflect important decisions and issues in the

Native Americans' efforts to regain sovereignty, strengthen tribal cultures, and build economies. The site preserves hundreds of documents from native peoples in the Americas, Africa, Asia, Europe, Melanesia, and the Pacific. They include essays, position papers, resolutions, organizational information, treaties, United Nations papers, speeches, and declarations.

Asian Americans

Asian American Resources (http://www.mit.edu:8001/afs/athena.mit .edu/user/i/r/irie/www/aar.html) should be your first stop if you're looking for links, events, connections, electronic magazines, and other material of interest to the Asian community. The page was brought online in 1994 by Brian Yamauchi, a member of the Asian American Graduate and Professional Organization. Since then, it has been passed to Robert Irie, a graduate student at the artificial intelligence laboratory at the Massachusetts Institute of Technology.

Covering topics as diverse as Asian movies and arts, business opportunities, and religion, the site also provides links to specific organizations such as Brown University Korean Students Association, the Filipino Club of Honolulu Community College, National Asian American Telecommunications Association, and Ohio State University Asian American Medical Student Group.

For fact-gathering, see the page's links to the Anti-Asian Violence Page, the Asian American Census Statistics, reports on Asian American small businesses, and, from the University of California's Asian American Studies Center, reports on political and social trends in the community.

The site invites calls for action. The last time we were in the digital neighborhood, the Asian American Legal Defense and Education Fund was seeking volunteers to assist in weekly naturalization clinics, voter education workshops, and translation services. Online applications were provided for those interested in helping out.

PART II

CYBERCIVICS
DATA TOOLS

Chapter 5

Power Up

Getting Government Data, Locally and Globally

Driving in Washington (DC) used to be an excellent metaphor for the federal government. Trying to navigate the city's thicket of narrow, one-way streets, or just plotting a course along the spokes of its dizzying circular design seemed to foreshadow the frustration that awaited anyone who had come to town to try to get some information from the government bureaucracy. But no more. Capitol Hill now connects with a superhighway of data and hypertext links. Nowadays, you can rocket around a cyberspace version of the nation's capital. Traffic jams on the arteries of information are not as likely as they are on the asphalt and concrete ground routes.

For long-time Washington watchers, this new accessibility takes some getting used to. No one could ever say our federal government was built for speed, so it was a surprise when Washington rapidly embraced the Web. It took less than two years for virtually all of the U.S. government to get online. First came the White House, in late 1994. The House of Representatives followed soon after the midterm election. By the beginning of 1996, the U.S. Senate had opened its site. And today, as you read these words, each branch of the federal government is accessible through a modem call to the Internet's World Wide Web.

Will the Internet be a cure for government bureaucracy and put an end to official obfuscation in our lifetime? Of course not!

Government agencies and political entities have hundreds of years' experience in manipulating information. Innovations in computer technology, no matter how earth-shaking they are, will not make our leaders suddenly forget everything they've learned about putting their best spin on the data they are sharing with us. On the contrary, the Web will make them even better at creating a good spin. Wired Washington already is using cool and pretty home pages to display its facts faster and more smoothly than ever before. Individual members of Congress and entire federal departments have learned to use the Net to put the best face on their accomplishments, to downplay their failures, and to dramatize The Challenge That Lies Ahead.

But the digitizing of the District of Columbia has put more power in *your hands*. This chapter starts by examining the online offerings of the federal government's three branches—the executive, the legislative, and the judicial—and then shows you how you can use your computer connections to your best advantage. These are the four goals you can expect to achieve.

1. *Get the facts*, including copies of proposed legislation. Suppose you work at a utility company whose profits could be affected by a proposed new environmental law. In the "old days" (the era that ended about two years ago), just getting a copy of a Congressional bill was a hassle. You had to call your Senator's or Representative's office and hope to be able to talk someone into putting some printed pages into an envelope and mailing them to you. By the time the package finally reached you by U.S. Mail, the text could be outdated because the bill went through revisions until a compromise version emerged from subcommittee hearings. These days, the Web gives you copies as quickly as you can make your printer print, *and* it enables you to follow a bill's progress through the entire legislative process. You can stay up-to-date on where a bill stands in the House or the Senate, through all its revisions, right up to the time it arrives on the president's desk.

2. *Check the facts*, by getting multiple documents for comparison. The problem with political animals is that they learn to speak out of different sides of their mouth. If you live in a town that is economically dependent on, say, a military base or a major government contractor, you know how frustrating it can be whenever the talk in Washington turns to cutbacks and closings. Now, through the Net, you can sort out the

facts from all the rumors that will inevitably float around your town. Online search options specially geared for government documents let you find all recent statements that even *mention* a specific business or military base. Thus, in one sitting, you can see precisely who's proposing what.

3. *Put government databases to work,* on *your* projects. As federal departments have come onto the Web, they have introduced interesting tools for solving myriad problems, from finding a nine-digit zip code or a telephone area code to searching by keyword or phrase through the entire collection of federal laws or recent court decisions, or getting help with preparing a tax return. Most of this chapter focuses on The Big Picture—the White House, the Congress, the courts, and the scores of federal departments, commissions, and agencies. But we also take time out for some interesting side trips. Utilities you discover along the way may become some of your favorite Net resources.

4. *Reach out beyond the feds.* Uncle Sam's alightment on the Web, the big Internet story of recent years, has overshadowed local and state governments' discovery of cyberspace and the fact that the international community has become modem literate as well. At the end of this chapter, we'll look at what's happening in governmental sectors of the cybersphere that lie *outside* Washington's Beltway.

This chapter also launches Part II of our cyberspace journey. We'll begin here to locate the educational and research "data tools" that you can rely on long after the current campaign rhetoric is archived. The sites discussed in this chapter are valuable for students of *all* ages, whether they're still in school or not. The president's cabinet departments are among the nation's top fact-gatherers on subjects ranging from crime and punishment to international affairs, economics, employment, and environmental issues. If you want the latest statistics and news on topics like these, the links you'll meet in this chapter stand ready to serve you.

Finally, *empowerment* is the "in" word during the political campaigns of the 1990s, as if we must wait for this candidate or that platform to grant us political clout. In a free democratic society, voters empower themselves, and, for those of us with access to the Net, the empowerment begins with powering up the computer. Wouldn't Thomas Jefferson have *loved* the Modemocracy, where ordinary citizens have ready access to government information, activities, and assistance! It is fitting that one of the hottest grassroots power tools online has been named in Jefferson's honor. Using the Library of Congress's slick new Thomas system, we can search the *Congressional Record,* get Congressional reports, track pending legislation, and receive within seconds the full text of bills being debated in either Capitol chamber. In imitation of Thomas, other branches of the federal government—and other levels of government—are racing to achieve an equal range of searchability.

GILS and the Mandate for Data

"Every year, the federal government spends billions of dollars collecting and processing information (e.g., economic data, environmental data, and technical information). Unfortunately, while much of this information is very valuable, many potential users either do not know that it exists or do not know how to access it. We are committed to using new computer and networking technology to make this information more accessible to the taxpayers who paid for it."

So says the Paperwork Reduction Act of 1995, a mandate for new federal databases. Out of this mandate has come a directive (from the Office of Management and Budget) for the Government Information Locator Service (GILS) (http://info.er.usgs.gov/gils/index.html), and related servers (the Defense Department's DefenseLink, and the Commerce Department's Commerce Information Locator Service (CILS), for example) intended to help with finding federal facts and figures.

GILS is still in development at this writing. Its designers' goals are: to identify and describe information resources throughout the federal government, and to provide assistance in obtaining specific information. As a supplement to other government and commercial information dissemination mechanisms, GILS will use international standards for information search and retrieval so that information can be accessed in a variety of ways.

The site also is intended to provide online training; to show electronic visitors how to use resources that have "samplers"; and to illustrate the use of GILS to retrieve federal, state, and international information for various sites around the Web.

Some day, a future generation enjoying the full benefits of the innovations that are now underway may think that the government has *always* worked this smoothly.

THE PRESIDENT AND HIS EXECUTIVE BRANCH

In 1992, the Clinton Administration inherited an in-house computer communications system that lagged behind the equipment that moderately technoliterate high school students were using at that time. Two years later, the newly wired White House was the cover story of tele-computing's prestigious *Boardwatch* magazine. The article proclaimed the executive branch's hot new home page on the Internet's World Wide Web "simply superb in all respects." Editor/publisher Jack Rickard commented: "Given the boost the entire Internet and the Information Superhighway concept received when Vice President Gore got behind it a bit, we have to believe the addition of a White House web server will signal most of institutional America to get a website up or be left out of the information age."

Unveiled in October 1994, Welcome to the White House: An Interactive Citizens' Handbook (http://www.whitehouse.gov) is ready with information about the president and vice president and their families, schedules, policy statements, speeches, photos, and transcripts of daily press briefings, as well as the full text of more than 3,000 documents. (The Report on the National Information Infrastructure may be a good starting point for perusing the documents.)

Taking reporters on a "virtual tour" by keyboard at the page's rollout, Vice President Gore described the site as an attempt to further cut government costs and red tape.

Whether you're researching topics on agriculture or on veterans affairs, the White House page will give you fast, easy links to all fourteen Cabinet-level departments and more than two dozen independent agencies. Subject-searchable indexes of federal information have been compiled. The site's "White House Virtual Library" invites visitors to enter a term or phrase in order to search the White House press releases, scripts of the president's Saturday radio addresses, captions of online photos, and other federal Web pages. Come here if you're looking for information on how to start and finance a small business, get a

White House Forums Featured on America Online, CompuServe

Months before the White House website opened its doors, the Clinton Administration's technocrats were haunting the commercial services, especially CompuServe and America Online (AOL). (Both still have active White House forums.)

Off the Web

On AOL, use the keyword WHITE HOUSE to access press statements issued by the White House Office of Media Affairs, and discussions with other visitors about Clinton Administration issues. The forum contains transcripts of all of Clinton's speeches plus his remarks at special meetings and summits and during TV and radio appearances. Also included are the transcripts of White House press briefings and statements on important issues. At this writing, the forum had five message boards—(1) "Domestic Policy," (2) "The Economy," (3) "Foreign Policy," (4) "Social Issues," and (5) "The Washington Scene"—and two download libraries: (1) "From the White House," which contains longer-text documents and recently released White House files, and (2) the "Information Exchange," which allows AOL members to carry on their own discussions about national issues and the Clinton Administration.

On CompuServe, enter GO WHITEHOUSE to reach the forum devoted to the Administration's policies and activities. The only files permitted in the forum's libraries are those provided directly by the Office of Media Affairs for the White House. Message sections exist for each cabinet post and responsibility. CompuServe members can exchange information and opinions with each other on a broad range of topics, including international and United Nations activities, the budget deficit, housing and urban development, and education.

farm loan, apply for a federal job, or learn about Medicare, retirement, or veteran's benefits. With the "Publications" option, you connect to material that you can browse or search by keyword. Documents in this section include briefings on specific topics such as economic policy, environmental policy, foreign affairs, jobs, health care, and science and technology. The White House page also offers some chuckles, such as Gore's gallery of self-deprecating political cartoons.

Arguably, the White House was the first big hit on the Web's political wing. In the first eighteen months after its 1994 opening, it hosted more than 5 million electronic contacts, and some 200,000 visitors took time to "sign" the online electronic guest book.

Responding to criticism that virtual touring of the White House left some of the younger visitors cold and disinterested, the president's advisors expanded the program and created a new White House for Kids site (http://www.whitehouse.gov/WH/kids/html/home.html) in early 1996. Meant for elementary-school-age children, the new site has sections on the history of the First Family's official home, and other children who have lived there, beginning with Tad Lincoln. Another highlight is the "First Pets" that have lived on the premises. Articles written for children cover basic economic issues such as the deficit and banking in general. A digital rendering of Socks, the first cat, greets new arrivals. Socks leads them on a tour and encourages them to send electronic mail, directly from the site, to the president, vice president, and first lady.

Department of Agriculture

Abraham Lincoln created the U.S. Department of Agriculture (USDA) in 1862, characterizing it as "the people's department" because, in those days, 90 percent of the nation's population lived and worked on farms. Lincoln said he needed the USDA to "acquire and to diffuse among the people . . . useful information on subjects connected with agriculture in the most general and comprehensive sense of the word." Today, the department still supports productive farming and ranching, but, with only 2 percent of the population living on farms, the focus has changed dramatically. The USDA is responsible for environmental and land-use issues, food safety, the well-being of rural Americans, domestic marketing of food and other farm products, increased exports, biotechnology and other research, and food assistance to those who need it.

On the Agriculture Department's home page (http://www .usda.gov/) are details of the text and status of farm bills, guides to farming resources online, press releases, fact sheets, backgrounders, relevant speeches, and information related to agriculture in the United States. Publications about USDA and its programs, media events, and periodicals also are available. "A Topical Guide to Agricultural Programs," an alphabetical index to USDA offerings, provides an easily searchable database. To contact a particular person at the department, click on "How to Get Information from USDA," which lists specific phone numbers, addresses, and e-mail addresses for key personnel in the department's Office of Communications.

History buffs should note the page's gallery of historical photos and an overview of milestones in the department's history.

Department of Commerce

The U.S. Department of Commerce, considered by many to be the most versatile agency in the government, has promoted American business and trade since 1903. Its responsibilities cover a broad spectrum: expanding U.S. exports, developing technologies, granting patents, disseminating statistical data through the Census Bureau, measuring economic changes, promoting minority entrepreneurship, and predicting the weather through agencies like the National Oceanic and Atmospheric Administration and the National Climatic Data Center.

The Commerce Department's page (http://www.doc.gov) provides an online calendar of significant Commerce happenings, news reports, press releases, conference announcements, and speech texts. Details on the federal budget, the Economic Conversion Information Exchange, and the Information Infrastructure Task Force can also be researched here.

More importantly, this is the hub for links to the home pages of all key Commerce divisions. They are among the most influential agencies in American business and society.

▶ The Bureau of Export Administration oversees exports of goods from the United States. Come here for information on licensing, export seminars, and hotline numbers for reporting illegal export activities.

▶ The Economics and Statistics Administration includes the Bureau of the Census and other fact-gathering agencies. Among them are business statistics units such as STAT-USA (formerly the Office of Business Analysis) and the Bureau of Economic Analysis.

▶ The Economic Development Administration is a source for grants to nonprofit organizations and local governments for projects that alleviate unemployment and underemployment. Use the site's

Economic Conversion Information Exchange to look for grant opportunities for communities, businesses, and individuals.

▶ The International Trade Administration helps U.S. companies sell their products and services abroad. This site is a must for international marketers because it has the government's latest word on emerging markets, the status of markets in the Western Hemisphere and Latin America, and business opportunities in new markets like Russia.

▶ The Minority Business Development Agency is the only federal agency specifically created to encourage the growth of minority-owned businesses in the United States. The site lists the locations of the agency's centers and provides online sign-up for a free subscription to the agency's electronic bulletin. It also points the way to other minority business sites on the Web.

▶ The National Oceanic and Atmospheric Administration is assigned to promote global environmental stewardship and conservation of the nation's marine and coastal resources. Environmental issues can be researched here. Among the associated agencies are the Environmental Information Services, the National Geophysical Data Center, the National Climatic Data Center, and the National Ocean Service.

▶ The National Telecommunications and Information Administration is the Commerce Department's primary voice on domestic and international telecommunications and information policy-making. Make this a frequent stop if you want to see the White House's position on telecommunications measures that are before Congress, the Federal Communications Commission, or international agencies. This is also a good resource for the "little issues." The last time we surfed through, the site offered "Safeguarding Consumers' Interests in Cyberspace," a speech by an assistant secretary during a recent symposium on law in cyberspace, at the University of Chicago.

▶ The Patent and Trademark Office offers general information on copyrights, patents, and trademarks; searchable databases of patents; and links on the Web for other patent and trademark information. Check this site for the Clinton Administration's position on "hot button" cyberspace issues, as stated in its reports on intellectual property and the national information infrastructure. Whether you want to find out how to register a patent or just need an update on questions of copyright in the cybersphere, the site has much to browse.

▶ The Office of Air and Space Commercialization is a new agency. Its mission is to assist in forming and implementing policy on the "international competitiveness of the U.S. commercial space sector" and promoting the commercial use of outer space by U.S. private industry. What used to be science fiction is daily business here. Emerging market trends in space transportation, direct-broadcast TV and radio, mobile communication, and commercial manufacturing in space are tracked and projected.

▶ The Office of Business Liaison is the Commerce Department's primary contact for the business community. Details on the office's efforts to deliver news of the Commerce Department's policies and programs to the public are accessible.

▶ The Office of Consumer Affairs provides consumer bulletins and special reports. As discussed in a later chapter, the office provides details on how to resolve consumer complaints and on consumer conferences and e-mail newsletters.

▶ The Technology Administration has connections to the National Institute of Standards and Technology, the National Technical Information Service, the Japan Technology Program, and the Office of Technology Policy. These sites give the Administration's positions on assorted high-tech issues, from development of flat screens for computers to support for U.S.-made semiconductors.

▶ The U.S. Travel and Tourism Administration measures international visitation to major U.S. cities and states, and the social impact of tourism to and within the United States. Regular topics include the effect of the devalued peso on tourism to Mexico, and estimates for international travel in the coming year.

Department of Defense

Want to surf in the Pentagon?

DefenseLink (http://www.dtic.dla.mil/defenselink), the home page of the Defense Department, provides direct connections to information about the Joint Chiefs of Staff, all the military services and reserves, the National Guard, and specialty agencies such as the Inspector General, the Department of Defense Field Activities, the Advanced Research Projects Agency, the Ballistic Missile Defense Organization, and the Defense Mapping Agency.

Besides press releases, answers to frequently asked questions, and details of recent appearances by the defense secretary and others, this excellent resource updates information on current U.S. military operations. As this book was being prepared, the U.S. armed forces joined "Operation Joint Endeavor," a NATO peacekeeping effort in Bosnia. In conjunction with the operation, DefenseLink set up BosniaLINK (http://www.dtic.mil/bosnia/index.html), a website specifically designed to provide operations maps, news releases, photos, biographies of key commanders and leaders, and transcripts of recent briefings. Similarly, GulfLINK (http://www.dtic.mil/gulflink) is a site for the latest findings of the Persian Gulf War Veterans Illness Task Force, set up to investigate illnesses affecting veterans as a result of that operation.

DefenseLink also has a guide to defense organizations and functions and a searchable database called DefenseLINK Locator, which can give access to information on defense contracts.

Students and researchers, take note: The site has assorted "fact sheets" on topics such as active-duty military personnel strengths, by region and by country, and updates the figures monthly. Other topics are: Persian Gulf War veterans' medical research issues, an overview of overseas military base realignments, and results of recent recruitment efforts.

Department of Education

This department was set up in 1980 to supplement educational efforts by state and local governments and by the private sector, and to coordinate assorted federal education programs. The Education Department page (http://www.ed.gov) can give you an overview of what's going on with education nationwide. "What's New" provides copies of the latest studies, such as a Biennial Evaluation Report on the purpose, funding, target population, services, administration, effectiveness, management improvement strategies, and sources of information for 154 programs administered by the department. "Progress of Education in the United

States of America: 1990 through 1994" summarizes national data during the period.

Come to this site for teachers' and researchers' guides to the department's resources, general descriptions of programs and their location within the department, and information on grants and fellowships. Also available are newsletters and updates on budgets, legislation, financial aid, and research; educational statistics; press releases; speech texts; and links to other educational resources.

The site lists some of the department's "national goals":

▶ By the year 2000, the high school graduation rate will increase to at least 90 percent.

▶ American students will be first in the world in mathematics and science achievement.

▶ Every adult American will be literate and "will possess the knowledge and skills necessary to compete in a global economy and exercise the rights and responsibilities of citizenship."

To reach a specific official in the Department of Education, check out the site's "People and Offices" option. Its organization chart can guide you to information about program offices, key staff, and a listing of programs and who manages them. There is a searchable phone directory of offices in Washington and elsewhere in the nation.

Department of Energy

The Department of Energy came into being in 1977, when the government's nuclear and nonnuclear policy agencies were combined under a single banner. Today, the department offers technical information and the scientific and educational foundation for technology policy. Current focus is on efficient energy use, diversity in energy sources, environmental quality, and national security and defense.

OpenNet (http://apollo.osti.gov/home.html) is the Department of Energy's database of press releases, statements, policies, speeches, and related data. The text of the National Environmental Policy Act, as well as assorted material from recent press briefings, can be accessed. The site has links to a large number of the department's specialty agencies:

the Office of Civilian Radioactive Waste Management, the Energy Efficiency and Renewable Energy Network, the Office of Environmental Management, the Office of Environment, Safety and Health, the Office of Fossil Energy, and the Office of Science Education and Technical Information.

Online notices of upcoming public meetings, conferences, speech and training seminars, and pollution data are available. The site's Pollution Prevention Information Clearinghouse provides files on policy, success stories, and government assessment standards. A searchable database of officials' phone numbers and addresses and an organization chart are available.

Department of Health and Human Services

This department is the principal government agency for protecting the health of Americans. It oversees more than 250 programs devoted to medical and social science research, prevention of infectious disease, assurance of food and drug safety, Medicare, financial assistance to low-income families, child support enforcement, the Head Start education program for preschoolers, prevention of child abuse, domestic violence, and substance abuse, and development of services for older Americans, including home-delivered meals.

The department's website (http://www.os.dhhs.gov) is built around links to a number of related units. Most prominent are:

▶ The National Institutes of Health (http://www.nih.gov), the world's premier medical research organization, which supports, nationwide, some 25,000 research projects on cancer, Alzheimer's disease, diabetes, heart disease, and AIDS. The site provides health data and research results on many conditions.

▶ The Food and Drug Administration (http://www.fda.gov /fdahomepage.html), which safeguards foods, pharmaceutical products for humans and animals, medical devices, and cosmetics. The site provides current news, such as fact sheets on children and tobacco use and on prevention of lead poisoning in children, and recent actions, such as the approval of specific products for marketing.

▶ The Centers for Disease Control and Prevention (http://www.cdc
.gov), which offers nationwide health surveillance to monitor and
prevent disease outbreaks. This is *the* source for the latest government research findings on chronic disease, HIV and AIDS, tuber-
culosis, and other infectious diseases, and for fact sheets and
statistics on injury, violence, and disabilities. One section covers
health risks involved in tobacco use, environmental factors and
toxic substances, occupational health and safety, and oral health.

▶ Indian Health Service (http://www.tucson.ihs.gov), which provides health services to 1.4 million native Americans and Alaska
natives.

Consumer health bulletins, data on grants, national health policy,
and related information are available. You can click into the online links
to reach the department's lesser known agencies and related resources.
Among them are the Office of Grants and Acquisition Management, the
Administration for Children and Families, the Office of Child Support
Enforcement, the Administration on Aging, the Health Care Financing
Administration, the Agency for Toxic Substances and Disease Registry,
the National Center for Food Safety and Applied Nutrition, the National
Center for Toxicological Research, the Division of Computer Research
and Technology, the Office of Information Resources Management, the
National Institute on Aging, the National Heart, Lung, and Blood Insti-
tute, the National Cancer Institute's Frederick Cancer Research and
Development Center, the National Institute of Allergy and Infectious
Diseases, the National Institute of Environmental Health Sciences, the
National Institute of Mental Health, the National Library of Medicine
(and the NLM Health Services/Technology Assessment Text), the Sub-
stance Abuse and Mental Health Services Administration, the Office of
Disease Prevention, Health Promotion, and Health Planning and Evalu-
ation, the Office of Research Integrity, and the Parklawn Computer
Center.

Department of Housing and Urban Development

This very visible department is a multifunctional agency that touches
our lives through these activities:

▶ Insures or guarantees mortgages made by local lenders to low- and moderate-income people.

▶ Investigates housing discrimination complaints.

▶ Manages programs for funding public housing, rental housing assistance, and housing for people with special needs, including the elderly, handicapped, and persons with AIDS.

▶ Oversees grants to revitalize cities and neighborhoods.

▶ Helps mortgage lenders sell "pools" of loans so the lenders can originate new loans for new borrowers.

On a more personal level, the HUD Page (http://www.hud.gov) has information on how to buy a home and on programs that might assist home buyers (see the "Places to Live" option). Pamphlets can be read online or ordered in print versions. A mortgage counseling service is offered for people who have lost their jobs and can't make mortgage payments; details tell how to avoid foreclosure.

The page also has lots of *local* information. Want to see a summary of your own community's housing plans, with online maps that show where HUD dollars are being spent in your town? See the "Cities, Communities and Neighborhoods" option. Information on programs available for communities, requirements to qualify for funding as a HUD "Empowerment Zone" or an "Enterprise Community," HUD success stories around the country, and details on job opportunities and training programs are all worth a click.

The HUD site publishes press releases and policy statements, as well as information on programs available under its umbrella organization: Community Planning and Development, Federal Housing Administration, Public and Indian Housing, Fair Housing and Equal Opportunity, Policy Development and Research, and the Government National Mortgage Association ("Ginnie Mae").

If your company does business—or would like to do business—with HUD, check out the page's list of current NOFAs (Notices of Funding Availability). These notices are issued whenever the department has funds to distribute through a competitive application process. Asset sales and information on the activities of the Inspector General are posted.

The "HUD Tool Kit" option gives 800 numbers for department information on buying and improving homes, applying for community improvement grants, filing fair housing complaints, and finding programs for native Americans.

Department of Interior

As the government's principal conservation agency, the Interior Department manages most of the nation's public lands and natural resources. It also is responsible for American Indian reservations and for the people who live in island territories under U.S. administration. If you need information about federal lands, parks, conservatories, forests, reservations, or preserves, visit the Interior Department at (http://info.er.usgs.gov/doi/doi.html).

The site also can be a quite useful resource for keeping up on current events. For instance, during the Pacific Northwest flood, in February 1996, the page provided links for the latest streamflow conditions in Oregon. A "top story" is presented each week; recent examples are Secretary Bruce Babbitt's testimony about federal land ownership by public land management agencies, and environmental issues regarding oil drilling in the Arctic region.

Beyond the breaking news, the site is the home of the National Park Service, which manages federal parks such as Yellowstone and the Grand Canyon, and it provides details on the department's other

---

Notorious! FBI Digitizes Its Most Wanted

Making a quantum leap from the old post office bulletin board, the FBI now uses the Net to spread the word about its ten most wanted fugitives. Log into its site (http://www.fbi.gov/toplist.htm) and the FBI will give you the rundown on each.

Names on the Net

The Bureau operates its own main home page (http://www.fbi.gov/homepage.htm) to provide information about its various operations and projects.

bureaus and offices, education and outreach programs and training, and employment and volunteer opportunities. This is your Net source for details on land, parks, public works, natural hazards, and natural history museums.

For the geographer in all of us, this page is a great resource for maps of states and regions throughout the country—printed maps you can order, and electronic maps you can see on your screen—all prepared by the U.S. Geological Survey. Online information tells you how you can volunteer to help the Earth Science Corps and participate in the National Mapping Program.

Other links from here are the bureaus of Indian Affairs, Land Management, and Mines and Reclamation, as well as the Minerals Management Service, the National Biological Service, the Office of Surface Mining, and the U.S. Fish and Wildlife Service. An "Agency Customer Satisfaction" option gives you the latest government "report card" on how each bureau was rated by its clients.

Department of Justice

Think of "DJ" as the nation's largest law firm. The Department of Justice is mandated to be the counsel for the nation's citizens, representing them by enforcing laws in the public interest. Cases range from charges of fraud and subversion to the rights of free entrepreneurs, anti-trust statutes, and enforcement of drug, immigration, and naturalization laws. The Justice Department conducts in federal courts all cases in which the U.S. government is a plaintiff or defendant, and it represents the government in legal matters generally. Upon request, it renders legal advice and opinions to the president and the heads of the executive departments.

The Justice Department home page (http://justice2.usdoj.gov) gives visitors background and direct links to its executive direction and management offices, litigation organizations, investigatory and law enforcement offices (such as the Federal Bureau of Investigation), and legal and policy offices. It also provides an alphabetical listing of all forty subsidiary organizations, such as its Anti-Trust Division, Civil Rights Division, Drug Enforcement Administration, Immigration and Naturalization Service, Office of the Inspector General, Tax Division, and U.S. Marshals Service.

If you're a student or a researcher, there is fertile ground here. Suppose you are a high school student preparing a paper on the federal prison system. You can link to a page on the Federal Bureau of Prisons and cull some statistics. (For instance, at this writing, there were 79 federal prisons housing more than 95,000 inmates, 34 percent of whom were in minimum security prisons and only 7.5 percent of whom were women. It costs $58.50 per day to house each inmate.) The same page could give you a copy of the Civil Rights of Institutionalized Persons Act, links to current research into the correction system, and an overview of the

Job hunters, surf this way.

The Labor Department has a Web resource that can help you find employment. America's Job Bank (http://www.ajb.dni.us), operated by the U.S.

Finding a Job Online

Department of Labor and some 1,800 state public employment service agency offices around the country, contains information on about 250,000 jobs. Most are full-time positions in the private sector; about 5 percent are in government. The openings, from around the country, represent all types of work: professional, technical, blue-collar, management, clerical, and sales.

Best of all, there's no charge to the employers who list their vacancies or the job seekers who use the database to look for work. (The system is funded through federal unemployment insurance taxes paid by employers.)

The database enables you to search using specific nine-digit job codes (which the government has assigned to specific occupations). If you don't know a job's code, you can select the "Self-Directed Search" option. It lets you narrow the possibilities by answering several questions about the kind of work you're seeking (such as choosing between "managerial and administrative" or among "professional, paraprofessional, and technical") until you've zeroed in on specific openings. Ultimately, the database provides the location of the job, the job title (such as "switchboard operator"), the salary ($6.67 an hour), education and experience requirements, hours per week, whether the job is full-time or part-time, and a summary of duties ("will operate switchboard to assist customers and callers to the plant. Must have some typing and telephone experience. Hours of work are 8 A.M. to 5 P.M. Monday through Friday."). If a listing appeals to you, other options tell you specifically how to apply.

Bureau of Prisons facilities, training centers, and regional offices. The same depth of data is available for other Justice Department bureaus.

Are you interested in what happens to crime victims in this country? The department's Office for Victims of Crime has a page detailing its programs and activities to help victims cope with personal and financial devastation resulting from victimization. It also provides information and links to Net resources for victims of domestic violence, child abuse, elder abuse, and bias-related violence, as well as facts on victim compensation laws.

The Justice page is a prime site for law enforcement documents. Want a copy of the Violent Crime and Law Enforcement Act of 1994? Or a list of "The 84 Policing Agencies Awarded Funds to Redeploy Officers"? This site has both—and more. The site has gained national attention from time to time for its rapid publication of information, such as the rewards offered in the bombing of the Oklahoma City federal office building and the latest clues in the UNABOM mail-bomb case. The site links to resources that list attorney vacancies within the Justice Department and at other criminal justice-related sites around the Net.

Department of Labor

Created in 1913 to "foster, promote and develop the welfare of working people, to improve their working conditions and to enhance their opportunities for profitable employment," the Labor Department continues to focus on many of the concerns of its founders: wages, hours, working conditions, job opportunities, discrimination, cooperative labor–management relations, and labor's role in the nation's industrial productivity.

If you're looking for employment/unemployment data, come to this site (http://www.dol.gov). The "Labor Related Data" option can link you to the Bureau of Labor Statistics, the principal federal fact-finding agency for the broad field of labor economics. The database contains a wide range of statistics, including employment/unemployment figures, consumer price index, producer price index, wages, and productivity. Data are provided in the form of news releases with high-level aggregates as well as detailed historical time series. If you're a first-time visitor, select the Bureau's "Most Requested Series" option, which probably contains the information you're seeking. An online form lets you simply check a box beside each reported subject (civilian labor force, total payroll, employment/unemployment rate, hourly earnings, output per hour, and consumer price index). Another useful report, "The Economy at a Glance," gives monthly figures for the national labor force, unemployment, hours and earnings, and prices, in both tabular and graph forms.

Another primary link for Labor Department data is the Occupational Safety and Health Administration, which has archived information on regulations, investigations, inspections, citations, and penalties, as well as figures on occupational injury and illness. The most frequently violated OSHA standards (improper scaffolding on job sites, improper electrical wiring, absence of portable fire extinguishers, and so on) are described.

Department of State

The U.S. State Department, the lead U.S. foreign affairs agency, is responsible for implementing the president's and Congress's foreign policies. It maintains diplomatic relations with more than 170 countries and operates some 260 embassies, consulates, and missions around the world.

In cooperation with the University of Illinois at Chicago, the State Department's Bureau of Public Affairs operates a home page (http://dosfan.lib.uic.edu/dosfan.html) to provide a broad range of foreign policy data. Called DOSFAN (for Department of State Foreign Affairs Network), the site is topped with a "Hot Topics" list of current events. As we were passing through, this section made available: copies of documents relating to U.S. policy on Bosnia—a summary and the official text of the Dayton Agreement, maps of implementation-force dispositions in the contested area, and speeches, statements, and testimony from State Department officials on the controversial boundaries and land claims. Similar data on the Middle East peace process were also accessible.

History buffs and anyone interested in current events should not miss the site's "International Affairs" section. Highlights include:

▶ Background notes on foreign countries and selected international organizations (describing the people, history, government, and political conditions), foreign policy, and bilateral relations with the United States. A search by name of country yields the latest information.

▶ Country Reports on Human Rights Practices, an annual report to Congress on human rights and worker rights; released by the Bureau of Democracy, Human Rights, and Labor Affairs.

▶ International Narcotics Control Strategy Report, required by the Foreign Assistance Act; an annual report on more than 130 countries.

▶ Patterns of Global Terrorism, an annual report from the Office of the Coordinator for Counterterrorism, on foreign countries in which significant terrorist acts have occurred and countries that repeatedly have provided state support for international terrorism.

If you're planning a trip abroad, be sure to visit the page's "Travel Information" option for tips, foreign entry requirements, security concerns, and the link to the bureaus of consular affairs and of diplomatic security.

The "America's Desk" option links you to the State Department's key services for Americans in business abroad. Phone contacts and publications are only the beginning.

The site also has summaries of historic and current declassified documents on foreign policy activities, biographical data and pictures of the Secretary of State and his principal officials, and a photographic tour of selected areas of the department's Washington facility. Also online are texts of speeches, daily press briefings, and publications such as *Dispatch,* a weekly foreign policy magazine.

Department of Transportation

Since its creation in 1967, "DOT," the Department of Transportation, has been responsible for transportation safety improvements and enforcement, international transportation agreements, and preparation of all legislation on the subject.

DOT's Web home page (http://www.dot.gov) offers an online directory of contact phone numbers for its employees, details of recent DOT events and announcements, grants and procurement information, details on regulations, pertinent legislation and policy, vacancy information, and travel tips.

The site also can provide news. In February 1996, less than a week after a fatal train wreck in Silver Spring, Maryland, DOT announced an emergency order requiring rail operators to implement tougher safety measures. Full text of the order was online at the site within minutes of the press conference.

The site can link you to assorted DOT agencies, including these major organizations:

▶ Bureau of Transportation Statistics, where the National Transportation Library has press releases and figures on topics such as bicycles and pedestrians, congestion management, freight, parking, and travel demand forecasting. A search option lets you enter a key phrase (such as "MOTORCYCLE HELMET LAWS") to find specific data.

▶ Federal Aviation Administration, for links to technical, environmental, safety, and business data relating to air travel. The *FAA Aviation News* magazine is available in electronic form, as are news releases, texts of official speeches, and details on FAA regulations, research, and educational programs. Also online are directories of FAA employees and contact phone numbers for assorted FAA computer bulletin board systems.

▶ Federal Highway Administration, with information on the latest highway-related legislation (full text and summaries), details on major federal aid and federal land programs, and program announcements.

▶ Federal Railroad Administration, with links to the agency's offices of public affairs, safety, and policy. There are also files for railroad students and hobbyists here. For instance, an entire home page is devoted to the Gage Restraint Measurement System, a track-strength evaluation program intended to improve safety and efficiency. For statistics hunters, the "Office of Safety" option links with tables on accident reports.

▶ Federal Transit Administration, for information on buses, subways and the like, with links to funding data, planning and policy files, research and technology, and safety issues and stats.

▶ Maritime Administration, for information on American shipping and the U.S. Merchant Marine, text of the new Maritime Security Act, and history files, such as details of the heroic contribution of the Merchant Marine during World War II.

▶ National Highway Traffic Safety Administration, where the "Research and Development" section can give the latest crash statistics and biomechanics data (the crash-test dummies of TV public service announcement fame are used in the page's introduction). The site also provides information on programs to combat drunk driving, and links to other automotive information sites around the Web.

▶ Research and Special Programs Administration, for details on research in safety and transportation systems, especially in conjunction with oil pipelines and hazardous materials.

▶ U.S. Coast Guard, for details on the agency's recruiting efforts, the Coast Guard Academy, and general boat and navigation information. The extensive recreational boat safety material gives details on marine communications, such as what radio equipment boaters need, lists of VHF marine radio channels and frequencies, current tides and tidal predictions, and interactive marine weather observations. For marine students, "The Cutter, Aircraft & Boat Data Sheets Index" provides text and photos of all the Coast Guard's fleet.

Department of Treasury

This department forms and recommends economic, fiscal, and tax policies, advises the president and other officials on government and national money matters, serves as the financial agent of the U.S. government, collects the federal taxes, and manufactures coins and currency. The department also oversees firearms, tobacco, and alcohol regulations.

At the department's website (http://www.ustreas.gov/treasury /homepage.html), you can gather information on business-related topics. The "Small Business Program" option has data on how to do business with the Treasury Department through the Small and Disadvantaged Business Utilization Office and through events such as the Small, Minority and Women-Owned Business Conferences. The site also gives details of other Treasury activities, such as auctions of seized property. If you're in a shopping mood, a "Mint Gift Collection" lets you examine catalogs of coin sets, jewelry, and medals available for sale.

The major Treasury Department bureaus accessible from the site are:

▶ Bureau of Alcohol, Tobacco, and Firearms. Want more information on the "Brady Law" on gun control? This site has answers to frequently asked questions, Treasury Department decisions on the gun-control issue, and a list of states that have adopted the Brady Law.

▶ Internal Revenue Service, which provides online assistance for tax preparation, as well as downloadable tax forms, bulletins, summaries of tax law changes, and press releases.

▶ U.S. Customs Service, with press releases and statements. Come here for information on the sale of seized property, including cars, airplanes, boats, real estate, jewelry, electronics equipment, and clothing. The site tells how to stay informed about these public auctions.

▶ U.S. Mint and the Bureau of Engraving and Printing, with data on current and historic coins and currency, special gift collections, and an online video that shows how currency is printed.

It may not be the sexiest site on the Internet, but it becomes one of the most useful between January 1 and April 15 every year.

Tax information of all kinds is available from the new Internal Revenue Service (IRS) home page (http://www.irs.ustreas .gov). Some 600 different tax forms and publications, for businesses and individuals, and a summary of changes in tax rules can be retrieved.

Getting Tax Help Online

An interactive section called "Tax Trails" answers basic questions; or, you can search among simple summaries of 150 tax topics and answers to frequently asked questions. At this writing, plans call for adding a hypertext version of the IRS comprehensive tax guide for individuals—Publication 17, "Your Federal Income Tax"—on the home page.

Electronic filing of tax returns is *not* yet available through the site—but keep watching. That feature is planned as an addition in a future tax season.

▶ U.S. Secret Service, providing general information about the bureau's duties, which include protecting the person and family of the president, the vice president, and former presidents, and keeping designated public buildings and grounds secure. Some criminal violations of banking laws, currency and stamp laws, and computer fraud are investigated.

Elsewhere on the Treasury site are links to the Office of Thrift Supervision, the Office of the Comptroller of the Currency, the Federal Law Enforcement Training Center, the Bureau of Public Debt, and the Financial Crimes Enforcement Network.

The "Treasury Electronic Library" (with speeches, press releases, and related data) and "Who's Who" (with photographs and biographical information on treasury officers) are additional features.

Department of Veterans Affairs

The Veterans Administration was established in 1930, when Congress authorized the president to consolidate and coordinate government activities affecting war veterans. The VA health care system grew from 54 hospitals in that year to today's network of 171 medical centers, more than 350 community/outpatient clinics, 126 nursing homes, and 35 domiciles. The Department of Veterans Affairs has been a cabinet-level agency since 1989.

The VA Home Page (http://www.va.gov) offers answers to frequently asked questions about veterans benefits, and tells where to go for help, news, and announcements. (The last time we were in the digital neighborhood, the site included a warning about a national veterans insurance hoax.) Also online are the Veterans Benefits Manual, state-by-state listings of VA facilities, and information on legislation, case appeals, policies, and miscellaneous articles. Additional data are available on compensation and pensions, education and training, home loan assistance, insurance, medical care, and medical research.

The site enables comparison of any local VA Medical Center with others around the country in terms of average appointment times, how many doctors and nurses are on staff, and what services and specialties are performed. Elsewhere are links to other pages of interest to veterans. One page is devoted to Vietnam Vets and another includes a database of all the names on The Wall, Washington's Vietnam War memorial.

Before there was the Web and its hundreds of thousands of links, there was FedWorld (http://www.fedworld.gov/), still a fertile site for digging up government information.

FedWorld: The Granddaddy of Data Meisters

Created in November 1992 by the National Technical Information Service (NTIS), FedWorld accepted the challenge to help Netheads keep afloat in the flood of data, even as more and more government agencies come paddling out into the data stream. Now that FedWorld is on the Web, it is even easier to use as a comprehensive central access point for locating and acquiring government information.

FedWorld offers the public one-stop shopping for locating, ordering, and having delivered U.S. government documents. It links with some 50 agencies and provides access to more than 130 government dial-up bulletin boards, most of which are not available via the Internet.

The resources are sorted by alphabetized subject categories. For instance, in the "U" section, click on "Urban and Regional Technology and Development" and you'll be whisked away to a variety of sites, from the Federal Emergency Management Agency to the National Science Foundation Bulletins or the Occupational Safety and Health Administration.

You also can search abstracts of recent government reports and studies, and related data received by the NTIS in the past 30 days.

Independent Federal Agencies and Commissions

The White House page links to dozens of independent federal commissions and agencies. The best known are noted here.

▶ Central Intelligence Agency (http://www.odci.gov), with press releases, transcripts of speeches and testimony, and agency answers to frequently asked questions ("Does the CIA give a tour of its headquarters?" No. "Does the CIA spy on Americans?" No; an Executive Order prohibits the agency from domestic surveillance. "Who decides when the CIA participates in covert actions?" The president.). The site has a keyword-searchable database of documents and CIA publications, such as the *CIA World Factbook,* the

Factbook on Intelligence, details on CIA maps you can order, lists of chiefs of state, and cabinet members of foreign governments.

▶ Commodity Futures Trading Commission (http://www.clark.net pub/cftc), created by Congress in 1974 to regulate commodities futures and option markets in the United States. The site's "Commission Information" feature offers advice to new commodities traders as well as a primer on the ABCs of the future traders' language. (Can you converse about "arbitrage," "backwardation," and "chooser options"?) For experienced traders, the site offers a database of its weekly advisory newsletters and publications such as *Commitments of Traders' Reports* and *CFTC Letters.* For news beyond press releases and official statements, the site has details of its latest enforcement actions in fraud and misappropriations cases.

▶ Consumer Product Safety Commission (gopher://cpsc.gov), with articles on the background and goals of the commission and its jurisdiction over some 15,000 products. (Some products are covered by other agencies. For instance, vehicles are covered by the Department of Transportation, drugs and cosmetics come under the Food and Drug Administration, and alcohol, tobacco, and firearms are regulated by the Treasury Department.) The site provides current press releases, alerts, notices of publications and events, hotline information, a current budget and annual report, and other items.

▶ Corporation for National Service (http://www.whitehouse.gov /White_House/EOP/cns/html/cns-index.html), the site for several of the current administration's jobs and services programs— AmeriCorps, Learn and Serve America, and the National Senior Service Corps.

▶ Environmental Protection Agency (http://www.epa.gov), with a database for locating documents and EPA people. At the site are press releases, calendars, announcements, speech texts, addresses for regional EPA offices, statements on policy, regulations, rules, and standards. Reports on research and technology, information on grants, contracts, and job vacancies with the agency, and newsletters and journals round out the list. The site has connections to other environmental sites and related Internet resources.

A "What's New" option gives you reports on EPA actions around the country, such as details on new proposed water-quality standards applicable to surface waters in Arizona, or a proposal to exempt a gold mine project near Juneau, Alaska, from the usual "de-watering" regulations. A "What's Hot" option lists the 20 files that have been the most popular retrievals among fellow Net surfers over the past week. These usually include EPA press releases, details of research grants and graduate fellowships, and Federal Register entries on air- and water-quality reports. Take a look at the "Highly Recommended" option to see the electronic library of consumer and environmental booklets and pamphlets you can retrieve. Data range from do's and don'ts of how to protect the ground water around your house, pesticide safety, and what you can do to reduce air pollution, to "The Plain English Guide to the Clean Air Act," data on acid rain and the ozone, and "Environmental Planning for Small Communities: A Guide for Local Decision-Makers."

▶ Federal Communications Commission (http://www.fcc.gov), with a daily digest of its agenda, and details on auctions. On the Web, the FCC seeks public comment on issues and conducts public forums. At this writing, an online forum had been established to solicit comments on television violence and the government's role, if any, in reducing it. The conference is *not* in real time, but the FCC says its executives do periodically review and comment on the ongoing discussions. In the aftermath of the enactment of the Telecommunications Act of 1996—the massive bill authorizing the overhaul of U.S. phone, cable, and online computer network businesses—the site presented reactions from various commissioners, text of selected portions of the measure, and the FCC's schedule for implementing the Act. The site provides links to FCC bureaus on common carriers, the wireless industry, mass media, cable, international issues, engineering and technology, compliance and information, and other issues. Other links connect to current auctions and the commission's agenda. Finally, for die-hard FCC-watchers, the "Current Rulemaking" option provides text of what the commission calls "Notices of Proposed Rulemaking" (NPRMs), which are changes in telecommunications regulations. The site lists NPRMs in fields of common carriers, mass

media, cable, wireless, international communications, and engineering and technology.

▶ Federal Deposit Insurance Corporation (http://www.fdic.gov),
with a "Corporate Library" feature that gives a number of guides
for the banking industry and interested citizens. Weekly updated
information on FDIC-insured institutions, quarterly reports on the
status of FDIC-insured facilities, and their supporting financial
statements, are standard offerings. For statistics on the banking industry, check out the site's Division of Research and Statistics. The
page links to two lists: "Bulksale" announces FDIC-held loans
being sold in bulk, and "FDIC Announce" stores press releases and
statements from the agency.

▶ Federal Emergency Management Agency (http://www.fema.gov),
where disasters are daily life. The site provides tips on preparing
for a disaster and on getting help after it's too late for preparation;
a collection of press statements; news of FEMA career opportunities; and updates on current situations. When Hurricane Erin
howled across western Florida and the Gulf Coast in the summer
of 1995, this site provided situation reports, maps, news releases,
information on hurricane preparedness, and instructions for filing
a flood insurance claim. The FEMA pages include data on disaster assistance programs and how the public can help disaster victims.

▶ Federal Trade Commission (http://www.ftc.gov), with information
on current hearings and statements and the FTC's organizational
structure. You might especially like the page's "ConsumerLine,"
which has full text of some 140 consumer and business publications
in categories such as credit, investments, health and fitness, telemarketing, homes and real estate, products and services, cars and
buying, and working at home. The site also has articles on trade
rules, how the FTC brings an action, where to get additional information, and details on its regional offices.

▶ General Services Administration (http://www.gsa.gov), a lively
website that explains the policies the agency has set on federal procurement, real property management, information resources management, and so on. Information is given on the GSA's diversified
government-wide operations involving buildings management,

telecommunications, consumer information, distribution, child care in the federal workplace, and the Federal Recycling Program. Among its more popular features are "Consumer Information Center" (with data on topics such as health, housing, car-buying, food, and federal benefits) and "Federal Information Center," which answers frequent questions about the U.S. government.

▶ National Aeronautics and Space Administration (http://www.nasa .gov), covering recent NASA and space news, history, and strategic plans. Space program images and transcripts, maps of space centers around the country, databases of documents and contact numbers, information on NASA's procurement programs and forecasts, and links to other space and aeronautics resources on the Net make this a popular site. Especially useful is the site's option for details of NASA's online educational resources, which include, for example, an atlas of Mars, "Basics of Spaceflight" (an electronic workbook on various aspects of spaceflight and solar system exploration), a pilot program to enhance science and mathematics curricula, and assorted other initiatives intended to encourage schoolchildren, teachers, and parents to discuss space colonization, astronauts, space telescopes, and more.

▶ National Archives and Records Administration (http://www.nara .gov), connected to the nation's main repository of historical documents. This site has material about genealogy, the Federal Register, assorted exhibits and events, training courses, tours, and a feature called the "Online Exhibit Hall," which creates changing displays. Interested in studying the investigation of the John F. Kennedy assassination, in 1963? The index to the collection that is housed at the archives can be searched online. Want to see history exhibitions—perhaps "The Mississippi and Her People" or "The American West Online"—with actual photos? Click on. The site also provides tutorial guides for genealogical research at the Archives' historical records collection. The site links with a database, combining its collections of information with easy access to diverse electronic resources elsewhere on the Net.

▶ National Endowment for the Humanities (http://ns1.neh.fed.us), operated by the agency that makes grants for projects in history, languages, philosophy, and other areas of the humanities. Online are articles that provide an overview of various available grant and endowment programs for the humanities, and how you or your organization can apply for a program. The site is home to scholarly discussions on topics such as "American Identity and Pluralism," and details of the agency's deadlines, awards, and events.

▶ National Performance Review (http://www.npr.gov), linked to Vice President Al Gore's program aimed at cutting government waste. The site outlines the history, goals, and accomplishments of the effort, as the page says, in "creating a new customer service contract with the American people." The site's highlight is its "ToolKit to Help Reinvent Government," which lists contacts and relevant Net sites, and presents status reports on earlier performance reviews. A database of some 800 documents and announcements includes a hypertext version of the *Reinvention Roundtable* newsletter, and text versions of the NPR Reports, Agency Performance Agreements, and executive orders.

▶ National Science Foundation (http://stis.nsf.gov), with guides to grant and research opportunities, funding request deadlines, science trends and information, news media material, and science education resources. Also detailed are results of NSF-funded research in science and engineering, press releases and breaking science foundation news, and links to federal research centers, federal laboratories, selected NSF-funded projects, and related federal agencies.

▶ National Security Agency (http://www.nsa.gov:8080), which is assigned to protect U.S. government communications and to intercept foreign communications. Considering that the NSA is the largest and most secret of the federal intelligence agencies, are you surprised that it has a public page on the Web? Well, it *doesn't* have a handy electronic phonebook of its employees (though the site does provide data on NSA employment opportunities). Most of the NSA website is devoted not to current activities, but to how the agency was created by President Harry Truman in 1952, as a part of the Defense Department, and its work with agencies such as the FBI, the CIA, and the Secret Service. The site has background on the NSA's code-breaking activities, and gives details on its National Cryptologic Museum, including a sample of its exhibits. If you're interested in the history of the Cold War years, be sure to see the page's extensive display on the documents of "The Venona Project." This was an agency project started in 1943 to secretly examine and possibly exploit thousands of encrypted Soviet diplomatic telegrams that were intercepted as they were sent between Moscow and its diplomatic missions around the world. If you love spy novels, you'll enjoy this true-life tale of code-breaking and international intrigue. The NSA says online that the "sweat-of-the-brow" effort led to the decoding of some 2,200 messages concerning Soviet operatives in the United States and abroad, atomic bomb secrets, and the role of the Soviet KGB in U.S. Communist Party activities in the United States.

▶ National Technology Transfer Center (http://www.nttc.edu), the hub of a national network linking U.S. companies with federal technologies that have potential for commercial application. The site provides contact information for the federal laboratory system and for information on materials, computers, information systems, biotechnology, agriculture, transportation, energy and environmental innovations, electronics, and defense-related research and development. The wide-ranging agency has worked with private developers of such diverse products as new clothing material, an improved on-screen captioning system, improvements in dry cleaning technology, and new engineering software. The site can give you details on upcoming seminars on marketing and technology assessment.

▶ Nuclear Regulatory Commission (http://www.nrc.gov), which, unlike some government agencies, uses its website as a teaching aid. Links to additional pages provide information on nuclear material safety, the location and operation of the nation's uranium fuel fabrication facilities, the licenses (about 22,000 annually) issued for medical, academic, and industrial uses of nuclear material, how nuclear material is transported, the operation of radioactive waste disposal facilities, how nuclear reactors work, and where they are located.

▶ Peace Corps (http://www.peacecorps.gov), with details on the program's humanitarian efforts in Africa, the Middle East, Asia, the

Pacific, South and Central America, the Caribbean, and Central Europe. If you're interested in participating, the site can give you information on how to volunteer, including how you might qualify in any of about sixty skill areas in the fields of agriculture, business, the environment, education, and health. You can fill out an online request form and have an application packet sent to you. There's also information on reaching your nearest Peace Corps recruiter if you want to talk to someone in person. The site has details on the World Wise Schools education program, which links approximately 4,500 classrooms around the country with Peace Corps volunteers around the world. Participating classes can correspond with their volunteers and receive videos and study guides.

▶ President's Council on Physical Fitness (http://www.whitehouse .gov/WH/PCPFS/html/fitnet.html), with information on the activities of the council: special observances, speeches, and calendars of events. An electronic version of the "Get Moving, America!" brochure gives tips for getting an organization to participate in the fitness program. Ideas include a fitness/health fair, lectures and films, distance runs and walks, and testing.

▶ Railroad Retirement Board (http://www.mcs.net/~taxation), which administers the Railroad Retirement Act and the Railroad Unemployment Insurance Act, and assists in administering the Social Security Act. The site provides information on available publications, details of eligibility for railroad retirement benefits, and what those benefits are.

▶ Securities and Exchange Commission (http://www.sec.gov), whose EDGAR database provides the public and business communities with free access to its vast library of corporate records. The database, covered in detail in Chapter 7, distributes records (ranging from quarterly earnings reports to notices of corporate takeovers) and shareholder proxy statements, as well as documents filed with the U.S. Patent and Trademark Office. Founded in 1994, the system distributed some 3.1 million documents in its first two years, an average of 16,700 per day. During the same period, 1.59 million patent documents were distributed. A keyword prompt enables visitors to enter the name of a company that is of interest. As part of a resulting display, specific reports mentioning that name are listed, and the user clicks on those that are relevant. Another section provides definitions of the various reports that are available. If you are a newcomer to stock trading, you might explore an educational file, such as "What Every Investor Should Know," which will link you to online publications such as "Invest Wisely," a guide to selecting a broker, choosing an investment, and identifying signs of trouble.

▶ Small Business Administration (http://www.sbaonline.sba.gov). Want to start your own business? Or expand the one you already operate? Stop here for reams of electronic data on these and related subjects, as well as information on SBA workshops, individual counseling, publications, and videotapes. The page has background on related groups, such as the Service Corps of Retired Executives, and Small Business Development Centers and Institutes. Also online is information on the various SBA loan and credit programs and on assistance for business expansion.

▶ Smithsonian Institution (http://www.si.edu), a largely educational site. You'll get answers to frequently asked questions about the Smithsonian and other topics, tips and ideas for visits to the

The Federal Emergency Management Agency maintains a huge (and growing) collection of disaster- and safety-oriented Net resources called the FEMA Global Emergency Management System (http://www.fema.gov/fema/gems.html).

Disaster Preparedness Can Begin Online

Visitors will find details on disaster management agencies around the world and in the United States, as well as data on disaster mitigation, risk management, emergency services, and search-and-rescue operations. The site has Net links for some police and fire departments around the country, the Red Cross, the United Nations, nongovernment agencies such as CARE, Save the Children, and Doctors Without Borders, and key federal agencies (Army Corps of Engineers, Environmental Protection Agency, and National Oceanic and Atmospheric Administration).

Of special interest to students and reporters is the page's material on natural disasters (with data and links about earthquakes, forest fires, volcanos, and severe storms) and medical emergencies.

famed Washington museums, transcripts of relevant speeches and articles about the facilities, details on current museum and National Zoo exhibits, and information on how to become a member. A "Perspectives" section of the page provides educational material on broad social, cultural, political, and organizational subjects such as African American culture, Asian culture, computers, mammals, oceans, and other topics. A "Products" section gives information about electronic shopping for goods from the museums' various gift shops.

▶ Social Security Administration (http://www.ssa.gov), which combines news (rulings, policies, announcements, legislation), history (how the agency is strongly linked with the Great Depression era dreams and goals of President Franklin D. Roosevelt), and education (how to "read" your Social Security card: the code behind the numbers). The site has material on the future of Social Security, including the status of the old-age, survivors', and disability insurance and the Medicare insurance trust fund, and health issues. (A fact sheet on chronic fatigue syndrome is part of its Disability Program Page.) At tax time, the site provides information on the amounts that employers must report to the Social Security Administration. A calculation of the cost-of-living adjustment is regularly updated (http://www.ssa.gov/OACT/95COLA/FR.sum .html), enabling you to take into account the effects of inflation when comparing dollar figures over a period of time. Much of the site's data can be displayed in Spanish, and the page has electronic versions of its most requested forms.

▶ U.S. Agency for International Development (http://www.info .usaid.gov), operated by the federal government agency that conducts foreign assistance and humanitarian aid. Want to know where the U.S. foreign aid money goes? This site can tell you. Linked to the page are the International Development Page and the Humanitarian Response Page. Also available is information on business opportunities and the agency's procurement policies. The site has strong environmental sections. Its "Protecting the Environment" option provides files on the "Famine Early Warning System," the "Productive Sector Growth and Environment Page," and the "Environmental and Energy Study Institute," as well as reports on the effects of U.S. aid in places like Tunisia, Madagascar, and Thailand. Statistics on its "Record of Accomplishment" page indicate that less than 1 percent of the total U.S. budget goes to foreign assistance, and that each year some 3 million lives are saved overseas through U.S. immunization programs. A "Population and Health" option can give you the agency's take on global population growth and on problems in specific countries such as Kenya and Bangladesh.

▶ U.S. Information Agency (http://www.usia.gov), provided by the agency charged with explaining to overseas audiences the details of American foreign policy through broadcasts and publications. Electronic versions of the agency's *USIA World* publication are here, as are details on various educational and cultural exchanges, and facts about the USIA's budget, goals, people, history, and activities. Information relates to its international broadcasting activities (including WorldNet Television, and Radio and TV Marti broadcasts to Cuba) and its assistance to foreign journalists assigned to cover U.S. politics and society.

Consumer Information Center Catalog (http://www.gsa.gov/staff/pa/cic /cic.html) is the General Services Administration's highly popular website for distributing all kinds of consumer data. It operates from what is (because of extensive televised public service announcements) one of the best known addresses in America ("Consumer Information Center, Pueblo, Colorado 81009"). Millions of booklets published by more than forty federal departments and agencies have been distributed since the Center was launched in 1970. Much of those data are now online.

Free Consumer Information from the Feds

Featured online are hundreds of government booklets and pamphlets on diverse subjects. At the site, you can download the entire catalog or selected booklets. Topics on the main menu include cars, children, employment, federal programs, food and nutrition, health, hobbies, housing, money, small business, and travel.

- U.S. International Trade Commission (http://www.usitc.gov), operated by the quasi-judicial federal agency that determines the impact of imports on U.S. industries, helps set the nation's position on exports, and directs actions against unfair trade practices, such as patent, trademark, and copyright infringement, and against exports that are a threat to national security. The site discusses the commission's analyses, economic investigations, and reports on U.S. industries and the global trends that affect them. Provided are news releases, meetings, and events. The latest on current trade investigations can be found here.

- U.S. Postal Service (http://www.usps.gov), used to augment basic information on the post office and its various offices around the nation. Topics of articles are: stamps and stamp collecting, doing business with the U.S. Postal Service, news of latest rates, and Postal Service documents, such as charts of current domestic and international postage. If you're a retailer, you might be able to turn the Postal Service into a customer. A "Selling to the USPS" section offers electronic versions of its *Let's Do Business* publication and its *Procurement Manual,* which gives details of what the agency is in the market for. Printable electronic versions of first-, second-, third-, and fourth-class postal business forms, as well as the Statement of Ownership, Management and Circulation, are available.

- Voice of America (gopher://gopher.voa.gov/1), which offers transcripts and sound files on Voice broadcasts, Chinese radio scripts, information on WorldNet and Radio Marti, and related material. Voice program schedules and radio frequencies around the world can be reviewed here.

- White House Fellows (http://www.whitehouse.gov/White_House /WH_Fellows/html/fellows1-plain.html), detailing a program under which, each year, 11 to 19 young men and women are selected to serve for a year as full-time paid special assistants to senior White House staff and Cabinet officials. The site gives the history of the program, its current working assignments, details of the selection process, and its educational opportunities. Also featured are comments from alumni of the program, including Colin Powell (1972–1973), former chairman of the Joint Chiefs of Staff.

want to perk up your postal efficiency by using your full nine-
but can't figure out what those last four digits ought to be. Say
Net knows.

The U.S. Postal Service's website includes a nifty
zip code lookout database (http://www.usps.gov
/ncsc). Simply input your delivery address, city, and
state, and within seconds it will figure out the nine
numbers for you.

Other options let you input a five-digit zip code and find out what city it
represents, or input a city and state and receive the five-digit zip code and
other information for that location.

THE LEGISLATIVE BRANCH

The nation's lawmaking machinery—the Senate and the House of Representatives, as well as their formidable information reservoirs at the Library of Congress and Government Printing Office, just for starters—is
thoroughly online these days. Washington's primary product always has
been data, but it has never been as searchable and sortable as it is now.

Need a copy of a law? Want to track a bill through the House or
the Senate? Have to find something in the *Congressional Quarterly?*
Want to know what your representative has been sponsoring these
days? As you'll see in the following sections, your computer can tell you
all this and much more.

House of Representatives

The House of Representatives Home Page (http://www.house.gov) is
steeped in data that are quite specific (biographical information about
House members, committee assignments, schedules and organizations,
as well as other U.S. government resources), but it is also rich in the
kind of broad-based general information that makes it a prime site for
teachers and students. For instance, you'll find comprehensive articles
on how laws get written and passed. An entire "Legislative Process"

section is dedicated to bills and resolutions being considered in Congress, current information about what's happening on the House floor, and a record of how individual members voted on specific measures. Another section reports on parliamentary controls, for example, resolutions defining the rules of debate for consideration of a particular bill on the House floor, and the associated committee report.

Options on the House's main page can give you details of recent House action (usually the most recent three days' floor votes) and a searchable database that lists the status of bills, amendments, and the like. Other options provide transcripts of committee testimony; details on committee votes; resolutions; and summaries of floor debates.

The *Congressional Record* is searchable here, as is a database of names, addresses, and phone numbers for members, committees,and House leadership. Electronic editions of key House publications, such as the *House Ethics Manual* and Thomas Jefferson's *Manual of Parliamentary Practice*, are available.

The Senate

When the White House and the House of Representatives were neck and neck in the race to reach the Web, it appeared that the Senate wasn't even going to make it to the post. Early in 1996, the Senate, the last major federal government body to reach cyberspace, finally got its World Wide Web site up and going.

The site (http://www.senate.gov) is still evolving; new features are being added regularly. A directory of senators lists the links to the fifty or so who have their own individual home pages, and the e-mail addresses of the 70 percent of senators who have them at this writing.

If you're a civics student, the educational files available on the Senate page are useful. The site not only provides the names of senators serving on the various committees, but gives valuable background information in an "About the Committee System" option. Because of the high volume and complexity of bills and issues, Congress divides its tasks among some 250 committees and subcommittees. Standing committees generally have legislative jurisdiction, and subcommittees handle hearings and research in specific areas. Select and joint (Senate and House) committees are chiefly responsible for oversight and housekeeping

Dedicated to "the spirit of Thomas Jefferson," Thomas quickly has become one of the hottest political sites on the Net—and with good reason. This site at the Library of Congress (http://thomas.loc.gov) can hook you up with:

Thomas the Data Tracker Is an Online Star

▶ Full text of all versions of bills in the House and the Senate, searchable by keywords or by bill number.

▶ Full text of the *Congressional Record,* the proceedings on the House and Senate floors—again, searchable by keyword.

▶ Connection to the "House Gopher," which provides directory information on House members and committees, the yearly calendar, the latest daily committee hearing schedules, the current week's House floor schedule, visitor data, and so on.

▶ The "Senate Gopher," similar to the "House Gopher" and including searchable committee and member documents.

▶ An e-mail directory of House members and committees.

Other features include the C-SPAN (Cable-Satellite Public Affairs Network) Gopher, with program schedules, press releases, election results, and online essays and pamphlets, such as "How Our Laws are Made," by Edward F. Willett Jr., House law revision counsel.

Thomas's search facilities in the legislation database and in the *Congressional Record* are easy to use. Select the desired search option. You will be prompted to enter a keyword or a phrase in a query box, for example, HAZARDOUS MATERIALS TRANSPORTATION. The search system then brings back results in relevance-ranked order, based on the search words entered. For more comprehensive retrieval, you can do an additional search on synonymous terms or phrases.

Regarding the database of bills, the search you type into the query box will be run against the text of all bills in the database for that Congress. However, you may elect to limit your search to the text of bills for which floor action has occurred or to the text of enrolled bills. The system then presents, in ranked order, a brief display of the first 100 most relevant items that match the search criteria. Although 100 items is the standard cutoff, you may opt to see more bills by adjusting the number, up to 1,000, in the "Maximum Number of Items to Be Returned" box. If fewer than 100 items match the search criteria, then all of the items will be displayed. By selecting the link entitled "List

---

Thomas the Data Tracker (continued)

of Bills by Bill Type," you may elect to "browse" a sequential numerical listing of bills by bill type, for example, all House bills numbered from H.R. 1 to H.R. 500, or all Senate Concurrent Resolutions starting from S.Con.Res. 1.

    The page includes links to the Library's LOCIS system (telnet://locis.loc.gov), for federal legislation summaries and status, and to its LCMARVEL database (gopher//marvel.loc.gov), for additional legislative information.

---

chores. You can learn how committees are funded, how bills move through the committees toward the Senate floor, and what actions committees can take. "The Legislative Process," a 55K electronic-text document, describes the rules and the body of precedents under which the Senate operates on a daily basis. It can teach you about debates and filibusters; how legislation is introduced, amended, and enacted; and the functions of quorum calls and roll-call votes.

If you're planning a trip to Washington and want to see the Senate in session, a "Visiting the Senate" option provides tips for viewing Capitol artworks and historic rooms, spending time in the Senate galleries, and visiting your own senators and representatives. Other items give specific dates and times when the Senate is in session, and the schedule for other Senate activities outside of the Senate chamber, including details of special services available for disabled visitors. "A Virtual Tour of the Capitol" lets you join a predetermined guided room-by-room tour, via captioned color photos on your screen; or, you can wander on your own with the help of an on-screen electronic tour map.

Library of Congress

Used primarily as an educational resource for students and history buffs, the Library of Congress site (http://lcweb.loc.gov/homepage/lchp.html) displays samples from assorted exhibits. During our electronic visit, for instance, "American Memory" featured a digitized collection of historic drawings, photos, and mementos. Other displays offered material on the Gettysburg Address.

This is an outstanding resource for learning about copyright. Linking to the home page of the U.S. Copyright Office (http://lcweb.loc.gov/copyright), the site teaches the basics of the copyright law: what can be protected and how. Electronic versions of its circulars show various copyright registrations from written works of fiction and nonfiction and from the performing and visual arts.

The site's LC Online Systems (http://lcweb.loc.gov/homepage/online.html) gives you search tools for trolling LOCIS (Library of Congress Information System).

The Vietnam Era Prisoner of War/Missing in Action Database (http://lcweb2.loc.gov/pow/powhome.html) contains the known information on those still listed as missing in action in the Vietnam War. This massive resource, containing more than 121,000 records, was set up to assist researchers investigating federal government documents pertaining to service personnel killed, missing, or imprisoned in Southeast Asia.

U.S. Government Printing Office

The U.S. Government Printing Office distributes publications of the Congress, the executive departments, and the federal government in general, through its website (http://www.access.gpo.gov). Here, you can examine documents such as House and Senate reports that contain committee findings on matters under investigation; the reports of the Committee on Foreign Relations, relating to treaties and trade relations with foreign nations; and monthly economic indicators published by the Joint Economic Committee.

The site also catalogs printed materials available from the thousands of federal depository libraries around the country. Books, maps, posters, periodicals, and electronic information products from numerous federal agencies are listed, along with information on the nearest U.S. Government Bookstore and alternative sellers.

Office of Technology Assessment

If technology is your search goal, you can see major assessment reports, background papers, briefings, and testimony on a variety of complex issues involving science and technology at the Web home of the Office of

Technology Assessment (OTA) (http:www.ota.gov). An online statement at the site notes that the OTA does not advocate particular policies or actions, "but points out their pros and cons, sorts out the facts,
and provides options."

The OTA's ongoing studies in energy, transportation, ·infrastruc-
ture, international security, space, industry, telecommunications,
commerce, education, human resources, environment, and health are
available via options at the site. Many of its publications are available
in electronic form online.

Congressional Quarterly

If you want to think the way Washington insiders think, you have to
read what they read. You can start with the *Congressional Quarterly*.

Founded in 1945 by newspaperman Nelson Poynter, the *Congressional Quarterly* has set up online facilities (gopher://gopher.cqalert
.com) to share regularly updated news and analysis on current events,
perspective pieces on state and local government, and information on
seminars, publications, and directions to related sites.

CapWeb (http://policy.net/capweb/congress.html), a straightforward, even-
handed guide to the Legislative branch, has links to features in the Senate,
the House of Representatives, the Library of Congress,
the U.S. Constitution, and other resources.

CapWeb's Political Page (http://policy.net/capweb
/political.html) provides fast links to other sites with political content. Although most of CapWeb is nonpartisan,
the gloves definitely come off in the Political Page. It

**CapWeb: A Guide to
the U.S. Congress**

links to House and Senate Democratic and Republican pages, as well as features by the Libertarian Party and pages by presidential candidates and others. Don't miss its "Parody and Play" section, with features from The Capitol
Steps, "The World According to Helms," and others.

The lively "Presidents and Presumers" section is the page's Campaign
'96 section. You'll find information on the convention plans of the major parties and the latest from the primaries and caucuses.

The Capitol Steps: Clickable Parodies

Say you're cruising for cutting-edge political comedy. You probably can't do better than The Capitol Steps, who have been spoofing official Washington with wickedly wonderful song parodies since the Reagan era.

Names on the Net

All the members are current and former congressional staffers who monitor events and personalities on Capitol Hill, in the Oval Office, and in other centers of power and prestige around the world. The troupe performs at Chelsea's, in the Georgetown area of Washington, most Fridays and Saturdays, and also appears on campuses around the country and, occasionally on National Public Radio.

At its website (http://pfm.het.brown.edu/people/mende/steps/index .html), the group offers online sound files of their latest compositions, as well as information about their tapes, CDs, and personal appearances. For instance, on the site during our recent surf-by was this new Valentine's Day politically correct complaint: "You Don't Bring Me Floriculturally Diverse Polyfragrant Soilistically Challenged Multipetaled Victims of Pesticidal Food Chain Chauvinism."

Most Web browser software is already designed to play the Steps' online files, but if you're in doubt, a "Sound Check" option enables you to verify your setup. If necessary, the page can link you to software that you can retrieve to bring your browser up to spec.

The site has documents and cover stories from current and past issues of five publications: (1) *CQ Weekly Report,* (2) *CQ Special Reports,* (3) *The CQ Researcher,* (4) *CQ's Weekly Alert,* and (5) *Governing* magazine. A recent issue of *Governing* focused on state governments and the effects of term limits. In a story called "15 Babes in Power," the mandate for "handing control of legislatures over to people who are just learning the ropes" was explored.

"Washington Alert" includes a database on the status of major legislation, appropriations, and congressional votes from recent years. For instance, if you need to see the House vote on the Motor Voter Registration bill in February 1994, this site can give you the yeas and the nays.

CompuServe Offers Congress Member Database

If you find yourself on CompuServe with a sudden pressing need for the address of your congressional representative, relief is just a few keystrokes away.

A Members of Congress database (enter GO FCC-1 on CompuServe) provides the names and addresses, state by state, of congressional representatives, plus the president and the vice president. Each listing includes: name, party affiliation, Washington telephone number, hometown, and committee memberships.

Off the Web

THE JUDICIARY BRANCH

The U.S. Federal Courts Home Page (http://www.uscourts.gov) is maintained by the Administrative Office of the U.S. Courts as a clearinghouse for information from and about the judicial branch. You can also find features like "Understanding the Federal Courts," a description of how the federal courts operate, and *The Third Branch*, the electronic version of a monthly newsletter of the federal courts. Instructions are given for automated access to U.S. federal court information and records, to press releases covering issues such as funding for the court system, and to statistics, such as a rise in the number of bankruptcy filings.

Come here also for statements from the justices. During a visit at the beginning of a new calendar year, we found text of Chief Justice William Rehnquist's annual report on the federal judiciary. Providing an interesting insight into the daily workings of the bench, the report is a traditional vehicle for the courts to "speak" to the Congress, the president, and the public, primarily on the administration of the judiciary, the salaries of judges, and the caseload.

Occasionally, the site seeks input from visitors. In October 1995, for example, the Judicial Conference's advisory committees on the rules of appellate, bankruptcy, and civil and criminal procedures proposed amending a wide variety of rules on how attorneys could present evidence and arguments in federal courtrooms. The site summarized

An electronic mail bulletin provided by Cornell University Law School's Legal Information Institute is an ideal way to stay current on the latest U.S. Supreme Court decisions. Since 1993, the Institute has distributed, within hours of a ruling, its "liibulletin," an electronic syllabus of the Supreme Court's decision.

Having the Court Come to You

To subscribe, send e-mail to listserv@lii.law.cornell.edu; as the text of your message, write:

subscribe liibulletin [your first and last name]

You then will receive an electronic bulletin containing summaries of all decisions of the Court shortly after they have been handed down. The message will contain instructions on how to access the decisions in full text or receive them by e-mail.

the proposed amendments and gave detailed examples, then sought comments from interested parties.

Elsewhere, the Library of Congress offers a gopher site of Supreme Court data (gopher://marvel.loc.gov/11/federal/fedinfo/byagency/judiciary). The site links to material on the justices, information on the requirements for U.S. court clerkship, a manual on the judicial branch, and searchable text of the U.S. Code.

Searching Supreme Court Decisions

For more extensive options, including searches of actual court decisions, you must turn to other resources, provided mostly by university law schools.

Brian Shelden of Cornell University Law School's Legal Information Institute has created software that gives the Net community near-instant hypertext access to archived Supreme Court decisions. Rulings are archived at Case Western Reserve University on the day they are handed down by the court. They are then automatically indexed and entered on access documents by the software available at the Cornell site (http://www.law.cornell.edu/supct).

Visitors can search rulings issued since May 1990 by keyword, words in a case name, year, or docket number. A search may consist of:

- Single words (such as *copyright*).
- Combinations of words: you want all decisions that include them (e.g., *copyright* and *fair* and *use*).
- Combinations of words that are alternatives: you want decisions using either (*forfeit* or *forfeiture*).
- Ranges of words that are alternatives: you want decisions within the range (*forfeit-forfeiture*).
- Words that operate to exclude (*forfeiture not 1993*).

The material can be searched by selecting specific topics from a far-ranging list of subjects. Here is a sample:

abortion	due process	labor
animals	elections	Medicare
antitrust law	employment	military
attorney fees	environment	Miranda rights
bankruptcy	FCC	obscenity
capital punishment	firearms	obstruction
civil rights	Freedom of Information Act	patent
clinics		pension
communications	habeas corpus	police
competition	harassment	reasonable doubt
confidentiality	health	reporters
conspiracy	housing	schools
copyright	immigration	Social Security
disclosure	immunity	speech
discrimination	impeachment	tax
disease	imprisonment	workers' compensation
double jeopardy	Indians	
drugs	infringement	

Elsewhere on the site are pre-1990 decisions on some "hot button" topics, including decisions bearing on school prayer, administrative law decisions, patent law decisions, copyright cases like *Feist Publications Inc. v. Rural Tel. Serv. Co.*, and *Roe v. Wade*, the landmark

1973 case that upheld a woman's right to an abortion. Another section of the Cornell location (http://www.law.cornell.edu/supct/justices /fullcourt.html) features profiles and related material about the Supreme Court justices.

Selected Supreme Court cases can be browsed in the "law center" of the new Court TV Home Page (http://www.courttv.com/library /supreme). The site provides "hot" cases from lower courts, on topics such as the death penalty, computers and technology, government documents, and tobacco. (More on the Court TV site is given in Chapter 6.)

Appeals Court Decisions

To find rulings and other information from the federal courts one level below the U.S. Supreme Court, check out Kenneth P. Mortensen's work at the Center for Information Law and Policy, at Villanova University's

---

Peter Adams: The Political Science Handbook

Peter Adams believes the Internet is "the most powerful form of media that the world has ever witnessed." He says it even has "the editors of the world's leading newspapers questioning the viability of the printed word." But, he says, the Net can use a hand in sorting out its treasures.

Names on the Net

That's why Adams—who works by day at a New York advertising firm, in charge of its Web development work—launched his Political Scientist's Guide to the Internet (http://www.trincoll.edu/pols/home.html), a particularly Net-savvy electronic handbook to direct students and political professionals alike to the wealth of information online that pertains to politics, government, and law. This is excellent one-stop shopping for political wonks. Come here for resources on the mechanics of government, issues, political research sites, and international political affairs.

The *Trincoll Journal,* a weekly multimedia magazine (http://www .trincoll.edu/tj/trincolljournal.html), and Harnessing the Internet (http:// www.trincoll.edu/harnessing/home.html), an interactive Internet training facility, are also recommended.

School of Law. Mortensen, a teaching fellow and director of operations at the Center, maintains the Federal Court Locator (http://ming.law .vill.edu/Fed-Ct/fedcourt.html), which is especially adroit in linking resources for decisions from the U.S. appellate court. The site is built around an interactive map of the United States that shows the eleven federal circuits and the District of Columbia. Click anywhere on the map to be transported to that particular circuit's home page. If you want to see decisions of the federal appeals court that represents Maryland, North Carolina, South Carolina, Virginia, and West Virginia, click inside that portion of the map and you will be taken to the home page of the Fourth Circuit, which happens to be maintained by the Emory University School of Law. Home pages for other circuits are managed by other regional law schools. Most pages offer browsing and keyword searching of recent decisions.

The Villanova Center for Information Law and Policy (http:// www.law.vill.edu), a project sponsored by the National Center for Automated Information Research, probes wide-area-networking needs for legal and accounting information from governmental sources. The site has links to publications and online tools that are of interest to the legal community.

Other Sites

Suppose you're looking for a more academic overview of the court system and its status. Check in with the Federal Judicial Center. Established by Congress in 1967 to study the courts' operations, and ways to improve the court system, the Center maintains a home page (http:// www.fjc.gov) devoted to education and training, with strong emphasis on computer technology and the courts. Here too are publications on assorted legal issues (sentencing guidelines, scientific evidence, voluntary arbitration, and mandatory minimum prison terms).

If you're a working lawyer or paralegal—or a layperson interested in the field—the Seamless WEBsite: Law and Legal Resources (http:// seamless.com/index.html) might be your ticket. The site has four components:

1. The Chambers contains introductory news and messages about the site.

The Internet is at its best when it is producing text. Whether you're panting to read the U.S. Constitution, the Mayflower Compact, or some other historical document, you can almost always find it somewhere online. Here are some Net sites for documents:

Getting Government and Historical Documents

▶ The Declaration of Independence, an enacted by the Second Continental Congress on July 4, 1776, declaring the USA's independence from England (http:www.house.gov/Declaration.html).

▶ The U.S. Constitution, the heart of federal law (http:www.house .gov/Constitution/Constitution.html); Amendments (http:www.house.gov /Constitution/Amend.html); Amendments considered but not ratified (http:www.house.gov/Constitution/Amendnotrat.html).

▶ The U.S. Code (http://www.pls.com:8001/his/usc.html). This is the official text of the federal laws, compiled in order of subject matter, under fifty alphabetically listed titles (such as arbitration, banking, education, highways, labor, and so on). Each subject is subdivided into sections. The site provides facilities for keyword searching.

▶ Code of Federal Regulations (http://www.pls.com:8001/his/cfr.html). This code, promulgated by agencies of the government, compiles regulations of general applicability. Like the U.S. Code, it is organized under subject titles and subdivided into sections.

▶ General Accounting Office reports (gopher://dewey.lib.ncsu.edu/11/library /disciplines/government/gao-reports).

For assorted historical documents from the United States and around the world, don't miss the massive Historical Text Archive (HTA) (http://www .msstate.edu/Archives/History/index.html). Operated by Mississippi State University's College of Arts and Sciences, the HTA stores historic documents from the U.S. colonial period, the American Revolution, the early republic period, and the 19th and 20th centuries, as well as documents relating to wars, immigration, Native Americans, and African Americans. Click on "Pre-Colonial," and you can retrieve the Magna Carta of 1215, the Mayflower Compact of 1620, or the first Thanksgiving Proclamation of 1676. Revolutionary War-era documents include Patrick Henry's "Give me liberty or give me death" speech (1775), the Articles of Confederation (1777), and the Treaty of Paris (1783). The site has archived the inaugural addresses of U.S. presidents from Washington to Clinton; biographies of leaders; and the flags of the nation since its founding. Important international documents are relevant to the history of Africa, Asia, Canada, Europe, Latin America, and Mexico; the history of women; and the history of African Americans. A history buff could take up permanent online residence here.

David Wuolu: Tracking Federal Agencies

David Wuolu, electronic services librarian at Louisiana State University, is one of the online heroes who save us all so much time by compiling guides to extensive sections of the Net. Wuolu's U.S. Federal Government Agency Directory Scope (http:www.lib.lsu .edu/gov/fedgov.html) is perhaps the most comprehensive list of assorted government organizations available anywhere on the Net.

Names on the Net

Intended for people who know where they want to go but just don't know the Web address, the resource has sections devoted to the executive, legislative, and judicial branches of the government, as well as to independent and quasi-official agencies. The depth of detail makes Wuolu's compilation especially useful. For instance, besides links to the Department of Agriculture, Wuolu's page has online connections to assorted services dealing with farming, food services, animals and plants, natural resources, agricultural research labs, extension services, and rural economic development agencies.

---

2. The Commons offers original articles and writings on law-related topics.

3. The Shingle links with home pages of lawyers and law-related businesses on the Net.

4. The Cross-Roads sends you along to more than 1,000 other law-related sites on the Net—law firms, law schools, international legal sites, and pages devoted to state and federal law resources.

CITIES AND TOWNS

The "space" syllable in *cyberspace* suggests a medium that is infinite, omnipresent, like air—existing in all places and in no one place exclusively. That simile is true enough, but, in another sense, the Net also is a largely local experience. Chances are that, even as you read these words, someone employed in your local government is working on a

America Online Offers Capital Connection

American Online's Capital Connection (use the keyword CAPITAL on AOL) provides various political information services as well as discussion areas. Among the offerings are congressional names, addresses, phone numbers, and fax numbers. Active features are related

Off the Web

to current national and local campaigns and elections. Evolving from a feature originally called "Issues Forum," the site invites debate on controversial topics and current events. Administered by Brian Carlisle, the forum provides space for:

▶ The Freethought Forum, which promises to "promote reason over superstition and provide a platform where leading thinkers can present their concepts of self-reliance."

▶ *Policy Review Magazine,* published by the conservative Heritage Foundation.

▶ The Libertarian Party, which spins out information about its operations.

home page on the Web devoted to the activities of his or her department. An increasing number of cities and towns are staking out residences on the Net. They're catching on: the same site that can provide residents with copies of tax forms, schedules of public hearings, and contact numbers for various departments can also serve as a welcome mat for out-of-state tourists thinking of visiting. For businesses considering relocation, a community's very presence online in these early days of our collective Net life can convey sophistication and worldliness to some observers. Beyond those public relations advantages, local government officials are finding the Internet very useful when they need to communicate with their counterparts in other parts of the region, the nation, or the world.

Public Technology Inc.

Public Technology Inc. (PTI) is the nonprofit technology wing of several urban planning/management groups, including the National League of Cities, the National Association of Counties, and the International City/County Management Association. Charged with bringing computer technology to local government, PTI has created an online site (http://pti.nw.dc.us) that is rapidly becoming a major electronic clearinghouse for city and county data.

If you want to see what some cities are doing on the Web, PTI can show you. It is leading the way, getting local communities to set up their own home pages by providing a central location for reaching PTI. The site has a regularly updated list of links to pioneering efforts of local governments as they explore Internet's potential, from Long Beach, California (http://www.ci.long-beach.ca.us), to Hennepin County, Minnesota (http://www.co.hennepin.mn.us), to Atlanta, Georgia (http://www.atlanta.com).

If you want a local perspective on topics such as energy, environment, transportation, or telecommunications, visit the site's research center. It also gives information about state municipal leagues and county associations on the Web; key contacts in federal environmental, energy, and criminal justice offices; details on getting government-related news; and downloadable articles on the role of local government in expanding information technology. If you are a salaried or elected local government official, you might be interested in the site's "Access Local Government," a private online forum that lets government professionals share information in an informal online setting.

CityLink

The USA CityLink Project (http://www.usacitylink.com/citylink) is a comprehensive service dedicated to becoming a starting point for Web surfers who need information about U.S. states and cities. Project coordinator Carol Blake says that the site, which started in mid-1994, attracted more than 2 million online visitors in its first year, including students, tourists, and businesses.

She says the product, which links to city home pages, state pages, and others, invites links to towns and cities outside as well as within the United States. Blake provides online facilities for local and state governments to send details of their pages for inclusion. Someone on the staff will log in and see whether the transmission meets the CityLink requirements for listing. The site provides a pro forma press release that can be shared with local media about the city's or state's inclusion in the project.

BEV: America's Most Plugged-in Citizens?

In the Blue Ridge Mountains of Virginia, you'll find America's most thoroughly wired town: BEV—Blacksburg Electronic Village—Bell Atlantic's $7 million test site for new communications technology. BEV has introduced computers to many of Blacksburg's businesses and more than a third of its 36,000 residents. Among the early findings is that, for all the talk of globe-hopping through cyberspace, computers also can help us talk to our next-door neighbors in the real world.

Names on the Net

BEV (http://www.bev.net) is a first-of-its-kind cooperative venture involving the town of Blacksburg, Bell Atlantic (a regional phone company), and the local university, Virginia Tech. The mountain village has been turned into a test site for new technology (such as modems that communicate at 100 times the speed of conventional units). So far, home computers in 13,000 of the town's 36,000 residences have linked into the subsidized network (each residence pays $8.60 a month to get connected), nurturing a large base of advanced users for future product tests.

But beyond all the technology, "BEV is really a communications project, a social project," says system director Andrew M. Cohill, a Virginia Tech professor. And one of the things he is seeing is that, for all its global goodies, the Internet also can be a hometown sensation.

"Sure, there's a certain novelty item when you first get connected," he says, "but if you think about what people do in their daily lives, they tend to be focused on activities close to home. So, here, they do 'Blacksburg stuff.'"

Such as? Electronic shopping with local merchants. Buying food. Ordering flowers. Finding out how to get various permits and licenses from Town Hall. Soon, residents will be able to pay taxes and utility bills through the network.

BEV is bringing the world to Blacksburg. Residents like to tell the story of Wade's, the local grocery store chain, which was using the system to sell only flowers. Someone in Kuwait, just out surfing the Internet one day, found the store's online kiosk and used it to ship flowers to friends in Pennsylvania.

But BEV also is bringing Blacksburg to the world. "We're not xenophobic," Cohill says. "BEV is not only a local project. What I hear over and over is people in Blacksburg wanting to sign up so they can send and receive electronic mail to families scattered all over the country."

BEV (continued)

So, could it be that communications is that long-awaited "killer application" the computer industry has wished for, the promise that will put a computer in every home?

"Well, I don't know about that," Cohill says, "but I call it the 'glue application,' because it's what holds everything together."

Names on the Net

The site also offers marketing opportunities for cities. For instance, as Mardi Gras approached, the site offered a Mardi Gras '96 promotion for New Orleans, with links to hotels and motels, a message from the mayor, contests, on-screen maps and guides, events schedules, a recipe for New Orleans' famous Mardi Gras King Cake, sound files of Bourbon Street jazz, and a glossary of seasonal terms (to keep the flambeaux away from the boeuf gras).

REGIONAL CENTERS

Realizing that many computer users surf the Net as preparation for taking a vacation or business trip "in real life," some regions of the country are beginning to use the Internet as a kind of never-ending travel bureau.

For instance, the Southeast Information Depot (http://www.southeast.org) is a collection of information about the southeastern United States and links to other southeastern WWW servers. For each state in the database, there is information on:

▶ Business: the climate for agriculture, economic growth, employment/unemployment, federal job opportunities, industry, real estate, and trade, and how to reach its chamber of commerce.

▶ Government: the various agencies, census data (population and per-capita income), the legislature, a directory of congressional representatives, and maps.

▶ Education: major colleges and universities, and primary and secondary public schools.

▶ Leisure: museums, sports teams and activities, travel attractions,
average weather and temperatures, and related material.

The Southwest Scout (http://www.swscout.com) provides information on topics such as tours available for the Four Corners and
Navajo Reservation, data on Navajo trading posts and arts and crafts,
and online photos and paintings.

The New England Online site (http://ftp.std.com/NE), which
focuses on the six northeastern states, delivers general travel, tourist,
and economic information. The site provides general resources (census and weather) along with information on New England's skiing re-
sorts, water activities, tourism highlights, and some general-interest
ecopolitical data, such as "The Nukes of New England—Reactors in
New England" and "Northeast River Forecast Center: Floods and
Droughts in New England."

Also covering New England interests is the Yankee Web Explorer
(http://www.tiac.net/users/macgyver/ne.html), which connects to assorted regional/state indexes, specific state home pages, the Cape Cod
Information Center (featuring a real estate database and a photo

---

From Here to There, as the Digital Crow Flies

In the tradition of great inventors, Darrell Kindred has made something new
out of something old.

The Carnegie Mellon University computer science student's "How Far
Is It?" Distance Server (http://gs213.sp.cs.cmu.edu
/prog/dist) calculates the distance between *any* pair
of U.S. cities. It automatically uses the University
of Michigan's Geographic Name Server (telnet://
martini.eecs.umich.edu:3000) to find the latitude and
longitude of the two places named. After completing its figurings, it logs into
the Xerox PARC Map Server (http://pubweb.parc.xerox.com/map) to provide
a map showing the two places.

gallery), a Boston restaurant list, and tips on metro hot spots, vacation ideas, and the like.

Out west, the Pacific Northwest Travel Page (http://www .shore.net/~adfx/2398dir/pntp.html) currently is focused on the Seattle/Tacoma area, but has plans to expand to encompass all of Washington, Oregon, and Idaho, part of Montana, British Columbia, and perhaps part of Alberta. Return here for expanded tourist and travel tips for the region.

STATE GOVERNMENTS

StateSearch (http://www.state.ky.us/nasire/NASIREmain.html) is a wide-ranging database maintained by the National Association of State Information Resource Executives. Members are senior officials from various state executive, legislative, and judicial branches who have executive-level and statewide responsibility for information resource management. (Associate members of the organization include representatives from federal, municipal, and foreign governments, as well as state officials who are involved in information resource management but do not have chief responsibility for that function.)

Serving as a clearinghouse for online resources (from documents and studies to websites, phone numbers, fax numbers, and addresses), the site can tell you how to reach state officials in two dozen different areas:

auditors

criminal justice

economic development and
    commerce

education

employment services

energy

environment and natural
    resources

executive branch

finance and administration

governors' offices

health

human services and
    welfare

information resource
    management

judicial

The health and fitness of a state or a metropolitan area usually are determined through demographics. The Net is a never-ending source for these vital statistics. Want to determine the changes in the population of your city, county, or state—or the nation? Gauge the economic health? Find the latest crime figures? Determine whether the poverty situation is improving?

Getting the Facts on States and Cities

For these and other statistics, your first stop has got to be the U.S. Census Bureau (http://www.census .gov), which makes selections from the Statistical Abstract of the United States, the County and City Data Book, and other resources. Specifically linked are:

▶ Population and Housing Data (http://www.census.gov/pop.html), including the latest briefs on social and demographic topics such as homeowners and home vacancies; income and poverty figures; the labor force; and estimates of population change. A "PopClock" feature estimates the U.S. population as of today.

▶ Economy (http://www.census.gov/econ.html), with highlights from the latest U.S. economic indicators. Specific economic and trends data on agriculture, manufacturing, and construction are offered, as well as the bureau's County Business Patterns, statistics of U.S. businesses, current industrial reports, economic data programs overview, economic census, and surveys. Data on income and poverty, international trade, the North American Industrial Classification System, and financial reports for manufacturing, mining, and trade corporations are also available.

▶ Geography (http://www.census.gov/geog.html), including the Data Maps (http://www.census.gov/stat_abstract/profile.html). You're invited to click on a portion of a U.S. map to get profile information on selected states.

Beyond the Census Bureau, there are other demographic resources. Suppose you question what the governor of your state said about unemployment locally, in his State of the State address. You can check the facts for yourself at the U.S. Bureau of Labor Statistics site (http://stats.bls.gov /blshome.html). Are you wondering what impact, if any, tourism is having on the economy? The U.S. Bureau of Transportation Statistics (http://www .bts.gov) deals with data on that subject every day. Perhaps the local mayoral race is heating up over the issue of crime. You can check on regional crime figures with the Bureau of Justice Statistics (gopher://uacsc2.albany.edu /11/newman).

libraries and records
   management
lieutenant governors
procurement
regulation and licensing
revenue

state home pages
state legislatures
tourism
transportation
treasurers

Suppose you need to contact the governor's office in Hawaii. Selecting the "Governors" option on the main page and "Hawaii" from a subsequent list, you are transported to the home of Governor Benjamin J. Cayetano. You can give a message to the governor, get a biography and a copy of his latest State of the State address, and link to the general Hawaii state government page. Or, if you need to talk to someone about traffic accidents in Alaska, you could select the "Criminal Justice" option, pick "Alaska's Department of Public Safety" from the resulting list, and get whisked away to the state commissioner's own home page and the Public Safety Department's divisions.

Also, don't miss a page called Piper Resources' State and Local Government on the Net (http://www.piperinfo.com/~piper/state/states.html), an index of Net links divided into three main groups:

1. Federal resources related to state and local governments, such as state-run rural development councils and the U.S. Advisory Commission on Intergovernmental Relations, a direct link between the federal and local governments.

2. Organizations, such as the National Association of Counties, the Council of State Governments, the National Conference of State Legislators, and the National Center for State Courts.

3. Other links, such as state capital newsletters, insurance and tax resources, and groups like Innovations in American Government.

The site can connect you with home pages operated by and about all the states, and it provides a keyword search option for fast look-up. *The Piper Letter,* intended to provide computer and technical advice to public agencies and governments, is also available.

Several other sites serve primarily as indexes to state government links around the Web. The most comprehensive of these sites are:

▶ The home page of the Council of State Governments (http://www.csg.org), which links users with the group's States Information Center. A database of tens of thousands of documents makes publications, such as the Council's *State Government News, Spectrum,* and *Innovations,* available in full-text format. Details on conferences, other government sites, and related Net resources are also provided.

▶ The WWW Virtual Library of State Government Servers (http://www.law.indiana.edu/law/states.html), listing Web resources from specific states—from Alabama's Government Services Home Page to Wyoming's State Library. Many of the cited links are to states' legislative sites.

▶ State Government Information Servers (http://www.trincoll.edu /pols/us/states.html), compiled by Peter Adams. Arranged alphabetically by state, the list links to a potpourri of data—general state home pages, sites of state courts and legislatures, public schools, election pages, and various state departments.

INTERNATIONAL RESOURCES

The *world* now has a home page. IanWeb (http://www.pitt.edu /~ian/ianres.html) was launched in 1994 by the International Affairs Network to assemble and simplify access to Internet global information resources.

The service—a collaborative venture by the University of Pittsburgh's Graduate School of Public and International Affairs, its International Management Development Institute, and others—is funded by a grant from the Pew Charitable Trusts. An international affairs archive stores research papers and documents for immediate access worldwide. This site links to resources elsewhere on the Net, organized by source and subfield.

Make this your first stop when you need to find Net links to sites provided by specific countries—perhaps the Australian government's

defense information, or the Virtual Embassy of Finland, an embassy in
Spain, Hungary, the UK, or other countries. IanWeb also links to the
primary U.S. federal government resources for international affairs:
the State Department's Foreign Affairs Network (http://dosfan.lib
.uic.edu/dosfan.html), the Commerce Department's Economic Conversion Information Exchange (http://ecix.doc.gov), the National Trade
Data Bank (http://www.stat-usa.gov/), and the U.S. Information Agency
(http://www.usia.gov).

Other sections of IanWeb provide resources from academic institutions, inter- and supranational organizations, think tanks, associations
for independent research, periodicals and working papers, and international news sources. The site has data and connections for material on
international economy, foreign policy, security, peace and conflict resolution, economic development, technology, science and environmental
policy, international law, teaching and curriculum development, career
resources and new positions, and grant opportunities.

For researchers of international topics, the site links to electronic
editions of important academic documents. Need information on agreements pertaining to world trade? Foreign and international law? Treaties
in international security? This is the place. Also found here is a link to
the archives of documents on the Arab-Israeli conflict and on the activities of the United Nations and the International Red Cross.

United Nations

The United Nations home page (http://undcp.or.at/unlinks.html) provides not only background on the organization, situation reports, and a
large collection of international data links, but also keyword searching
for General Assembly and Security Council resolutions, and connections to related sites on activism, women, conferences, human rights,
and international affairs.

From this site, you can reach many other UN organizations: the
Food and Agriculture Organization, the International Atomic Energy
Agency, the International Telecommunications Union, the United Nations Children's Fund, the UN Conference on Trade and Development,
the United Nations Development Fund for Women, the United Nations
Educational, Scientific and Cultural Organization, the UN Environment Programme, as well as various UN commissions and committees.

CompuServe and AOL Offer Visas and Travelers' Advisories

American Online and CompuServe both have several databases that are of interest to international travelers.

Off the Web

On CompuServe, the Visa Advisors and Electronic Visaguide (GO VISA), provided by a firm based in Washington (DC), expedites the process of getting passports and visas, and supplies applications and information on the travel requirements of more than 200 countries. It offers same-day service for passports to persons able to submit copies of their round-trip tickets.

On both AOL and CompuServe, the U.S. Department of State's Travel Advisory Service (enter GO STATE on CompuServe; use the keywords TRAVEL ADVISORIES on AOL) is maintained by the Citizen Emergency Center as a continuously updated information service to Americans traveling abroad. The database includes advisories and warnings on conditions such as warfare, political unrest, hotel/motel shortages, currency regulations, and other information of interest to the American traveler. To locate travel advice about a particular country, select the country's name from an alphabetical menu. In dealing with conditions of risk that might affect travelers abroad, a program offered by the U.S. State Department's consular information unit has these categories of information:

▶ Consular Information Sheets, available for every country in the world. They show the location of the U.S. Embassy or Consulate in the subject country, unusual immigration practices, health conditions, minor political disturbances, unusual currency and entry regulations, crime and security information, and drug penalties. If an unstable condition exists in a country but it is not severe enough to warrant a warning, a description of the condition may be included under an optional section entitled "Areas of Instability." Consular Information Sheets generally do not include advice. Instead, they present information in a factual manner so the traveler can make his or her own decisions concerning travel to a particular country.

▶ Travel Warnings are generally issued because of civil unrest, natural disasters, or outbreaks of serious disease. Warnings are issued when the State Department decides, based on all relevant information, to recommend that Americans avoid all travel to a country, particularly to its problem areas. Temporary advisories will be canceled as soon as the situation improves. Countries where travel is not recommended will have Travel Warnings as well as Consular Information Sheets.

Other International Data Reservoirs

The Intelligence Consulting Group (ICG) is a Chicago-area research firm specializing in international topics such as defense, economics, and econometrics analysis, but ICG is best known on the Net for OLIN, the Online Intelligence Project (http://www.icg.org/intelweb /index.html).

Visiting this site sometimes can give you a hint as to *tomorrow's* headlines. For instance, in 1995, well before the United States had committed peace-keeping troops to Bosnia, this page was highlighting data on the deteriorating situation there. Beyond the political hot spots, the page provides resources, news, and commerce and security data on Europe and Russia, Asia and the Pacific, Canada, Latin America, and the Middle East.

For a tamer view of international affairs, visit the Electronic Embassy (http://www.embassy.org), the Net home for Washington's Embassy Row. You'll find information on some 160 foreign government embassies and the countries they represent, from Afghanistan to Zimbabwe. Some entries list only the embassy's address and phone number, but, increasingly, there also are home pages. As an example, the Embassy of Norway page (http://www.norway.org), provides the

---

Canada's Quaker community is online with the Peaceweb (http://www .ottawa.net/~peaceweb), a source of information on a number of affiliated pacifist organizations: Peace Brigades International, Project Ploughshares, Peacefund Canada, Conscience Canada, and Quaker Peacemakers. The site proudly traces the Quaker history in peace and politics, offering text on historical Quaker testimony as well as a modern position statement.

The Quakers Come Online with Peaceweb

Also online are excerpts from writings by Mohandas Gandhi, Martin Luther King Jr., and others. Connections to other resources link you with the Peace and Conflict Resolution Archives at the University of Colorado, and the U.S. Institute of Peace, a federally funded U.S. agency devoted to peace research.

Foreign Affairs Magazine Goes Electronic

Foreign Affairs, perhaps the most influential periodical on the subject, has an electronic presence now.

At its website (http://www.enews.com/magazines/foreign_affairs), you can find the full text of major feature articles, paragraph summaries, and other excerpts from the most current issue. Keyword searching of an article—by subject, author name, or date of publication—is available.

ambassador's spin on the nation's cultural, political, and travel scene; a history-and-culture lesson on Norwegian food; Nobel Prize-winning author Sigrid Undset; and how the Vikings discovered America. The Electronic Embassy also offers information on passports and visas and on connections to other international sites around the Net. Details on foreign affairs personalities, committees, and issues, and links to nongovernmental organizations involved in foreign affairs can be accessed.

Students and travelers should check these out:

Websites Predicted to Increase Fivefold in Six Months

Seattle's Internet Solutions Inc. keeps an up-to-the-second Internet statistics estimator running on its Web page (http://www.internetsol.com). According to this source, the number of websites still is doubling about every two to three months, as it has for the past year. The company estimated that the Web would hit the 100,000-site mark in mid-1995, and was predicting nearly a half-million locations by year's end.

A company statement noted that, if the current rate of growth continues, there will be 17 billion sites by the year 2000.

What's wrong with this picture? Project manager Matt Jensen observes, "Since that would imply three computers for every person on the planet, I think we can expect the growth to taper off quite a bit before then."

▶ Social studies goes electronic in the Library of Congress's Country Studies/Area Handbook Program (http://lcweb.loc.gov /homepage/country.html), a collection of online books. Each book is about a particular country, describing and analyzing its political, economic, social, and national security systems and institutions, and examining the interrelationships of those systems and the ways they are shaped by cultural factors. Studies are written by a multidisciplinary team of social scientists.

▶ For a quick, current profile of any nation in the world, click into the Central Intelligence Agency (http://www.odci.gov) and select its "World Factbook" option. The CIA produces its factbook annually for use by U.S. government officials. Its own data are merged with information from the Bureau of the Census, the Defense Intelligence Agency, the Defense Nuclear Agency, the Department of State, the Maritime Administration, the National Science Foundation (Polar Information Program), the Naval Maritime Intelligence Center, the Office of Territorial and International Affairs, the U.S. Board of Geographic Names, the U.S. Coast Guard, and others.

▶ Before you take that trip to Tunisia, drop in at the U.S. State Department's Travel Advisories (http://www.stolaf.edu/network /travel-advisories.html). It will give you the latest travel warnings and consular information sheets on countries around the world, as well as maps, health tips, and related data. By reading the reports, you'll know what to expect in terms of medical facilities, crime, security checks, and currency registration. Many of the reports have electronic mailing lists you can subscribe to, if you need to stay up-to-date on volatile situations in specific countries.

Chapter 6

Netting the News and Commentary

News and commentary have always fueled government and politics, but even they have a new spin in the cybersphere: commentary on the commentators. Where else but on the Net would you find an Anti-Rush Limbaugh Page or electronic journals, original cyber columns, and bulletin boards established to present alternative views on the day's events?

And, because cyberspace is a very large place indeed, there is room for traditional news organizations as well. Rapidly, the print giants are setting up shop in Cyberia. *The Wall Street Journal, The New York Times, USA Today,* the *Chicago Tribune,* and magazine giants like *TIME* are reaching out to a new breed of readers who are becoming accustomed to getting their news from a screen rather than a printed page. Along with newspapers and magazines come newsletters, wire services, broadcasters, and press release services, all ready to stake out a spot on the electronic newsstand.

In this chapter, we sample the journalistic juice of the modem nation. You'll see how to:

▶ Stay on top of the news. Special sites are dedicated exclusively to the year's big, complex, long-running story: the thousands of national and state political races taking place in 1996.

With some 10,000 electoral contests across the nation, just about everybody has a horse in the political races of 1996. A run for the presidency always gets top billing, but all kinds of regional and state races have kept us interested. Ballots will be cast for 33 U.S. Senate seats and for the entire 435-seat membership of the U.S. House of Representatives, not to mention 11 governor's offices and thousands of state legislative positions.

1996 Elections Offer Net News Providers a Proving Ground

Because voting usually makes the nation hungry for data, 1996 also has become a perfect year for *another* kind of race: national news organizations have been competing to make a place for themselves in cyberspace in hopes of discovering how best to cover the world from the Web.

The Net is a natural as a medium for reporting complex, long-running news stories like elections. Because it is able to reach a global audience instantly, the Internet is ideal for reporting the daily breaking stories through words, sounds, and pictures. In addition, the Net's enormous data storage capacity enables it to provide massive amounts of background information—facts and statistics, a backlog of previous statements and position papers, and earlier news stories. For us, as consumers, it's like having a newspaper, television, radio, and library all rolled into one. The same electronic publication that gives you a daily shot of campaign news can also let you "check the record" by looking through a database of the latest polling results, delegate counts, electoral college tallies, details on advertising expenditures, and campaign finance reports.

No wonder some of the top names in the news business have tapped into the Web's electoral energy. Even before the first caucus vote in Iowa and the first primaries in Louisiana and New Hampshire in February 1996, election-watch sites were popping up all around the Web, offering daily updates from the campaign trail.

As the election year has progressed, several news sites have emerged as the front-runners for the facts. And just as the primary season was wrapping up in the spring, two of the best on the Web—ElectionLine and Politics USA—announced they are merging, creating a super-site to cover the conventions, the general election campaign, and politics beyond 1996. Let's tour some of these studioless news studios.

ElectionLine (http://www.electionline.com), produced by ABC News, *The Washington Post,* and *Newsweek* magazine, was launched as a broad-

1996 Elections (continued)

based resource for election news and campaign background information, and developed an early reputation for accuracy. For instance, on the day of Arizona's primary, but many hours before the votes were counted, this page opened with a story headlined, "Steve Forbes Says He is Going to Win the Arizona Primary Today." That prediction came true, surprising many who thought the race would be another showdown between Bob Dole and Pat Buchanan. The page also has featured commentary from ABC political director Hal Bruno and analyst Dwight Morris of the Campaign Study Group. ElectionLine tries to share some of the spirit of election campaigns in general, through a collection of "Defining Moments" video clips. Need a refresher on who said, "Where's the Beef?" or "You're no Jack Kennedy"? It's all here. You can also turn to this site if you need primers on election subjects such as state primaries, caucuses, and conventions, or if you're hazy on state demographics (population, health, education, labor, and income figures) and voting histories. For even more research, check out the page's links to the American Association of Retired Persons' '96 Voters Guide (http://www.electionline.com/AD/AARP/home.cgi). It has meticulously detailed sections on some of the campaign issues—Medicare, Social Security, tax reform, long-term care, and campaign financing reform.

Politics USA (http://PoliticsUSA.com), which provides breaking election news from primaries and conventions, has won praise for its analysis and commentary and for its campaign "buzz," the kind of insider information that makes politics such a great spectator sport. For example, the page—operated by Washington (DC) magazine and book publisher National Journal and Virginia newsletter publisher American Political Network—early in the campaign was carrying articles like "White House Insider: Mondale's Advice Is to Stop Slinging Mud," adding, "Campaign '96 has become too personal and ugly, says our ambassador to Japan . . . where's the rewind button?" The page lets you review the candidates' schedules, use e-mail to send questions and comments to the candidates' staffs and to lawmakers and journalists, and register your opinion in a daily "Voter Booth" feature. For research, check out its databases of the Almanac of American Politics and assorted polling data. The site invites you to sign up for an electronic bulletin that will be delivered to your e-mail mailbox.

All Politics (http://allpolitics.com), a site created by Cable News Network (CNN) and *TIME* Magazine, emphasizes not only its extensive election news resources, but also the interactive nature of the online medium, "which

1996 Elections (continued)

can make you a prime player in politics today," say CNN President Tom John-son and Time Warner editor Norm Pearlstine in an online statement. "Ameri-cans have long felt disconnected from their leaders and the political process; this new form gives you the chance to reconnect with your leaders and with everyone else at the grassroots, whether it's to discuss a presidential debate, find a way to balance the federal budget by playing a game, vote your con-science on issues and candidates or even discuss policy issues with key political players." To that end, the site offers polls and "talk-back" e-mail fea-tures as well as reports from the campaign trail, summaries of issues, pro-files of leaders and behind-the-scenes campaign workers, poll results, videos, and sound clips.

If commentary is your cup of tea, drop into the Doonesbury Electronic Town Hall (http://www.doonesbury.com), where they don't have to take the gloves off because the gloves were never *on* in the first place. After conser-vative Pat Buchanan had scored victories in early GOP primaries, the site's "Straw Poll" one morning asked visitors to select one of the following alterna-tives to complete the description: "Pitchfork Pat, with his low-budget bomb-throwing campaign, will be in this thing all the way to San Diego. So what to make of him? Pat Buchanan is (a) a dangerous, proto-racist, neo-fascist, anti-Semitic xenophobe, (b) a refreshingly honest—if controversial—outsider who can raise critical economic issues and build a new conservatism of the heart, or (c) ultimately irrelevant but good for a few laughs in an otherwise dull cam-paign." Not exactly the phrasing a Gallup poll would have used. Maintained by software company Mindscape Online Publishing in cooperation with Doonesbury cartoonist G. B. Trudeau, the site also offers a "Daily Briefing" on political news and analysis, and a "Chat Hall" to communicate with other online visitors. If you're a long-time Doonesbury fan, be sure to catch the "Flashback" section. It displays panels from the syndicated strip that were published on the current date during five previous election years (1972, 1976, 1980, 1988, and 1992), and it shows the headlines of that day.

▶ Link up with electronic editions of publications you probably al-ready know from their paper-and-ink incarnations. The Web has something for everyone, whether your tastes lean toward Doones-bury or *U.S. News and World Report.* Increasingly, the electronic data are not reheated leftovers from the print publication, but in-formation specifically cooked up for the Net community.

▶ Make electronic connections with real-world radio and television shows. E-mail lets you send your questions, ideas, and comments directly to the hosts.

▶ *Hear* as well as *read* the day's news. After you get the rundown on "real-time audio," one of the Next Big Things online, you can retrieve software from the Net that enables you to use the speakers of your personal computer to hear radio broadcasts, speeches, panel discussions, and campaign sound bites (not to mention rock concerts and soap operas).

▶ Put national wire services to work for *you*. Your computer connections enable you to "assign" top wire services to gather the news stories you want while you're not even online, and save them for you until your next visit.

▶ Research back issues of important publications. Starting in the early 1980s, some forward-looking publishers of newspapers and magazines began preserving their text in electronic form, even before the availability of technology for fast and easy searching of that text. In the 1990s, we've all benefited from their foresight. Online services have started rolling out massive databases of newspapers and magazines, many with issues dating back a decade.

▶ Read cool new electronic journals designed specifically for the Net. Called "zines," many of these electronic magazines, existing only on the screen and not on paper, provide fascinating insights into a new computing subculture being born online.

As usual, our journey takes us primarily to sites on the Internet's World Wide Web. However, because of the topic, this chapter also makes a few extra off-the-Web stops, especially to visit several sites on CompuServe. The oldest of the commercial online services, CompuServe has always had a fondness for reference databases, including the kind of newspaper and magazine resources we are seeking.

News(without)papers

Doomsayers love to characterize the newspaper industry as slow, wasteful, anachronistic, and lumbering toward extinction—the dinosaur of the Digital Age. Increasingly, though, it appears that only the "paper" part of the newspaper business is in peril; the news portion is healthy and happening online.

Literally hundreds of newspapers, large and small, have launched Net sites. Each has a different way of doing it. Some give us only a sample of their printed product each day and use the rest of their online space to hawk subscriptions. Others serve up all or most of their news stories but create on-screen publications that are entirely different from the print editions. Some have extensive, searchable archives of back issues; others, instead, carry into the cybersphere the adage about nothing being as dead as *yesterday's* newspaper. Often, a print publisher initially will provide its online publications for free—happy at the start to give away access time in order to gauge public interest in the site and to test

Need more details out of Washington than you're getting from your newspapers and broadcasters? Look into the Federal News Service (FNS) (http://www.fednews.com/), a private corporation that intensely covers the White House, Congressional sessions and hearings, the U.S. Supreme Court, the Federal Reserve, regulatory agencies, the United Nations, and more.

Federal News Service

For a fee, FNS can give you verbatim transcripts of speeches, testimony, rulings, and the like. Its Moscow office provides verbatim text (in English) of the Russian Parliament proceedings, President Boris Yeltsin's speeches, news releases of other government departments, coverage of prominent politicians, and newspaper translations. FNS's Spanish News Wire (Notimex) offers 150 to 300 stories a day, written in Spanish, by some 400 native Spanish-speaking correspondents from all over the world. FNS reports are transmitted to major media and foreign governments in more than 115 countries.

Rates are subject to change, but during the summer of 1995, the service was charging $285 a month for 100 percent coverage of all congressional hearings' prepared-text documents. Complete presidential election coverage was being offered on a month-to-month basis.

A "focus service" can be customized to collect and deliver only the information you want. An FNS calendar of activities around Washington lists appearances of the president and the speaker of the House, conferences, embassy events, and election coverage.

out the software on electronic passers-by—but most indicate their sites eventually are intended for subscribers only.

The number of newspapers offering some form of electronic service—online sites, fax services, audiotex phone lines, and so on— increased sevenfold in the first few years of the 1990s, according to the Kelsey Group, a Princeton, New Jersey, media consulting firm. The total jumped from 450 in 1991 to 3,200 in 1995, meaning that about a third of the daily papers in the United States are looking beyond paper for their new media.

Your hunt for newspapers on the Net ought to start with Steve Outing's excellent Editor & Publisher Interactive site (http://www .mediainfo.com/edpub). An "Online Newspapers" option can link you to some 300 papers across the country and around the world (North, Central, and South America, Europe, Asia, Australia, and Africa). Outing, who is founder of Planetary News LLC, a consulting firm specializing in online newspaper services, also includes information on consultants, organizations, and newsletters focused on online news. Details on conferences and workshops, job openings, and classifieds also appear, as well as information on off-websites, such as computer bulletin board services operated by newspapers.

Another good resource for finding Web connections for specific newspaper, magazine, and broadcast organizations is NewsLink (http:// www.newslink.org), a product of NewsLink Associates, an academic and professional research and consulting firm studying electronic publishing and visual journalism. Managed by Eric K. Meyer, a journalism professor at Marquette University and a media consultant, NewsLink is a comprehensive list of links for more than 50 newspapers (commercial and university), 500 magazines, and more than 350 broadcasters. The group also is preparing a report called "Tomorrow's News Today," intended as a resource for potential online publishers.

At this writing, some of the best known print newspapers were still feeling their way around the Web, trying to find out whether consumers were willing to pay for news online, and, if so, how much. As a result, some of the best contenders in the early run of electronic newspaper pages were not from The Big Guys at all.

For instance, would you expect one of Silicon Valley's premier newspapers to teach colleagues elsewhere how to *do* computers? That's precisely what the *San José* (California) *Mercury News* does daily. Its

CompuServe Provides Major Newspaper Databases

CompuServe has staked out territory in the online newspaper business. The following major surcharged archives can be searched by keyword to retrieve full-text newspaper articles.

Off the Web

▶ News Source USA (GO NEWSUSA) is a Telebase Systems Incorporated gateway to major U.S. magazines and about fifty newspapers from cities across the United States. (Classified ads are not included.) The database is updated daily, but there is a two-day lag before today's newspapers become available and (a month's lag on magazine articles). The resource incorporates a "Scan" feature intended as a quick way to locate articles from several sources at the same time. A "Search Specialist" (SOS) feature gives research assistance online. At this writing, SOS is available Monday through Friday from 8 A.M. to 10 P.M. Eastern Time, and Saturday and Sunday from 10 A.M. to 8 P.M. Eastern Time. The surcharges for the newspapers are: $1.00 for the first five headlines located, $1.00 for each additional five headlines, and $2.00 for each full-text newspaper article retrieved, regardless of length. For the magazines, the surcharges are: $3.00 for the first five titles located, $3.00 for each additional five titles, and $5.00 for each full-text newspaper article retrieved. There is a $1.00 charge for each search that retrieves no titles.

▶ Newspaper Archives (GO NEWSARCHIVE) gives access to the complete text of articles appearing in more than sixty U.S., Canadian, and U.K. newspapers. (Advertising and classifieds are not included.) Articles from the late 1980s to the present are available for most newspapers. New articles are added daily, one or two days after they've appeared in print. You can search each newspaper by topic of interest and within a specified date range. To access the Newspaper Archives, you must use the CompuServe Information Manager software, which is available from CompuServe (and usually comes "standard" with your CompuServe signup kit these days). In addition to the normal connect-time charges, each full-text article viewed or downloaded incurs a $1.50 charge.

Full text of many newspapers is available from Dialog Information Services, Inc., on the Knowledge Index (enter GO KI on CompuServe), where you can search for more than 100 popular full-text and bibliographic databases. The surcharged service promises affordable reference searches of Dialog databases during evenings and weekends. At this writing, the database is surcharged at 40 cents a minute ($24 per hour), and there is no extra charge on how many articles you retrieve in that period. The service is available only in evening/night hours (6 P.M. to 5 A.M. local time).

lively Mercury Center Web (http://www.sjmercury.com) offers both free and subscription-only features. Its electronic publishing venture is subsidized with the traditional newspaper solution: advertisers, especially those offering goods and services of specific interest to Net travelers. For free, you can read the day's headlines and article summaries plus a featured home page story, and then search classified ads and other advertising. For $4.95 a month (or $1.00 extra a month if you already subscribe to the printed paper), you have access to the full text of the day's news stories, updated throughout the day; wire service articles; comics; and other features, such as an archive of humorist Dave Barry's columns.

Other newspaper sites are worth noting:

▶ *USA Today* (http://www.usatoday.com) has made its full online service accessible to all Web users. (At its launch in April 1995, the paper's highly graphic, regularly updated news and information service was available only to users of a customized USA TODAY browser, at a cost of $12.95 a month for three hours of Internet access and $2.50 for each additional hour.) All visitors now have access to the Gannett Inc. newspaper's more than 12,000 pages of news, sports scores, graphics, and worldwide weather. The publisher has said it will be free of charge "for a limited promotional period," but did not specify how long that period will be.

▶ *The New York Times* site (http://nytimesfax.com) offers a daily eight-page digest of the paper, with highlights of front-page stories, the top foreign, national, and business news stories of the print edition, sports results, a selection of editorials and commentaries, and the day's crossword puzzle. TimesFax is available by midnight Eastern Time each day. Designed to provide the "look and feel" of a newspaper, TimesFax on the Web is presented in Adobe Acrobat format. If your Web browser doesn't already recognize Acrobat, you'll need to download the free viewer that is available on the site, then follow its instructions on how to modify your particular browser software in order to use it.

▶ *The Wall Street Journal* on the Web (http://wsj.com) features "Money & Investing Update," a continuously updated electronic publication containing business and market news. The publisher expects that eventually the entire paper, including Personal

Technology and all other extensive technology coverage, to be on-line in a full-blown Wall Street Journal Interactive Edition, which will be updated around the clock. Initially, the "Money & Investing Update" was free, but don't be surprised if eventually it is available to subscribers only.

▶ *The Washington Post* Digital Ink project (http://www.att.com /bnet/services/dink.html), launched in early 1996, is a subscription service that, at this writing, requires special communications software (available by calling 800/510-5104). Following a thirty-day trial period, users pay $5.00 a month for five hours of connect time, with overtime billed at $2.95 an hour. The system connects current and past news and features from the Post, including eight years' files of archived text and photos from the Washington home office as well as the paper's bureaus around the nation and the world.

▶ *Chicago Tribune's* Career Finder (http://www.chicago.tribune .com) includes recruitment advertising in five computer and electronics-related areas. Copied from the newspaper's classified sections, the ads remain on the Web for two weeks. Advertisers pay a premium to have their ads on the Internet. The site also provides articles and columns about employment and employers.

TRACKING TV

Television also has jumped on the Cyberian bandwagon. Among the TV-related sites that have appeared on the Web are the slick home pages of big networks like NBC (http://www.nbc.com/news/index.html) and CBS (http://www.cbs.com), which offer some breaking stories online and a little political coverage from the campaign trail. By and large, these are not news resources so much as marketing vehicles and teasers for the evening newscasts. If you need some history of a network, bios of on-air personalities, programming schedules, and details of new shows, the sites often can help, but most are not great reservoirs of daily news reports or commentary.

A pleasing exception is the new CNN Interactive (http://www.cnn .com), from the Cable News Network. Drop by and you'll find a news summary updated *hourly* (not daily, as are some print-oriented pages). You can read the full text of key stories, and search a database of earlier news reports in a number of departments, including U.S. and world news, business, sports, weather, politics, show business, food, health, technology, and fashion. The CNN site has its own staff of reporters and editors who produce text, audio clips, and graphics for the site and who locate links to other Web resources.

The search option invites you to hunt for earlier stories and/or pictures in the database by entering one or more search terms. You can connect two or more terms by adding AND, OR, or NOT, as in DOLE AND NEW HAMPSHIRE (to find stories that mention both "[Robert] Dole" and "New Hampshire"), ELECTION OR VOTERS (to find those that mention either "election" or "voters" or both), and CHICAGO NOT ELECTION (for all stories mentioning "Chicago" *except* those that also mention "election"). The site lets you check a number of topic boxes (such as U.S. News, World News, Sports, Weather, Business, Showbiz) to narrow your search to a particular area.

At its launch in autumn 1995, the CNN site was free, but the page managers indicated some sort of payment—through subscriptions or advertisements—was in the works.

Court TV Invites the Net's Legal Eagles

Court TV gained national prominence for its live gavel-to-gavel coverage of sensational trials like the California case of the Menendez brothers, accused of killing their parents, and later, the O.J. Simpson murder trial.

Online, the Court TV Law Center (http://www.courttv.com) provides not only schedules for upcoming broadcasts and updated still images from its live-TV video feed, but also stand-alone news reports and commentary on legal issues of interest to newshounds.

The site isn't shy about politics, either. For example, in late February 1996, even as candidate Pat Buchanan was riding high on the strength of early Republican primary victories in Louisiana and New Hampshire, Court TV's "Legal Times" newsletter presented an online article linking the conservative candidate with a "pro-Confederacy journal" called *Southern Partisan,* thereby putting the presidential hopeful "in league with those who favor the ultimate Southern strategy: secession."

Legal issues are analyzed here. The last time we stopped by, the site had, among its online articles, "When Death Comes Knocking at

CNN Establishes CompuServe Beachhead

Many people heard about CompuServe for the first time in 1995, when Judge Lance Ito would take the afternoon lunch recess in the O.J. Simpson murder trial. Then, on the screen, instead of the judge, the prosecu-

Off the Web

tors, the star defendant, and his "dream team" of defense attorneys, CNN's Susan Rook was front and center with her lively "TalkBack LIVE" call-in show. Featured prominently each day were members of the show's "cyber audience," typing in from CompuServe's Talkback LIVE Forum online. Considered the first daily interactive talk show, the forum (enter GO TALKBACK on CompuServe) enabled visitors to respond to Rook and her associates through either the forum's message boards or the daily, simultaneous online conference. Comments made by CompuServe users on both the message board and the conference were regularly incorporated in the television program, along with input from participants using phone, fax, U.S. Mail, and digital-compression video conferencing provided by MCI, one of the CNN "TalkBack Live" technology partners.

That was just one of the forums started in the CNN Online area. For a look at CNN's suite of interactive services, enter GO CNNONLINE on CompuServe and see news-related forums, operated by television's Cable News Network, enabling CompuServe users to interact with the network's viewers, newsmakers, and CNN staffers. Highlighting the area are:

▶ CNN Forum (GO CNNFORUM), urging users to discuss and debate current events, including science, sports, politics, MediaWATCH (for discussing how journalists do their jobs), ShowBiz (for celebrity gossip), and more. The forum's libraries have transcripts of many of the network's stories, along with contact numbers and resources.

▶ CNN Business Forum (GO BIZNEWS), which links you to timely business information, transcripts of key CNN interviews, daily market averages, and real-time conversations with business leaders, industry experts, and various CNN staffers.

▶ OJ Simpson Forum (GO OJFORUM), devoted to what has been called the most publicized, most watched, most discussed, most famous murder case in history. The forum, still operating to cover related matters such as the "wrongful death" civil suit, enables users to discuss the latest legal maneuvers and evidence, debate the social and ethical implications of the

CNN (continued)

trial, and praise or criticize the media coverage. The forum's library contains trial transcripts, graphics of evidence, and photos of trial participants.

Off the Web

CNN Online offers online versions of some of the network's standard features, including "Entertainment News"—daily coverage of the news in music, film, and theater— and CNN Online's "Hollywood Minute." Written by Dennis Michael of CNN Entertainment News, "Hollywood Minute" features Hollywood views and news. It is updated Monday through Friday. Previous issues are available in Library 22, "CNN Showbiz" of the CNN Forum. Also available are: CNN Sports Calendar, The Washington Notebook, Earth Matters, and Motor City Memo.

Your Door," a glimpse of Alabama's death row, contributed by a New Jersey lawyer; "When Will Whitewater End?" a commentary on the congressional investigation of Bill and Hillary Clinton's involvement in a failed Arkansas savings and loan; and "Testing the Court on Polygraph Evidence," news of a U.S. Supreme Court case seeking to push open the door that bars introduction of lie-detector evidence in trials.

NET-BASED ORIGINALS

The computer medium effectively mirrors and shadows the movers and shakes of the Real World, but it also has its own online originals, particularly in terms of news and commentary. News wire services such as Associated Press, United Press International, and Reuters News Service bring the world to us in print in our daily papers; the Net has homegrown its own news services. Commentators like Mike Royko and Ellen Goodman come to us in established print newspapers and journals; Cyberia has electronic columnists such as Brock N. Meeks, hundreds of original electronic magazines (called zines in geek-speak), and its own original daily "newspaper," the "American Reporter," started by a group of professional journalists from around the country who were looking for a new gig on the global Net.

Conventional wisdom suggests that television news is not *journalism of record* because, unlike printed news, it doesn't have "back issues" on file anywhere. But, as the archivists at Nashville's Vanderbilt University can tell you, that's not exactly so.

Vanderbilt's TV Archive Documents Network News

For more than twenty-five years, Vanderbilt's Television News Archive has been systematically recording, abstracting, and indexing national television newscasts. You can now search text of those abstracts on the World Wide Web. And, in addition to the archive's "Network Television Evening News Abstracts" (descriptive summaries of each item on network evening news programs), the website (http://tvnews.vanderbilt.edu/) has added these other online features:

▶ "Special Reports & Periodic News Broadcasts," descriptive summaries of other news shows collected at the archive.

▶ "Specialized News Collections," descriptive summaries of collections of news material relevant to major events.

▶ "The Vanderbilt Television News Archive Newsletter," printed reports published about the news collection over the years.

Abstracts, dating back to the early 1970s, can be browsed by date and/or by network, but most often you'll find it more useful to search the database by keyword or phrase. Suppose you are interested in learning when the national television news broadcasts first mentioned Bill Clinton and Al Gore in the same news story. After you select the "Search" option on the Web page, the site displays all the years covered by the database, asking you to click on the year or years you wish to search. For this example, you'd choose 1991 and 1992.

You then can fill in the search query box. (The administrators suggest you use lowercase letters to enter search terms; use of capital letters can lead to unpredictable results.) To create more complex searches, you also can use logical connectors (OR, AND, and NOT) as well as an asterisk for a truncation search (comput* to find computer, computing, computation, and so on). For our example, you enter "clinton and gore" as the search query.

About five or ten seconds after you click on the page's "Search" button, the database reports its findings. In our example, it locates abstracts of forty-three stories in 1991 and 1992 that mention both "Clinton" and "Gore." Looking down the list, you can find the earliest mention, on May 19, 1991, on NBC:

Vanderbilt's TV (continued)

(Washington: Andrea Mitchell) Senator Al Gore, who may run for the presidency on the Democratic ticket, profiled; scenes shown. (In several speeches, Gore comments on the party, the Persian Gulf War, education.) Gore's '88 campaign recalled. (In interview, Gore ponders the future.) Possible Democratic candidates named: Governor Bill Clinton & Senator Jay Rockefeller.

(Note that Gore got top billing and a complete profile, compared to Clinton, who was simply mentioned as a possible presidential rival.) Further down on the list of abstracts you would find that more than a year passed before Clinton was rumored, on July 1, 1992, to be eyeing Gore as a running mate. On that day, Charles Kuralt reported on CBS that Clinton was said to have narrowed his choice to either Gore or Representative Lee Hamilton. A week later, on ABC, Chris Bury reported the field also included Senators Bob Kerrey, Bob Graham, and Harris Wofford. From New York, Jim Wooten reviewed the Clinton running-mate candidates and gave "reason why Gore is the smart-money choice cited," according to the abstract of that broadcast.

The Vanderbilt page creates a separate database for each year, so you can search for a word in a specific year, or you can search all the years. The resulting list is ranked by "relevance," using a scheme based largely on the number of occurrences of the search term compared to the number of words in the document. The list is currently limited in size to nearly 200 items per database. If you get 200 items, there are probably more.

As the example illustrates, these are abstracts of what was said, not verbatim transcripts of broadcasts. If you need the actual words, the site gives details on Vanderbilt's videotape loan requests for reference, study, classroom instruction, and research.

ClariNet e.News

ClariNet e.News (http://www.clarinet.com/index.html), started by Brad Templeton in 1989, and produced by ClariNet Communications Corporation of San Jose, California, is the Net's first original news service. It gives Internet service providers around the world general, international, sports, technology, entertainment, and financial news, as well as special features, comics, and columns. You can even order an Internet joke book, when you want to catch up on your cyberhumor. A new feature, "ClariNet Tearsheets," carries the top stories of the hour, updated regularly throughout the day. ClariNet's customers include corporations, universities, and public access systems around the world.

ClariNet is an especially attractive feature for those interested in news that doesn't usually get attention in local newspapers: international reports, news of technical developments in scientific fields, obscure legal rulings, and so on.

Daily data on ClariNet e.News come from Reuters News Service, Associated Press, and, for computer news, NewsBytes. Also available are stock reports and syndicated columns by writers like humorist Joe Bob Briggs and etiquette writer Miss Manners. Most of its articles are delivered to Internet service providers through Internet's plain ASCII text newsgroups (often called "UseNet"). As many as 300 different ClariNet newsgroups are available, each on a different subject—the environment, personal finance, book publishing, taxes, animals, medicine, law, and so on. One group is dedicated to local news in the San Francisco area. ClariNet's website provides samples of the newsgroups for prospective customers.

One problem with the Net's Usenet newsgroup bulletin boards is the sheer volume and diversity of data. An answer to the data overload is Stanford Netnews Filtering Service (http://woodstock.stanford.edu:2000), which can give you a personalized Usenet news delivery service via e-mail, sorting through literally tens of thousands of documents daily.

Stanford Sifts Newsgroup Data

Stanford's filtering service allows you to express your interests "in finer granularity," says an online statement, by submitting profiles that describe your interests. The system automatically filters incoming data against topics specified by users, customizing all hits into a single page.

Online at the website are examples of such profiles and a tutorial on how they work.

The service charges Internet service providers a site license fee for its news feeds. Everyone using that server can then have access to some or all of the ClariNet newsgroups. Costs for site licenses, at this writing, are $1.00 per site user per month, with a minimum site license charge of $60.00 a month. If your Internet provider doesn't subscribe to ClariNet, you can sign up as an individual, but it's pricey ($40.00 a month at present).

NewsPage

It's hard to imagine anything online being considered "old-fashioned" already. However, to some Net navigators who arrived online in recent years with the popularizing of the World Wide Web, ClariNet and all its pedestrian text-based newsgroups look like black-and-white TV. By and large, Web weavers want a little more zippity for their do-dah, and Individual Inc. thinks it provides this twist.

Individual's NewsPage (http://www.newspage.com) is a slick, colorful site that filters some 25,000 news stories from more than 600 worldwide sources overnight and categorizes the stories on a main menu. A strong computer-industry orientation is evident in the industry breakouts: computer hardware and peripherals, computer professional services, computer software, data communications, interactive media and multimedia, and semiconductors. Other industries covered include aerospace and defense, automotive, banking, business management, consumer electronics, energy, environmental services, health care, hospitality and gaming, insurance, media and communications, telecommunications, transportation, and travel.

NewsPage enables you to "bookmark" topics you like; by 8 A.M. each day, you will receive news on the topics you've marked. Other options let you scan brief summaries, then select some for more details. At this writing, NewsPage's briefs are free, and full-text articles are available to subscribers only for a fee of $3.95 a month. The site also offers, at $6.95 a month, "NewsPage Direct," a service that provides an e-mailed edition of stories on topics you've requested in advance.

FYI Online's NewsView

As this book was being finished, MCI Communications Corporation, a telephone company, announced plans for its new NewsView e-mail

CRAYON is one of those new Net ideas you just can't look at without saying, "Waaaay cool."

An acronym for CReAte Your Own Newspaper, CRAYON (http://crayon.net) enables online visitors to customize their own news resource by linking to their choices among more than 100 news sites around the Net for national and international news, weather, business reports, technology updates, entertainment stories, sports, comics, "tabloid" news, and online developments.

A New Kind of CRAYON

Created as a free service by Bucknell University students Jeff Boulter and Dave Maher, the idea is simple. "Imagine going to your local paper office and telling them exactly what you do and do not read," they say in an online statement, "and then the next day they deliver to your door a newspaper that is customized just for you. Getting the information you need is now faster and more efficient. This is what CRAYON does."

The two students created CRAYON in the spring of 1995, literally between classes and labs and in late-night sessions, for a news-hungry audience they knew well. For college students, they wrote, "It is easy to get isolated from the real world. We have irregular schedules, and most of us don't have TVs." There is a real need for a regular source of daily information, and the Net can be turned into a virtual newspaper. Want to follow news from your hometown? Follow the campaign on your favorite candidates? Get sports results on your teams? You're in charge.

To create your own paper, start by choosing one or more links from the site's list of checkboxes. CRAYON connects to the site and displays the news. The links you selected can be saved (on your hard disk) as a single bookmark in your Web browser software; from then on, you can access the sources without having to go through CRAYON. The simple beauty of the idea is that the "paper" you've saved on your disk doesn't have to get updated; rather, the information that your paper is *linked to* is updated, and the information providers on the Web handle that for you every day. To make changes—adding and/or deleting information sources—click on the "Update" button at the bottom of your paper.

newsletters (http://www.fyionline.com). Subscribers can personalize the newsletters by selecting topics of interest.

The service gets the requested news from two dozen wire services (including Associated Press, Reuters, Knight-Ridder, and *PC World*

Magazine, as well as international services such as the Russian ITAR-TASS and the Chinese Xinhua); from some 4,000 business and trade magazines, journals, and newsletters in databases operated by Information Access Company; and from company reports and filings provided by Dun & Bradstreet, Standard & Poor's, and the Reference Press.

To customize a newsletter, subscribers complete an online profile that lists keywords and topics they want covered. At this writing, the rates for the service had not been announced.

Brock Meeks and the CyberWire Dispatch

Brock N. Meeks has more readers than most daily newspapers. At their request, some 800,000 people around the world—including many inside the Pentagon, the FBI, and the Commerce Department—receive installments of his CyberWire Dispatch, a cool, caustic, sometimes comic commentary on Washington political and government life as seen from the information highway.

Focusing primarily on issues affecting the world of computers and the Net, the 39-year-old Meeks—by day, an award-winning Washington (DC) bureau chief for a trade journal called *Interactive Week*—writes his newsletter in the evenings and distributes it free, by e-mail, to anyone who wants it. Back issues are preserved in an archive on the Web (http://cyberwerks.com:70/cyberwire.cwd).

Don't let his name fool you; Mr. Meeks is no journalistic shrinking violet. His blunt, tell-it-like-it-is style harks back to an age of crusading, advocacy reporting that now—partly because of his work—is more common in the cybersphere than in print.

For example, in a dispatch headlined "You Can't Fool All the People All the Time," Meeks began: "The brain-dead, ill-named Communications Decency Act was, as expected, folded into the Senate's telecommunications reform package today . . . ." And in a latter transmission on the same subject (this one with the headline, "Jacking in from the 'Damn the Torpedoes' Port"), Meeks identified "a posse of top House Republicans . . . riding into Cyberspace wearing White Hats and riding a horse called the First Amendment."

Meeks also is more than his verbiage. CyberWire Dispatch is making the man into a veritable cyberpolitical insider. After his coverage of last year's debate over the Clipper Chip (a government proposal to install, in every computer in America, a "back door" through which

CompuServe's Executive News Service Offers Computer Power

For daily news, it's hard to top CompuServe's Executive News Service, where you can have immediate access to up to 4,000 new stories daily, including those from:

Off the Web

- ▶ Associated Press (national, Washington, sports, and business).
- ▶ United Press International (national, regional, sports, business).
- ▶ Dow Jones News Service (stories from the current issue of *The Wall Street Journal*).
- ▶ OTC NewsAlert (press releases from companies).
- ▶ Reuters News Service (world, North America, sports, financial, and European Community reports).
- ▶ Deutsche Presse-Agentur (German-language reports).
- ▶ Associated Press France (written and displayed in French).
- ▶ Australian Associated Press.
- ▶ Press Association News (a United Kingdom news agency).

The Executive News Service (which you reach by entering GO ENS on CompuServe) also automatically can save, in personalized electronic *clip folders,* any stories containing keywords about subjects that you want to follow. You create one of these online holding areas by selecting a folder name, expiration date, and number of days to retain clipped stories. You also specify the news wires you want the system to monitor for you, and the subjects to watch for (in the form of keywords). These folders support up to seven keywords or phrases (or candidates' names). Phrases may contain up to eighty characters, and may be enclosed in parentheses (LEAGUE OF WOMEN VOTERS). An asterisk (*) is a wildcard, so VOT* clips stories containing "vote," "votes," "voters," and so on. You also may qualify your phrase with a plus sign (+) to require two or more words or phrases to be clipped. This means "AND" as in CLINTON+VOTERS and CLINTON+ELECTION. To indicate that a story should be clipped if it contains one keyword but *not* another, use a minus sign (−), such as ELECTION−NATIONAL. To clip a story that matches any of two or more phrases, use the I sign to mean OR, as in ELECTION I VOTE I RUN-OFF.

ENS, surcharged at 25 cents a minute, works around the clock, even when you are not online. It instantly clips stories to offer to you the next time you visit the feature. You also may browse ENS's wires yourself in "real time," or search for recent stories.

government agents could spy on private citizens), Meeks was summoned to a secret rendezvous by some government officials. "They wanted to make it known that they were paying attention," he told Elizabeth Weise of Associated Press. "It wasn't threatening, but it was all kind of Spy vs. Spy, at Georgetown at two in the morning."

Of his reporting style, Meeks says, "I tell people, 'If you took all the attitude out of the Dispatch articles, they could wind up in *The New York Times.*' I have a commitment to reporting the facts; I just go off with those facts as I see fit."

Although Meeks distributes his work for free, CyberWire Dispatch is not without its rewards. "If I told you I didn't enjoy the exposure and recognition that my work gets, I'd be lying. I like the fact that all the hard work and effort has created a brand and reputation that's respected. That's the payoff—it makes a difference. That's why I went into this business."

To subscribe to CyberWire Dispatch, send e-mail to majordomo@cyberwerks.com. On the first line of the message (no subject necessary) type: subscribe CWD-L.

American Reporter

The *other* dream of most American reporters (besides writing the great American novel, or, these days, the great American screenplay) is the "Let's-blow-this-joint-move-somewhere-new-and-start-our-OWN-damn-newspaper" one. Joe Shea did that—without leaving his keyboard.

Shea's The American Reporter (http://www.clickshare.com:9999) holds the record as the first daily newspaper to originate on the Net. Its founding, in early 1995, was inspired by a series of notes posted in the Society of Professional Journalists Internet discussion group, in the wake of the demise of *The Milwaukee Journal.* Online, reporters and editors around the nation were bemoaning the loss of yet another grand newspaper and, when inevitably the talk turned to the perennial why-don't-we-just-grow-our-own-newspaper topic, Shea, a Hollywood, California, journalist who has written for *The Village Voice* and was an editor with *L.A. Weekly* magazine, decided to act. As he later told writer Ryan J. Donmoyer, in *Internet World* magazine, "I wanted to do it. Other people wanted to talk about it." Since April 1995, The American Reporter has

NewsNet, the Newsletter Network

Some serious news consumers depend on specialty newsletters. The online king of newsletters, along with an assortment of news wire services, is NewsNet.

Off the Web

The 14-year-old computer network connects with more than 800 full-text industry-specific newsletters, trade publications, and magazines in some thirty industries, including electronics, computers, aerospace, public relations, education, law, and medicine.

Suppose you are interested in topics related to government regulations and regulatory agencies. On NewsNet, that category alone has 137 newsletters and wire sources accessible, ranging from the "Antitrust Freedom-of-Information Log" and "Federal Grants and Contracts Weekly" to "Environmental Issues Report," "Hazardous Waste News," "S.E.C. Today," "The Political Finance & Lobby Reporter," and "Washington Telecom Newswire."

In all categories, for both current and back issues, information is delivered in full text and in many cases is available online before it is available in print. NewsNet also offers access to more than twenty worldwide newswires, including Associated Press, United Press International, Business Wire, PR Newswire, Agence France-Presse, Reuters, Jiji, Xinhua, and Knight-Ridder.

NewsNet users also have access to commercial credit company research databases from Dun & Bradstreet, TRW, and American Business Information; company and industry reports compiled by market analysts such as Standard & Poor's; business opportunities from the federal government; and stock and commodity quotes.

Best of all, the NewsFlash electronic clipping service allows for continuous monitoring of unlimited keyword phrases. This means you can establish a profile of the kind of material you are interested in, specify industry groups you want monitored, and file the profile, online, direct to NewsNet, which will then gather and save incoming news for you while you are offline.

Until recently, NewsNet was a powerful but dull-looking text-based system. However, in early 1995, the company jazzed things up a bit with new communications software called Baton, bringing the service online with a much more engaging look.

appeared on the Net five days a week, featuring the work of a loosely affiliated volunteer staff of some 30 correspondents and editors from around the world.

They keep it tight—under 40K words, or about seventeen single-spaced pages of text, per issue—because the publication is ported around the Net each day by e-mail, and some sites have a limit on the size of incoming mail. A typical issue contains two or three news stories, several features, an editorial by Shea, and a humor piece or essay.

Shea and his colleagues are beginning to explore other ways in which a cyberpaper might differ from its paper-based ancestors. For instance, The American Reporter, operating on a shoe-string budget, takes pride in giving journalists around the world an opportunity to have a financial stake in their own work. Each story earns "equity" for the correspondent in terms of profits from advertising and subscriptions, and income when their stories sell to other newspapers. Initially, the equity has been theory more than hard cash, but there is hope among Shea and his core of believers. Subscriptions are $10.00 per month for publications such as electronic magazines or bulletin boards for "first-copy use." (Subscribers may select stories—remitting the quoted price shown below the byline—for republication or reposting.) Shea told Donmoyer he hopes other papers across the country will start buying the copy.

For a publication born in the inky infinity of cyberspace, The American Reporter has a pleasant, homey camaraderie with its readers. In the dog days of its first August, when California was being broiled in a seemingly endless heat wave, Shea wrote in his lead article, "Please accept our apologies for a late newspaper today. The heat here in Hollywood, where we have no air-conditioning, blew out our trusty 386 so often it became pointless to try to work on the newspaper until it became cooler. . . ."

MAGAZINES AND JOURNALS

Web wonks who think they invented the concept of data surfing need to spend a little more time at the newsstand and watch what happens at the magazine rank. For decades now, those rows and rows of bright, glossy pages have been inviting browsers to stop and look inside. No

Mike Sierra and Chuck Shepherd:
The First Word in Flummery and Weirdness

"Flummery," from the Welsh word *llymru,* originally meant a soft, sweet jelly or porridge made with flour or meal. However, since the market for porridge has been way down for the past century or so, that old word has been assigned a new meaning in our time: "nonsense, complete foolishness." In that context, Mike Sierra has become the Net's father of flummery.

Names on the Net

In 1992, Sierra, a production editor with technical publisher O'Reilly and Associates, started collecting, for his own "amusement and sanity," examples of "political correctness," which, he writes online, "aside from the alien seed-pod theory, I find difficult to explain without resorting to a drastic waving of the arms. Wherever it came from, I hope this helps drive a stake through the heart of it once and for all."

Sierra's popular Flummery Digest (http://jasper.ora.com/sierra/flum/) is a carefully indexed assemblage of anecdotes and quotations collected from a wide assortment of publications, including *The American Spectator, The Boston Globe, Chronicles, Esquire, Harper's, Heterodoxy, Insight, The National Review, The New Republic, The New York Times, Newsweek, Penthouse, Policy Review, The Progressive, Reader's Digest, Reason, Spy, TIME, TV Guide, The Wall Street Journal,* and *The Washington Monthly.*

Many items aren't so much about political correctness as they are the old "say-it-ain't-so" kind of news. For example, Sierra includes an August 1992 story about an Australian who was jailed five years ago "for stomping his mother to death at four o'clock in the morning after she objected to his repeatedly playing the Bob Dylan song, 'One More Cup of Coffee.'" The stomper was given a weekend furlough from prison to attend a Bob Dylan concert.

Sierra warns us, "Many of these items may cause offense if you align yourself with any of a number of grievance groups, or if you trust the government with your hard-earned paycheck. Some may cause offense simply because they're disgusting, so you may want to skip any item that contains the words 'National Endowment for the Arts.' They are not meant to offend, only to instruct. Lighten up and enjoy yourself. Be careful, though: reading too many of them at once may give you a bad case of the shakes."

After Sierra, if you still need some help with your flummery factor, you can get into some really strange stuff with Chuck Shepherd's News of the Weird. The column, now syndicated in hundreds of newspapers around the

Mike Sierra and Chuck Shepherd (continued)

country by Universal Press Syndicate, is saved in an online archive (http://www.nine.org/notw/archive.html); issues date back to 1992. The current column also is available, but the online edition is delayed two weeks, to give the newspapers (the paying customers) a chance to publish it first.

Names on the Net

Shepherd hunts the same daily papers for his material. This quote, from *The Washington Post* on September 21, 1995, was in a story about a Maryland assistant county attorney who admitted purchasing sexual favors from a courthouse prostitute, but disputed the price. "I paid her $60 a visit," he is quoted as saying. "I wouldn't have paid $100 to her for anything. In a contest between lust and frugality, frugality always won with me."

With Shepherd, you can even have weirdness e-mailed to you by subscribing to his electronic mailing list. To do that, send e-mail to notw-request@nine.org and put the word subscribe (without quotation marks) as the subject. No text in the message itself is necessary.

wonder the World Wide Web immediately seemed like home to magazines, which—with their covers like home pages and their tables of contents like clickable menus of additional services—probably are the Web's closest relatives in real life.

Hundreds of magazines have set up camp on the Net. Like television and newspaper sites, each magazine location differs from all the rest in terms of how deeply the creators want to go digital. Some are no more than shameless come-ons for print subscriptions; others put the entire current issue online, parsing out a full-text article for free, with the rest of the magazine being held back for the paying online public. The best sites provide searchable archives of back issues. A few produce original online features that, rather than merely mirroring their print incarnations, enhance them with bulletin boards for public comments, editor feedback, and displays of additional photos and text that perhaps didn't make the paper edition.

The Electronic Newsstand (http://www.enews.com) was launched in 1993 to afford the Net community an opportunity to try before they

CompuServe Forums Service Writers and Broadcasters

CompuServe, as the oldest of the commercial online services, created the first discussion forums and these days has a number of these online clubs devoted to print and broadcast journalism. Next time you're modemming in those parts, check out:

Off the Web

▶ Journalism Forum (GO JFORUM on CompuServe), established in 1985 by Jim Cameron, president of Cameron Communications, Inc., a New York City consulting firm specializing in radio news and program syndication. He also is the anchorman for newscasts on the United Stations (RKO) Networks several days a week. The forum is designed to serve professional journalists, those in related fields, and students considering careers in the profession. Featured in the forum is MedNews, a searchable database that offers medical research news releases from thirty universities and nonprofit research institutions. Among the sources are: Columbia University College of Physicians and Surgeons, Duke University Medical Center, Johns Hopkins Medical Institutions, Stanford University Medical Center, and Yale University School of Medicine, as well as the American Medical Association, the National Cancer Institute, the National Institutes of Health, and more.

▶ Broadcasters and Broadcast Engineers Forum (GO BPFORUM), operated by John Hoffman, a broadcast engineer at the NBC Television Network in New York. He also presents an electronic magazine called *InCue OnLine*. The forum is open to individuals and companies involved in radio, television, cable television, professional audio and video communications, and so on.

buy—or, in this case, subscribe to—new magazines. It is a central location for a selection of articles from some 300 magazines and journals in key categories: automotive, books and CDs, business, computers and technology, entertainment, health, news services, sports and recreation, travel, and related catalogues. Links to some 2,000 other magazine sites elsewhere on the Net are found here.

Like traditional newsstands, The Electronic Newsstand is a place where you can browse—for free—through many publications. Every

Newsstand publisher provides the table of contents and several articles from the current issue. Archives of previously featured material also are searchable by keyword. You may subscribe to the printed versions of any of the publications via e-mail or by calling 1-800-40-ENEWS.

The site also produces its own weekly electronic magazine, *Off the Rack,* about the magazine business, its people, and its products. "We're interested in what the media obsesses about," says editor Brian Hecht, "why it obsesses at all and why anyone else should care." To that end, a prominent feature each week is "Hype Heaven," with caustic comment on what made magazine cover stories that week.

Increasingly, though, the megamagazine publishers have opted to initiate their own Web works rather than rely on third parties, as described in the following sections.

TIME, *Sports Illustrated*, Other Time Warner Magazines

Imagine *TIME* magazine being updated continuously throughout the news day, *every* day. On the Web, you don't *have* to imagine it: it's here. And so are daily versions of other American magazine giants, such as *Sports Illustrated, Money Magazine, Fortune, People, Life, Southern Living,* and *The National Review,* as well as major newcomers like *Entertainment Weekly* and *Vibe.*

They are all part of Time Warner's gigantic Pathfinder site (http://www.pathfinder.com), set up as an outpost for the corporation's enormous stable of publications and entertainment products, which also includes Warner Brothers, HBO, Elektra and Discovery Records, and TV's The Weather Channel.

Best of all, the site, which is evolving into a publication in its own right, also provides daily news updates, Time Inc.'s corporate data and product announcements, links to related sites, and educational features such as a link to the Encyclopaedia Britannica. In an online statement when it was launched in early 1995, the site noted, "When Henry Luce and Britton Hadden founded Time Inc. 72 years ago, they spoke about how the glut of information in our daily lives created the need for a guide to what was important and interesting. We like to think that if they were alive today, among the first things they would do is build a website."

U.S. News Online

U.S. News and World Report, existing for years in the shadows cast by *TIME* and *Newsweek,* has made a big commitment to the online world. With electronic versions on America Online, CompuServe, and Microsoft Network, as well as on the Web (http://www2.USNews.com /usnews), U.S. News Online has won praise from Net critics. For instance, *Interactive Publishing Alert* magazine, which reports on Internet activities, recently ranked U.S. News Online as the best overall news website of any national print publication, beating out *TIME, USA Today,* and *The Wall Street Journal* in categories rating online design, performance, ease of use, interactivity, and advertising and sales.

What impresses most visitors is the site's relevance to the Net community. While visiting in early 1996, we found articles not only on the presidential primaries and the general news of the day, but also reports on the turmoil over freedom of speech online in the wake of the passage of a telecommunications bill that bans "obscenity on computer networks." Features included an in-depth interview with Netscape Communications Corporation chairman James Clark on topics such as the future of Microsoft Corporation's Windows operating system, how to make money on the Net, and questions about encryption of online messages to avoid government eavesdropping.

U.S. News Online routinely features the top stories from its printed edition and newly updated versions written for the Net in several categories, including News Watch, Washington Connection, News You Can Use, and Colleges & Careers. It also provides a search option to look up stories in back issues, and information on U.S. News products (books, CD-ROM disks, and videos).

Hearst's Multimedia Newsstand

Hearst Corporation's Multimedia Newsstand (http://mmnewsstand .com) shares a few selected articles from some of its publications. As we were touring the page, for instance, it offered text of a *Harper's Bazaar* article called "Lolitas OnLine: Should Adolescents be Protected from Sex on the Net?" and a brief review of Sherry Turkle's book, *Virtual Gender,* on the same general subject.

The site details links to other home pages operated by Hearst publications, such as Car Collector, Living History, Lotto World, and Home Arts.

However, at this writing, the site operates primarily as an online venue to facilitate magazine subscriptions, sell videos, promote contests, and seek electronic mail to its editors.

Finding Computer Magazines

It doesn't take much hanging around these parts to learn what a diverse bunch Net citizens are, but one thing we all have in common is the computers that brought us to the Web in the first place. Is anyone surprised that the Net is especially adept at putting us in touch with the publishers of computer-related magazines and journals? Here is an overview of three top Net sites for locating the work of the computer press.

▸ CMP Publishing's TechWeb (http://techweb.cmp.com/techweb) links with the publisher's sixteen publications, which include *Home PC, NetGuide, CommunicationsWeek, InformationWeek, Interactive Age, Windows Magazine,* and other computer magazines. It features a searchable database that can focus on a specific magazine or search all of the magazines at once and produce full text of articles. The site has daily news updates and "virtual newsletters," such as the current TechCareers and TechFile on Windows 95, and it offers TechLink, an e-mail newsletter.

▸ Mecklermedia iWorld (http://www.iworld.com) is the Web welcome center for a number of computer magazines well known in the Net community, especially *Internet World.* In fact, Mecklermedia was one of the first magazine publishers positioned on the Net with its MecklerWeb, sharing Internet news, tips, how-to information, product reviews, resources, directories, and expert commentary. The site provides a live "chat room" called "The Net House" for computer-related topics and bulletin-board subjects such as security, multimedia, and other technical concerns.

▸ Ziff-Davis Publishing's ZD Net (http://www.ziff.com) is operated by perhaps the best known name in computer publishing. The esteemed *PC Magazine* resides here, as do *PC Week, MacWeek,*

Irish-born Mary Harris Jones would love how her name is commemorated on the cover of rabble-rousing *Mother Jones Magazine*. The original "Mother Jones," Mary was a fixture in the American labor movement in the first three decades of the 20th century. She is best known for her comment, "Pray for the dead and fight like hell for the living." Today, her spirit lives on not only in the pages of the liberal publication that bears her name, but also in an feisty website that has come to be known as "MoJo" to its friends and its detractors.

Mother Jones and the Coin-Operated Congress

On a typical day at MoJo (http://www.mojones.com), you'll find articles such as "What do Newt Gingrich's supporters want for their money?" and "Why did presidential candidate Phil Gramm help get a drug dealer and repeat felon out of jail?" But more than echoing its printed articles, MoJo has begun launching some original electronic features, such as the new "Coin-Operated Congress" in connection with the magazine's Full Disclosure Project.

"Political campaigns cost money, lots of it," says an online statement from the magazine. "The cost of a winning race for a seat in the Senate has gone from $1.2 million in 1980 to $4.1 million in 1994. To an alarming extent, that money is provided—to Democrats and Republicans both—by large donors (both individuals and PACs), many with very specific interests before Congress. They pay for the races—and then expect to be paid back. Mother Jones and The MoJo Wire, in cooperation with other nonprofit research organizations, want to shine a light on the legalized bribery we all suspect but rarely see exposed in the establishment press."

Under the heading "The Best Congress Money Can Buy," the Coin-Op Congress Data Viewer enables you to do some data-digging on your favorite—and your least favorite—federal candidates. The MoJo Wire is making available, in an easy-to-use graphical format, data gathered from the Federal Election Commission (FEC) by the Center for Responsive Politics.

To look at the data, simply enter the last name of the candidate you want to probe, then check the boxes to indicate what you want to include in the search (1991 to 1994 Political Action Committee contributions and/or individual contributions over $200). When you are done, select the "Show Me" button. After taking a few seconds to look up the candidate's name and get his or her official FEC code, the site gives you a screen from which you can confirm your choice (or select a particular candidate if more than one has the same last name). You will then get a page with a bar chart showing how much

Mother Jones and the Coin-Operated Congress (continued)

money that candidate received from each of the fifteen industrial sectors that the federal government uses to classify all donations.

From that screen, you can select any individual sector and see its total contributions broken down by industries—agriculture, communications/electronics, construction, defense, health, labor, lawyers, lobbyists, and miscellaneous. These industries can be further broken down into more specific categories. Say your candidate got most of his or her money from "Labor." You might want to click on that portion of the graph to see precisely how much was reported from the buildings trade unions, the industrial unions, public sector unions, and transportation unions. Want even *more* detail? Click on one of those breakdowns to see how much came from federal employees unions, how much from police and firefighter associations, and so on.

MacUser, Computer Life, and *Yahoo Internet Life.* The site also provides some original material, such as audio clips of commentary by columnists Gina Smith ("Gina's Dirt") and Charles Cooper ("Coop's Corner"), as well as downloadable software, updates to printed stories, access to back issues, and links to other websites of interest.

ZINES ON THE SCENE

And then there are *zines* (pronounced "zeens"). More than just paper magazines and journals transported and transformed for the wide open (cyber)spaces, the best of these electronic publications play with the medium and explore how words might work differently on the Web. Some are direct descendants of the "gonzo journalism" of the late 1960s and early 1970s (the school of "demented involvement," as originator Hunter Thompson once described it) that just cry out for R. Crumb cartoons. Trucking in and out of the dark spaces between fact and fantasy, clarity and obscurity, this is jigsaw journalism at its 1990s-style best. Others are cybo-neobeatnik sandwiches of poetry and prose, served

AOL, CompuServe, Prodigy Offer Magazines Online

Off the Web

Many computer mags have been online for almost a decade, but, in recent years, America Online, CompuServe, and Prodigy all have made a big push to bring major noncomputer magazines to your computer screen.

Among those with specialized sites on AOL (followed by their AOL keywords) are *Atlantic Monthly* (ATLANTIC), *Backpacker Magazine* (HIKING, BACKCOUNTRY, or CAMPING), *Bicycling Magazine* (BICYCLING MAGAZINE or BICMAG), *Car and Driver Online* (CAR AND DRIVER), *Consumer Reports* (CONSUMER REPORTS), *Disney Adventures* (DISNEY), *Flying Magazine* (FLYING MAGAZINE or FLYING MAG), *Longevity Online* (LONGEVITY), *National Geographic* (NGS or NATIONAL GEOGRAPHIC), *New Republic* (TNR or THE NEW REPUBLIC), *OMNI Magazine* (OMNI), *Popular Photography Online* (PHOTOS), *Road and Track* (CARS), *Saturday Review* (SATURDAY, SRO or LITERATURE), *Scientific American* (SCIAM), *Smithsonian Publications* (SMITHSONIAN), *Stereo Review* (STEREO REVIEW), *TIME* (TIME), and *Worth Magazine* (WORTH). For the latest additions to this section, visit the AOL Newsstand (keyword: NEWSSTAND).

On CompuServe, special sites have been set up for several major magazines, including *Sports Illustrated* (enter GO SIMAGAZINE on CompuServe) and *People Magazine* (GO PEOPLE). However, more important is the Magazine Database Plus (GO MAGDB), provided by Ziff Communications Company. The database contains full text of articles from more than ninety general-interest magazines. Topics covered include arts and crafts, business, cooking, current events, education, the environment, family, news, people, personal finance, political and consumer opinion, science, sports, and travel. Also available are book and movie reviews. Coverage for most titles begins with 1986 and is updated weekly.

with large dollops of the same angst, cynicism, and wonder that have sustained undergraduates for centuries. Some play it straight; they're out to make a mark for themselves in the new medium of paperless publishing, with news and commentary, new literature, and criticism. Others . . . it's a little hard to know *what* they're about, but their names are fun to play with: Aunt Salli's Cyberkitchen, Chip's Closet Cleaner,

Et Tu Boo-Tay, Grilled Pterodactyl, Holy Temple of Mass Consumption, i can't tell you anything, My Screws Aren't Loose—I'm Just Wired a Bit Different, OBZINE, Outrageous Online Uncle Al, Pete and Bernie's Philosophical Steakhouse, Poop God, Raging Smolder e-News, Strange Ways, TikiZine: A Bi-Weekly Survey of All Things Cool, TwentyNothing, and Your MoM.

In other words, the coolest people online are not those simply surfing the Net; they're the ones who are out there making the waves. "Zines are generally produced by one person or a small group of people," says zines expert John Labovitz, "done often for fun or personal reasons, and tend to be irreverent, bizarre, and/or esoteric. Zines are not 'mainstream' publications. They generally do not contain advertisements (except, sometimes, advertisements for other zines), are not targeted toward a mass audience, and are generally not produced to make a profit." And they are distributed partially or solely on electronic networks like the Internet. No one knows for sure, but as many as 10,000 zines may be published nowadays (many erratically, but then, how often would you *want* to see Dead Pig Digest?).

In a land that has 10,000 such publishers, perhaps the man with an index to them is king. On the Net, several kings of list-keeping can help you locate zines for all occasions:

▶ The EText Archives (http://www.etext.org), operated by Paul Southworth, Rita Rouvalis, and Jason Snell, is located at the University of Michigan and contains details on hundreds of zines. The site offers a special section on political publications, legal and religious documents, and more. And, as Southworth comments in an online statement, "There are many controversial files on the site that I do not endorse in any fashion, and some that I hope nobody endorses. Readers are expected to be able to defend their minds with reason."

▶ John Labovitz's E-Zine List (http://www.meer.net/~johnl /e-zine-list/index.html) details nearly 900 zines around the world, accessible via the Web and elsewhere on the Net, and updated at the beginning of each month. At this writing, Labovitz was adding options to cruise the list by keyword, media type, and other navigation methods. He publishes his own zine called Crash, a magazine of "alternative travel."

▶ Virtual Library's Electronic Journals Lists (http://www.edoc.com /ejournal) lists electronic journals by a number of categories (including academic and reviewed journals, college or university, e-mail newsletters, magazines, newspapers, political, print magazines that maintain web resources, and publishing topics) and provides options to search the library by keyword.

▶ Computer Underground Digest (http://www.eff.org/pub/Publications/CuD), maintained by the Electronic Frontier Foundation, upholds the counterculture reputation of zines by including many controversial journals on computer cracking, phone phreaking, piracy, and related topics.

RUSH LIMBAUGH: CYBER CELEB

If you just awoke from a ten-year nap, brace yourself for this news: One of the biggest names on the new digital 21st-century faster-than-blue-blazes medium of the international computer networking is a radio star.

Radio? Like static-y old AM/FM, big-analog-knob-for-changing-stations, rock-a-day-johnny, dialing-for-dollars? *That* radio?

The same.

Rush Limbaugh didn't create the cybersphere—in fact, in the Net's decade-and-a-half history, he wasn't even among its pioneer settlers—but the nationally syndicated radio show host has found an affinity among a segment of the Web's regulars that still astounds some observers. The conservative pronouncements on Limbaugh's daily call-in show appeal to a bloc of telecomputerdom's prominently white, middle-class, male population, but there's more to his popularity than that. Limbaugh himself is a Nethead. From the earliest days of the radio broadcasts, he was singing the praises of CompuServe and urging his listeners to write to him by electronic mail. (He still receives e-mail at his CompuServe mailbox, which can be reached from the Internet by posting to 70277.2502@compuserve.com.) And his fans often dominate the discussions on CompuServe's Issues Forum (on CompuServe, GO ISSUES), where one offhand comment on the air can result in a month's worth of electronic argument on the message board.

On the Web, Limbaugh receives a kind of veneration usually reserved for dead rock stars. "Online, Rush is not just a single person, and interactivity is not just a matter of a phone call or two," say writers Gary Wolf and Michael Stein in their Aether Madness: An Offbeat Guide to the Online World (http://www.aether.com/Aether/limbaugh.html). "The aetherial Rush is a legion of devoted listeners ('ditto-heads,' as they like to be known) who echo, extend, and occasionally argue with their hero's worldview—along with a few sadomasochistic Rush-baiters."

Rush trivia abounds. On his Unofficial Rush Limbaugh Home Page (http://mail.eskimo.com/~jeremyps/rush), in Seattle, Washington, 16-year-old Jeremy Schertzinger offers a Rush Limbaugh FAQ (fact database) about the commentator and his various stations around the country. And he puts the database in Web format so that users can simply click on highlighted text for additional information to questions such as, "Why is Rush labeled 'the Most Dangerous Man in America?'" Incidentally, the answer is under dispute. One suggestion is that the label first appeared in print in a letter from Jon Kleinman of Los Angeles to the *Los Angeles Times Magazine* on March 3, 1991. The letter said, "Radio is powerful. Limbaugh's view go unchecked. It is my view that he's one of the most dangerous men in America." However, others say a radio caller dubbed him that in 1990 or even earlier.

Meanwhile, Limbaugh listeners know that a favorite regular feature of the radio show is his song parodies and fake "commercials." Rush Limbaugh: The Radio Show page (http://www.mcp.com/people /rwaring/rush.html) is devoted to sharing these parodies and put-ons in the form of sound files (or .WAV files) that can be retrieved and played on virtually any PC. The site, operated by computer game programmer Robert E. Waring, lists the song parodies he has used and the original songs on which they are based, such as "Born Free," as performed by Andy Williams. Except that when Rush does it, there are added sound effects and occasional additional lyrics in the chorus, such as ". . . EAT BEEF . . . for beef is de-li-cious . . . beef is nu-tri-tious. . . ." Other Limbaugh classics include "Bomb, Bomb, Bomb, Bomb, Bomb Iran," "Womb to the Tomb," "Reginald Denny's," and "The American Excess Card."

Limbaugh fans know their hero loves to make lists. For a sample, check out radio station WTAW-AM's Rush Page (http://www.rtis.com /nat/pol/rush) and Limbaugh's "14 Commandments of the Religious Left," among which are "Thou shalt not kill. With these exceptions: life forms under the second trimester, and those opting for medically assisted suicides." Or, "Thou shalt not make any graven image out of any

Got something you think Rush Limbaugh needs to know *right now?*
The Berkeley Republican Club's Grand Old Page (http://www.berkeleyic
.com/conservative/index.html) offers a feature that
enables you to send an instant fax from your Internet account to Limbaugh's office.

Automated Fax to Limbaugh

substances which cannot be recycled" and "Honor thy mother. If she is dysfunctional, it is thy father's fault."

Meanwhile, among Limbaugh's digital detractors is Mike Silverman, who has built a net-rep with his fiery Turn Left home page, described in Chapter 3. Silverman doesn't hide his distaste for Limbaugh. His Anti-Rush Home Page (http://www.cjnetworks.com/~cubsfan/rush/antirush.html) is topped with a doctored photo of radio's hefty host morphed into a pig. Under the image is, "Oink If You Love Rush" and the motto, "We gather here today not to praise Rush, but to bury him." A highlight is his *answers* to Limbaugh's "35 Unquestionable Truths." The page also provides text of a report by FAIR (Fairness and Accuracy in Reporting) on Limbaugh's accuracy, along with the commentator's reply and FAIR's rebuttal.

Silverman's data goodies include Nate Patrin's "Rules of Right-Wing Talk Radio Bombast," such as, "The only thing that deserves to be recycled is a joke," "When you can't find any substantial basis for attacking your opponents, question their sanity, appearance, sexual lifestyle, etc.", and "Contradict yourself often, just to see if they're listening."

Others Online: Linking with Liddy, Stern, and Hamblin

Following Limbaugh's lead, other radio stars are rushing to the Net, from the politically charged G. Gordon Liddy of Watergate fame to shock jock Howard Stern. And the modem medium is providing global exposure to newcomers, such as conservative African American Ken Hamblin, who calls himself "The Black Avenger."

The G. Gordon Liddy Home Page (http://www.rtis.com/nat/pol/liddy) provides reports of Liddy's schedule, details of his books, The Liddy Letter (a newsletter), and connections to his e-mail address (potent@aol.com). This is also a resource for news of the controversial talk show host. For instance, not long ago, the page opened with a report headlined, "The G-man Honored," explaining how Liddy, "who has come under fire for telling his radio audiences the best way to gun down federal agents," had been named winner of the 1995 Freedom of Speech Award by the National Association of Radio Talk Show Hosts. Quoting from *TIME* Magazine, the page noted, "The judges admit that they agonized over the decision, but concluded that Liddy 'has been adamant in exercising his right to freely express his opinions, particularly in voicing political speech which is critical of the government.'"

Because free speech is in the ear of the beholder, there are those who argue that today's real First Amendment battles on radio rage around, not Liddy, but the outrageous Howard Stern. Fans of New York's ne'er-demure "King of All Media," whose provocative language

---

America Online Links with Assorted Talk Shows

A number of talk shows on radio and television have cyber sites on America Online. Among the specific shows that can be contacted through the system are:

Off the Web

▶ Geraldo Rivera Show (GERALDO or GERALDO SHOW), featuring a message board and a "Local Listings" section, to find out what time and on what station the show airs in your area.

▶ The Ricki Lake Show (enter the keywords RICKI LAKE on AOL), with online data about the show and opportunities for input from viewers.

▶ OnLine Tonight with David Lawrence (enter ONLINE TONIGHT). Most of the talk revolves around personal computers. Topics include Macintosh, PowerPC, DOS, or Windows computing issues. The online feature gives schedules for the show and telephone numbers for participating.

▶ Computer America with Craig Crossman (COMPUTER AMERICA), covering various computer topics.

Net-based Radio Is a Reality

In the Information Age, *all* data—text, audio, and video—can be stored and transmitted in digital form. With ever-faster modems and an international computer network to which we can connect them, the possibilities for Net-based global audio and visual media are fascinating.

Off the Web

And they're no longer just "possibilities." In 1995, several start-up companies began releasing "real-time" audio players—software utility programs that allow the average personal computer with a sound board (standard equipment in most PCs these days) to listen to online sound files. This development is prompting media moguls to begin some fascinating Net-audio experiments.

First, some background. Audio actually has been available online for a long time. The problem lay in how we had to listen to it. Audio files are usually quite large and, traditionally (as "traditionally" as *anything* is in this medium), you had to retrieve (that is, "download") the audio file and then listen to it with other audio-playing software. The effect was not especially breathtaking: you could spend eight or ten minutes downloading a file that, when finally played, produced maybe a minute and a half of sound.

The big improvement offered by the new generation of players is that you listen to the data *as you download it.* In other words, you simply click on a screen option and up comes your real-time player, which fetches the audio file and begins playing the sounds as it receives and translates the data. Not only that, the player offers tape-player-like "buttons" for pause, rewind, fast-forward, and so on.

Without question, future versions of Web browser software will have real-time audio players built in, but, at this writing, the technology is all so new that the players must be downloaded and added manually to the browser. Two competing firms are offering players, and savvy Net surfers have *both,* downloadable free from the respective Net sites:

▸ RealAudio from Progressive Networks (http://www.realaudio.com). This was the first real-time player on the Net and is more widely recognized.

▸ StreamWorks from Xing Technology Corp. (http://www.xingtech.com), the newcomer with something to provide. Xing seems to be the player of choice for more music-oriented sites.

Net-based Radio (continued)

This play-as-you-go technology put a twinkle in the eyes of a lot of audio information providers out there. Suddenly, everyone from CBS, ABC, National Public Radio, and local rock and country stations sees an opportunity to rap, rag, rant, and rave in real time. For instance:

Off the Web

▶ The Internet Hourly News (http://www.RealAudio.com/contentp/abc.html) is an online version of ABC Radio's newsbreaks. New material is added around the clock, at fifteen minutes past the hour. Visit the page for all the day's reports, or hear just the latest news, sports, and commentary. Also provided are Johnny Holliday Sports and commentary from Peter Jennings Journal.

▶ National Public Radio (http://www.realaudio.com/contentp/npr.html) uses the audio from its daily shows, including Morning Edition and the evening All Things Considered, as well as special features.

▶ Internet Radio Nexus (http://www.nexus.org/Internet_Radio) specializes in European radio news feeds. Most programs are excerpted from IRRS-Shortwave on 7,125 kHz to Europe, United Nations News, Swiss Radio International, Radio Copan International, and UNEP-PRB's environmental radio series on the Global 500 Challenge awards.

▶ Bootcamp from WCBS NewsRadio88 (http://www.pulver.com/bootcamp) is a ninety-second report on computer news featuring WCBS technology reporter Fred Fishkin on assorted software and hardware developments.

All the talk is not news and commentary. For instance, Brentwood (http://www.hallucinet.com:80/brentwood) is an old-fashioned radio soap opera (with new-fashioned computer themes to keep us attentive), produced by Bill Reynolds of Bear Left Productions in Hollywood. Interesting alternatives to rock radio, such as iRock (http://www.irock.com) and Adam Curry and The Vibe (http://metaverse.com/vibe), have been focusing on the obvious music opportunities here. Also, by autumn 1995, the first play-by-play baseball coverage was being offered by an experimental site operated by the ESPNET SportZone (http://espnet.sportszone.com).

and topics push the FCC's buttons every day, have established a number of websites for their man, but the main one at this writing is The Interactive King of All Media Newsletter (http://haven.ios.com /~koam). Subtitled "Six Silly Years of Kissing Stern's Ass," Kevin Renzulli's page is cyberspace's prime source for Howard Stern stories, interviews, and pictures. Want a sample? Features in one edition included "The Best of Ponce De La Phone's Phoney Phone Calls," "An Open Farewell Letter to the Space Lesbian," "The Continuing Adventures Of Kross Kountry Karl: The San Diego Experience," and "A Rest Stop for the Few Fans of Melrose Larry Green."

From the other side of the political/social spectrum and another side of the country comes Denver-based talk show host Ken Hamblin, who says on his Black Avenger Home Page (http://www.globaldialog .com/hamblin) that he considers himself "an 'American Hero' and living proof that America works." Born the son of first-generation West Indian immigrants in the poverty of Brooklyn's Bedford-Stuyvesant neighborhood, Hamblin says he was an antiwar protester in the 1960s, but supported George Bush's drawing a line in the sand during the Gulf War. He supports capital punishment, fights gun control, and believes men have no right to join the abortion debate. His page also discusses his column in the *Denver Post* and his work as a photographer for the *Detroit Free Press* in the late 1960s. He moved to radio in the early 1980s and now has a three-hour dial-in show syndicated nationally by the Entertainment Radio Networks.

New among radio commentators who are finding their cyberlegs is Oliver North. The Ollie Home Page Home (http://www.north.inter.net /north) provides information about the conservative talk show hosted by the man most of us first heard of as the central operative in the Ronald Reagan White House's Iran-Contra guns-for-hostages controversy. Following his unsuccessful 1994 Republican bid to be a U.S. Senator from Virginia, North took to the airwaves on "the Common Sense Radio Network." These days, some 150 stations across the country carry his show, and the website provides a station list. You can fill in a "Cyber Call-In form" with any questions or comments about the show. North regular reads online comments on the air. Signing up with the "Listener Club" gets you on the mailing list for electronic bulletins that will be e-mailed to you.

Chapter 7

The Little-P Politics of Consumerism

Politics is not just P°O°L°I°T°I°C°S, our quadrennial adrenalized national passion play; it's also Little-P politics in the style and flavor we started learning at our mama's knee, before continuing our education at the knees (and hands, and feet) of all those mother institutions and individuals we've been dealing with ever since. We refine our Little-P political savvy day in and day out as we learn to better stand up for ourselves in our dealings with the boss, the police, the university, the military, our clubs and organizations, city hall, even our own children. But we especially hone our Little-P proficiency in our dealings with businesses of which we are the customers. Such politics of daily life often come down to the not-always-gentle activist art of *getting:* getting along; getting by; getting even or just getting through; getting back a little of our own. We've all seen the arrival of a new quid-pro-quo kid on the block, one with a defiant don't-trend-on-me/gimme-my-due kind of attitude that now seems to have worked its way into our national psyche.

This bold individualism may seem like a *new* development, but there actually is an old term for it: consumerism. Even before the rise of ultimate consumer advocate Ralph Nader (who burst onto the scene in 1965 with his exposé of the automobile industry, *Unsafe at Any Speed*), journalists, commentators, and other social observers already were starting to use that word in everyday speech. And in a sense, much of our history in the half-century since the end of World War II could be told in terms of this new view of capitalist politics.

At the heart of consumerism is a simple principle: Buying goods grants certain rights to the buyer. Power to the patrons, as it were. In our lifetime, the terms *citizen* and *consumer* have become virtually interchangeable. We've seen the rise of rigorous government regulations (to protect us), and the subsequent decline of rigorous government regulations (to liberate us). We've smiled as we watched both the rise and the fall of the regulators being characterized by politicians as victories for us, the consumers. Much of our current social debate (on health care, on welfare, on Social Security, and all the various "entitlement" issues) centers on the same basic consumer question: What needs to be protected, and how much regulation is appropriate for us to pay for with our tax dollars?

Consumerism—a movement intended to protect buyers from useless or dangerous products, misleading advertising, unfair prices, and outright fraud—is fundamental to the Net, where cybercitizens thrive on all kinds of potent information for solving their problems. In this chapter, you'll see:

▸ Net-based consumer protection. A brand new coalition allied with the National Consumers League and funded by Mastercard (the credit card company) is getting the skinny on online scams. This group can teach us how to avoid being victims on the cyber highway.

▸ Consumer advocacy as it is expressed on Web pages maintained by private watchdog organizations. The Better Business Bureau has arrived online. So have tenants' rights organizations, groups promoting environmentally safe products, and groups with all kinds of legal advice to share.

▸ Federal government services that have come to cyberspace to distribute their information on product safety and fair trade. Let them help you with everything from sorting out Social Security benefits to getting details on buying government property.

Finally, because consumer questions usually concern how we, as customers, can deal with businesses, the chapter wraps up with tips on how to get current information about companies and corporations. These resources may appear to be of use only to investors and stock analysts, but they also can be very valuable for basic consumer research.

THE LITTLE-P POLITICS OF CONSUMERISM

For instance, not long ago, my mom called to say that she had been approached by an insurance company with what seemed to be a pretty good deal. One problem: she was unfamiliar with the firm. Could I do anything through the computer to find out whether the company that had contacted her was really on the up and up? Yes. Logging on to sites such as the Securities and Exchange Commission's powerful new Edgar database of corporate records, we were able to determine that the firm was indeed legitimate. It had been selling health insurance since the mid-1960s. We got an overview of its recent business activity—it had been quite successful—and phone numbers that she could call if she wanted to verify anything the salesman had told her about the policy he was offering. In a matter of minutes, we were able to relieve her mind about doing business with these people.

Other resources can help avoid costly mistakes. A friend recently told us he had been contacted by a company that sold "environmental products" (mainly air and water filters). He was so impressed with the sales pitch, he was even thinking of applying for a job with the company. First, though, he wondered if we could do an online background check of the firm. The company was privately held (that is, it sold no shares on the public stock exchanges), so no documents about it were on file with the SEC database we had used for my mom's case. However, by searching old business news stories in databases maintained by publisher Dow Jones and Company, we discovered that a number of public complaints by both customers and former employees of the firm had been reported in regional newspapers around the country. The company had a very unimpressive history, one that would not have come to light for us without the Net. Our findings were enough to persuade our friend not to do business with the firm.

Incidents like this remind us that information is a powerful weapon. Like all weapons, it is at its very best when it is used to protect ourselves, our friends, and our loved ones from harm. The Net is an arsenal for data that can help us tell the bad guys from the good guys.

FOR THE NET, CONSUMER PROTECTION BEGINS ONLINE

Astute online citizens know that, these days, consumer protection must begin with the Net itself. In other words, the same Net that can arm us

Calling cyberspace "the new frontier for scam artists," the Federal Trade Commission (FTC) is warning electronic consumers that the scams aren't new. What's new is the online medium. Fraudulent sellers use computer services to promote familiar schemes: bogus stock offerings, credit-repair services, and exotic or high-tech investment opportunities such as ostrich farming, gold mining, gemstones, and wireless cable television. Promotions for ineffective weight-loss and health-related products and programs also regularly appear online.

How Not to Be a Net Victim

"Treat all ads or would-be ads with skepticism," advises an online statement from the FTC, "and never make an investment or health-related purchase decision based solely on information obtained from a single source in any medium—print, broadcast, or online."

The FTC advises caution in dealing with:

▸ Classified ads online. Many promote quick-and-easy weight-loss products and programs, or "business opportunities"—"Use your home PC to make money fast in your spare time." Other ads encourage consumers to invest in communications technologies, such as 900-number telephone services, with promises of high returns and low risk.

▸ "Disguised advertising," which is difficult to recognize because it is not always clear whether something is being advertised. The FTC cites at least two areas—bulletin boards and chat rooms—where comments or statements about the quality or the performance of products or services may be ads in disguise. "In some cases," says the commission, "individuals contributing [to bulletin boards or online chats] have financial ties to companies or businesses that sell products or services related to the bulletin board subject area. But, this may not be obvious to the online user. What may appear to be an open discussion could be a disguised sales pitch."

The FTC provided a half-dozen warning signs of a scam, online or elsewhere:

1. Overstated claims of product effectiveness, such as "Cures or improves 27 different conditions: Hypertension, some forms of cancer, age spots, ulcers, lowers weight . . . ."
2. Use of hype titles and frequent use of the word "hot" to describe an investment opportunity.

Net Victim (continued)

3. Exaggerated claims of potential earnings or profit, such as, "We target a return of 2% to 5% per month (up to 60% per year) . . . on your protected principal. That is, YOUR PRINCIPAL IS GUARANTEED . . . no loss is possible."

4. Claims of "inside" information. "Such information is almost always false," the commission says, "and, if true, trading on it is almost always illegal."

5. "Pump and Dump" promotions of cheap stocks, promising high returns.

6. Promotions for exotic investments such as ostrich farming, gold mining, or wireless cable television.

The Internet fraud watch coalition headed by the National Consumers League and Mastercard International adds its own tips to help you avoid those who want to put a "con" into "connectivity." The coalition suggests:

▶ Never disclose checking account numbers, credit card numbers, or other personal financial data at any website or online service location, unless you are sure that you know where this information will be directed.

▶ When you subscribe to an online service, you may be asked for credit card information. When you enter any interactive service site, however, beware of con artists who may ask you to "confirm" your enrollment in the service by disclosing passwords or the credit card account number used to install the service. *No reliable online service ever asks for your password in such a "confirmation."* Don't give out your password, and notify the service provider of the incident.

▶ Use the same common sense you would exercise with any offline, personal, or telephone credit card purchase. Always know whom you are dealing with. A flashy, professional-looking Internet website does not guarantee that the sponsor is legitimate.

▶ Be wary of "get-rich-quick" and "easy-money" schemes advertised in newsgroups.

▶ Report anything suspicious you see on the Internet or at any online service location by contacting the National Fraud Information Center or by forwarding complaints directly to the Federal Trade Commission or to your state attorney general's office. The fraud center can be reached at 1-800-876-7060. (Outside the United States, dial the U.S. country code, then 202-835-0159.) On the Web, the National Fraud Information Center can be reached at http://www.fraud.org.

Net Victim (continued)

For more information on Net scams, check out the website operated by Minnesota Attorney General Hubert Humphrey III. In 1995, in an effort to stop cyber scams, Humphrey filed suits charging six separate companies and individuals with operating illegal business activities on the Internet and on computer online services. Humphrey stored details of these and other cyber scams—ranging from peddling alleged cancer and AIDS cures to illegal betting and a credit-repair scheme—on his website (http://www.state.mn.us /cbranch/ag/).

with powerful information for protecting ourselves can also be a medium that defrauds us. As the online population grows, the Net is ripe for deceptive and misleading promotions, from bogus travel offers and phony investment schemes to innocent-looking contests and lotteries.

"The problem of fraud on the Internet is more difficult [to combat] than fraud by phone and mail," says director Susan Grant of the National Association of Consumer Agency Administrators. "It's difficult to pinpoint where the con artists are operating from. They don't even need a boiler-room operation. They can conduct this kind of fraud from their living room."

One of the newest good guys in cyberspace is a coalition of global businesses, consumer advocates, and law enforcement agencies, formed to curtail what many fear could be an epidemic of online fraud.

Launched in early 1996 by the National Consumers League, the campaign—backed by MasterCard International, the U.S. Federal Trade Commission, and the National Association of Attorneys General—targets credit card fraud, investment swindles, and new versions of the old Ponzi con games, that is, variations on "pyramid schemes" in which victims are lured into increasingly bigger risks by a quick return on initial investments.

At Mastercard, which provides funding for the new antifraud drive, Vice President Charlotte Newton noted, in early March 1996, that the group in its first few months already had uncovered 500 scams sent over the Internet. "Fraud has no boundaries," she recently told United Press International. "At this point we don't have a handle on how much [Net fraud] is costing consumers, but society as a whole pays when this type of fraud takes place."

The coalition has created an online database to track Net fraud complaints. Visit the site on the Internet's World Wide Web (http://www.fraud.org), and feel free to use it to report suspicious activities you encounter in your Net travels. Your tips will be passed on to federal and state law enforcement agencies for investigation.

Of the tips the coalition already has received, Grant said, "They are the same kinds of scams that we've seen promoted by telephone and mail. Credit repair, get-rich-quick schemes, investment opportunities—those seem to be the biggest categories of dubious offers you see right now on the Internet."

She told UPI the coalition's fraud database will "provide a gold mine of information to consumer protection agencies" such as complaints against a certain company, fraud complaints by type and geographic area and even by type of payment mechanism." It also will help law enforcement officials build cases for prosecution and determine approaches for curtailing fraud, such as creating or amending legislation that would halt certain types of activities online.

BETTER BUSINESS BUREAU

One of the best known names in consumer protection—the Council of Better Business Bureaus (BBB)—has come to the World Wide Web (http://www.igc.apc.org/cbbb) to spread the news of its investigations and monitoring programs.

This is an excellent resource for finding out the very latest on the fraud-stopping front, offline as well as online. Don't miss the site's "Alerts and Advisories" section. While we were visiting, in early March 1996, the site was already warning about Summer Olympic Games shenanigans, such as bogus offers for tickets, and travel services to Atlanta, starting the following July. The BBB advisory provided phone numbers in Georgia for checking out information on hotels, real estate agencies, and other local businesses. Other alerts in the same section listed names of specific companies under investigation for suspected scams, and gave general summaries on sweepstakes swindles, home-repair ripoffs, and gold investments. Still others warned of "look-alike

Because much of the cyber public is computing from home, the Net community is especially vulnerable to what the Better Business Bureau (BBB) characterizes as "work-at-home schemes," the fastest
growing category of the bureau's consumer inquiries.

**Watching Out for Work-
at-Home Schemes**

"Work-at-home schemes flourish during times
of economic uncertainty and continuing unemployment," the BBB says in an advisory on its the World
Wide Web site (http://www.igc.apc.org/cbbb). The
agency attributes the popularity of such scams to the lure of easy money and
a common belief that all work-at-home offers that appear in newspapers or
online must be true.

The bureau's online report cites its national investigation of fifty-five
work-at-home promotions, which revealed that ads promising hundreds of
dollars for a few hours' work all "were simply lures by the advertisers to sell
information on how to set up your own business or conduct the same scheme
as the advertiser's. No actual employment existed."

The scam doesn't stop there. "Would-be workers," says the report,
"would have had to first pay for details purporting to show how to make the
claimed income, and then invest more money in ads, envelopes, postage and
other items."

Here are some typical "come-ons" the Better Business Bureau has
found:

▶ The ad says, "$356 Weekly Guaranteed. Work Two Hours Daily at Home."
But it turned out the "guarantee" didn't apply to earnings, only to a refund
of $15 paid for how-to details if the worker's own efforts failed to produce
the weekly income.

▶ "Earn $1,000 to $3,000 Monthly Stuffing Envelopes." Investigators who answered the ad received no envelopes for stuffing. Instead, they received
promotional material asking for $8 to $25 just to order the details on the
money-making plans. To pursue the plan would have required spending
several hundred dollars more for advertising, postage, and printing.

▶ "Assembly Work at Home. Earn $600 Monthly Through Home Sewing."
Usually, you must invest hundreds of dollars in "instruction and materials,"
says the bureau, and "only after you have purchased the supplies and
done the work, the company may decide not to pay you because the work
you send back does not meet certain 'standards.'"

Watching Out for Work-at-Home Schemes (continued)

What are some of the warning signs? The bureau says that, online or off, the work-at-home con artist will:

1. Never offer you regular salaried employment.
2. Promise you huge profits and big part-time earnings.
3. Use personal testimonials but never identify the person quoted so that you can check with him or her.
4. Require money for instruction or merchandise before telling you how the plan works.
5. Assure you of guaranteed markets and a huge demand for your handiwork.
6. Tell you that no experience is necessary.
7. Take your money and, says the bureau, "give you little or nothing in return except heartbreak and grief."

'bureaus'" shilling as Better Business Bureaus for credit counselors, and of telemarketing fraud, which continues to plague small businesses.

Elsewhere on the site, you can find reports on advertising, alternative dispute resolution, consumer and business education, reliability reports on businesses, marketplace complaints and inquiries, and related matters, such as answers to frequently asked questions about the organization, press releases, and event schedules.

Besides the "Alerts and Advisories" section, perhaps the liveliest area is devoted to the National Advertising Division (NAD) and its activities. Late in 1995, for instance, its large collection of press releases and statements included details on the NAD's review of exaggerated claims for such diverse products as personal air purifiers, motor oil, and vegetable shortening.

For consumer guides of all kinds, check out the BBB's online "Publications" section where you'll find electronic editions of the bureau's "Tips On" pamphlets on 70 different products, as well as "Parent's Guide to Advertising," "Children's Advertising Review Unit Guidelines," and philanthropic advisory service publications (including

"Give But Give Wisely" and "The Annual Charity Index"). Business-people can get information here on how to protect their operations against fraud and avoid costly business scams, and advice on honest advertising techniques.

FREE LEGAL SERVICES ARE A CLICK AWAY

Has all this talk of scams and schemers got you wondering whom you can trust? Is there no place to turn on the Net for good, reliable advice on basic consumer issues and legal questions? You want to sell your house, write your will, reach a child support settlement, deal with a sticky divorce . . . or copyright the new country song you've just written about all these dire developments in your life. Is there anyone online you can count on to point you in the right direction?

There is. The con men haven't taken over the Net. Publicity surrounding their arrival in cyberspace is simply another indication of how much the online community has grown. Congratulations, Modem Nation—the crooks now think you're big enough to be worth victimizing!

Letting fear of fraud discourage you from exploring the Net would be like allowing apprehension about crime to inhibit you from traveling to see the wonders of New York, Chicago, or Los Angeles. For self-preservation, employ the same smart watchfulness on the Web that you would when visiting any real-world metropolis. You'll not only survive, but you may come to believe, as we do, that the good guys online still greatly outnumber the bad.

Nowhere is that ratio more obvious than in the Net's remarkable resources for helping with all kinds of everyday legal issues. At sites described in this section, you can find advice and assistance on matters such as divorce and child support, estate planning, home and car buying, small claims court, pensions and retirement, adoption, abortion, copyright and patents, and much more.

Court TV's Cradle-to-Grave Legal Advice

Court TV is best known for its live telecasts of sensational trials, such as the O. J. Simpson murder case. However, on the Internet, the television network has even bigger influence. In fact, since launching its

World Wide Web site in early 1996, Court TV has become the Net's premier legal reference center. You'll find it is an excellent resource for help with all kinds of family and consumer law issues.

Built around an electronic version of its printed *Cradle-to-Grave Survival Guide,* Court TV's legal center (http://www.courttv.com /legalhelp) has articles on everything from selling a used car to creating a prenuptial agreement, finding a lawyer, and filing a lawsuit. The online guide, which is regularly updated as the law changes, introduces you to important legal issues you're likely to encounter in day-to-day life and, in language that is easy to understand, outlines your rights and responsibilities. The source is not meant as a substitute for professional legal advice. In fact, although many of the articles suggest strategies for solving programs without a lawyer, "we don't believe you should pursue litigation, sign an important contract or face criminal charges without the assistance of an attorney," says an online statement.

The online survival guide has a quite impressive depth of data. For example, its material on divorce has additional sections on alimony, annulment, child custody and visitation rights, division of property, and separation agreements. The discussion on buying and selling a house has breakouts on a glossary of legal terms commonly used in real estate deals, checklists for buyers and sellers, details on buying an apartment, taxes, liens and insurance, foreclosures, and finding defects in the property. The site has similarly detailed entries on topics ranging from sexual harassment to Social Security and worker's compensation.

Besides the general legal issues covered in the survival guide, the Court TV site offers:

▶ A Family Law Center, for guidance on issues such as abortion, adoption, the appointment of a guardian for children, child abuse and neglect, foster care, parental obligations and liabilities, and surrogate parenting.

▶ An Elder Law Center, with information relevant to older citizens: estate planning, medical issues and Medicare, and pension and retirement plans.

▶ A Small Business Law Center, for data on topics such as business taxes, liability, and insurance.

Patricia Gima, a staff writer with Nolo Press in Berkeley, California, says that although there are wonderfully rich reservoirs of legal data online, it's important for Net explorers to remember one thing: Free legal advice is not necessarily legitimate. In fact, it may be worth every penny you didn't pay for it.

Writer Suggests Tips for Evaluating Online Advice

"There's nothing to keep people from giving incorrect or poor guidance," she wrote in a 1995 issue of *Nolo News,* the publishing house's own journal. "In other words, the electronic world is just like the real world: It's up to you to evaluate the advice you're given."

In an electronic reprint of her article on Nolo Press's Self-Help Law Center site (http://gnn-e2a.gnn.com/gnn/bus/nolo/), Gima suggests these tips for evaluating legal information you receive online in e-mail, on bulletin boards, and in legal resource databases:

1. Consider the source. Is the person a lawyer? Has the person been through the same kind of problem you are describing?

2. Is the information up-to-date? Don't rely on legal answers you've found online until you're sure the laws in question are still the same as they were when the data were put online.

3. Make sure the information is valid in your state. Many consumer issues—divorce, wills, and landlord/tenant questions—are controlled by state law. The Net is global, so be aware that legal information you find on a topic may not be valid in your state.

4. Get a reference. "Don't accept legal information on face value," Gima writes. "Ask for the number of the statute or the citation to the court case that makes this rule the law of your state. The next best thing is a reference to an article or a self-help law book."

5. Don't use legal forms unless you understand their language and how to fill them out. Online resources often have forms that can be retrieved and printed out—contracts, leases, wills—but if they are filled with legal jargon you don't understand, you could be courting disaster. Gima advises, "Look up unfamiliar terms in a legal dictionary or wait for a better form, written in plain English."

The site can even help you check up on your own lawyer. Are you worried that you might have hired an attorney who has run afoul of the bar association's disciplinary authorities? At this site, you can fill out an online form to e-mail the attorney's name and address to the Court TV headquarters. The staff will check with the appropriate state authorities to see whether there are any records of disciplinary actions taken. Later, you will get an e-mailed response stating the findings.

Finding a Lawyer

The Net can help you find an attorney. Lawyer Search (http://www .counsel.com/lawyersearch) is an electronic directory for locating attorneys in a particular firm, city or state, and/or area of specialization.

At this writing, all the lawyers listed in the database (about 25,000) are members of Counsel Connect, the online network of attorneys that operates the sites. However, the group says it plans to add other groups, such as academic and government lawyers, as well as non-CC members who request to be listed.

Each listing gives the lawyer's name, address, phone and fax numbers, and e-mail address. Some listings also include practice area information, a description of the attorney's experience, and links to other websites.

Nolo Press Self-Help Law Center

For 25 years, Nolo Press has been publishing plain-English "self-help" guides on consumer law subjects such as wills, small claims court, divorce, and debt problems. Now the Berkeley, California, publishing house has brought much of its material to the Web on the electronic pages of its new Self-Help Law Center (http://gnn-e2a.gnn.com /gnn/bus/nolo/).

For instance, in its "Intellectual Property" section are free articles such as "Can You Really Get a Patent Without a Lawyer?" "Copyrights in Cyberspace," and "Leggo My Logo: What Small Businesses Should Know About Trademarks." In the "Estate Planning" section, you'll find titles like: "Facing Your Fears: If You Die Before Your Kids are Grown," "Estate Tax Planning: A Scam for the '90s," "What Happens If You Die Without a Will," and "Leaving Final Instructions After

Death: Last Rights." Other sections of the site have articles on business and the workspace, family matters, senior citizen issues, home-ownership, landlords and tenants, immigration, and investments.

Nolo Press can give you details on how to order its books, tapes, videos, and software. An "Update Service" option provides a summary of important court decisions and new legislation that affects its existing books and programs.

TENANTS' RIGHTS: WORKING LOCALLY, SURFING GLOBALLY

Tenants' rights is an intensely local issue, especially in urban areas like New York City, where a perpetual shortage of living space has motivated renters to organize to make their case on issues involving rent

---

In our increasingly ecologically aware world, the "green" market has received a real boost lately. On the Web, the EnviroLink Network, a site that covers all manner of environmental topics, has begun the Internet Green Market-place (http://envirolink.org/products) to identify businesses on the Net that have passed its screening of their "social responsibility," according to an online statement.

Finding Environmentally Friendly Products

The EnviroLink Network says it will not list a corporation if the group "has an active progressive boycott against their products," adding, "These standards ensure that the consumer is not being misled in any way by the corporations listed in this directory."

At this writing, the backers were adding options to list firms by company name, product, and geographic location. Another option invites online businesses to apply for inclusion.

Also of interest is The Progressive Business Web Pages (http://envirolink.org/products/pbw.html), a clearinghouse of information about socially responsible businesses and investment opportunities on the Internet. The site provides connections to organizations, publications, electronic mailing lists, and government support agencies.

CompuServe's Consumer Forum

CompuServe's Consumer Forum (enter GO CONFORUM on CompuServe) is intended to help you avoid the latest ripoffs and scams, get information about your consumer rights, and gather money-saving ideas. Managed by Edgar Dworsky, an attorney with the Massachusetts attorney general's office, who has 17 years of experience helping consumers, and Phyllis Eliasberg, an attorney and Emmy-award-winning consumer reporter, the forum offers sections covering automobiles, banking and credit, buying advice, consumer rights, coupons and rebates, food, health, investment tips, insurance, scams, and more.

Off the Web

In addition, David Horowitz, who has produced his syndicated U.S. television show and newspaper column "Fight Back!" for twenty-five years, provides information and responds to member inquiries in Section 2, "Ask David/FightBack." The forum can be tapped for more than a hundred booklets and pamphlets from the Federal Trade Commission on topics such as how to obtain a new credit identity, how to fix your credit problems, how to deal with telephone scams, and more.

control, neighborhood safety, noise abatement, and other mutual concerns. In cyberspace, the concerns go global. Tenants in other parts of the country—and in some other countries—may discover they have much in common, and much to share, with renters everywhere. An idea for dealing with jackhammers and noisy traffic in Miami might be just what tenants are looking for in Dallas. Rent control guidelines under discussion in Newark might make sense in Cleveland as well.

"These are trying times for tenants," says the introductory page of TenantNet (http://tenant.blythe.org/TenantNet), a project of New York-based Tenant Watch, a coalition of tenant activists. "Landlords have mounted intense public relations campaigns filled with inaccuracies and misrepresentations about hard-won tenant protections and rent regulation. Tenants are losing basic services and being price-gouged at alarming rates. There is a very real chance tenant protections will be repealed in 1997, leaving over 2.4 million New Yorkers at risk."

The Web can help you plot a great escape.

Suppose you've grown weary of toiling in the orchards of The Big Apple, you're fed up with the traffic and the housing shortage, and you long to pull up stakes and relocate. But where? You've become accustomed to New York's wages and prices. How would those dollar figures translate to the cost of living in another part of the country?

Quick and Cool Calculations the Net Can Make for You

This question is pondered by many wage-earners in our ever-more-mobile America. It can be answered with The Relocation Calculator (http://www.homefair.com/homefair/cmr/salcalc.html). This nifty site on the Internet's World Wide Web is operated by the Center for Mobility Resources (CMR), a ten-year-old executive relocation service. CMR maintains cost-of-living indexes for more than 450 cities in the United States, and the online salary calculator enables you to figure out the income you will need to maintain your current living standard if you move to a new town.

You start by typing in your current salary. Then, from an online list, you enter the two- or three-digit codes for your current city and the city to which you might move. In our test of the site, we entered $50,000 as our salary and the regional code for Long Island, New York, as our current residence. We selected other cities around the country as possible destinations and let the site calculate the difference in costs.

We immediately had to rethink our plans for moving to sunny, sandy Hawaii. The calculator informed us we would need an income of more than $75,005 in Honolulu just to match an income of $50,000 in Long Island. Even staying in New York State could be difficult if we had our eye on Westchester County, where it would take a salary of $63,354 to match the $50,000 in Long Island. California was a little better, but still more expensive: it would take $52,762 in Los Angeles and $59,681 in San Francisco to maintain our Long Island lifestyle.

But the calculator also found opportunities for us. In Washington (DC), for instance, we could live a little cheaper ($48,394 would match our $50,000 in Long Island), and in Philadelphia, we could get by with just $47,861. Even better were Chicago ($45,275), Miami ($41,408), and Denver ($39,940). And we understood why they call New Orleans "The Big Easy" when we realized we would need only $35,403 there to equal the buying power of $50,000 in Long Island. To nearly double our buying power, we would have to consider

Quick and Cool Calculations (continued)

Bartlesville, Oklahoma, where $30,273 will go as far as $50,000 at our Long Island digs.

The calculator also can be used to examine shorter-distance relocations. Suppose you and your $50,000 income are currently living in Lexington, Kentucky, and plan to move to another city nearby. The site could tell your that costs would be about the same in Louisville, Kentucky (a $50,378 income would equal $50,000 in Lexington), a little higher in Indianapolis, Indiana ($52,430) and Nashville, Tennessee ($53,803), considerably higher in Cincinnati, Ohio ($55,244), but a little lower in Chattanooga, Tennessee ($48,543).

Elsewhere on the Web are other calculators to guide you in spending your money on all kinds of big-ticket items. For instance:

▶ Retirement Planning Calculator (http://www.altamira.com/altamira /rrsp_calc.html) helps to determine whether your current savings plan and future contributions will be enough to support your desired lifestyle. The site prompts you to answer questions on your desired annual retirement income, how many years you will be working before retirement, and the percentage of your retirement income that must come from the savings. It then reports the findings, taking into consideration the expected annual compounded investment return and estimates of inflation.

▶ Mortgage Calculator (http://www.majon.com/majon/estate.mort.html) prepares and prints out an amortization schedule for house payments, letting you play "what-if" games with the figures.

▶ Debt Calculator (http://www.uclc.com/consumer/debtcalc.html) lets you work out a schedule for payments to get out of debt. You're prompted to enter the debts you've incurred for cars, credit cards, mortgages, and other expenses, the interest rates you're being charged, and the estimated remaining balances you owe.

▶ Car Loan Calculator (http://www.motorcity.com/site/MC/AutoLoan.html) can help you determine the monthly payments you'll have to meet for loans on cars. You are asked to enter the loan term (in months), the loan rate (that is, the *annual* interest rate, such as 9.00% or 9.25%), and the projected purchase price of the car. Optionally, you can enter the down payment, the trade-in value of your current vehicle, and the sales tax.

"Put simply: We run your life. Free will is a carefully-constructed illusion. We are *the* conspiracy."

That's how they talk in The Electronic Bunker (http://rainbow.rmii.com/~tph/bunker.html), a weird, wonderful Web corner from which a group calling itself the Conspiracy of Normals Inc., reveals its plans for us. "We operate in all facets of modern life. Overt action is generally not necessary to achieve our goals, as most of modern society is more than willing to comply with our mass-media propaganda and consumerist ideologies. It has been observed that, in a perfect police state, police action becomes unnecessary."

Joining the Web of Conspiracy

Outlining its goals for world domination through mass consumerism, the Conspiracy says, "Ours is not the heavy-handed totalitarianism of Orwell's *1984,* but rather the seductive, pleasant totalitarianism of Huxley's *Brave New World.* Indeed, modern society goes far beyond tolerating our control; today's citizen clamors for our control, happily herded in whatever direction suits our needs."

The Conspiracy notes that it has always found the Internet "a major annoyance" ("We don't like it, as it has a nasty tendency to promote free speech and—god forbid—independent, nonconsumer thought") and for that reason has recently launched its Internet Suppression Plan. "The first stage . . . was the creation of the World Wide Web . . . a trap which has ensnared the Net and its users in the same way that a fishing net entangles dolphins." It is no accident, they say, that Web users are said to be "surfing" the web. "Just imagine what would happen to a surfer who encountered a commercial fishing net, and you begin to understand. It is a 'web' of surveillance and creeping consumerism. Already the WWW is crowded with companies advertising their wares, infiltrating every corner of the WWW with consumer-manipulation memes, urging viewers to buy more, to submit to our plan for society . . . ."

Says the manifesto, "It's all part of the grand Shopping-As-Entertainment meme which we've gradually been spreading through the population. It is our objective to make shopping as pleasurable as possible, so that this activity will eventually supplant all other forms of entertainment."

Does the Conspiracy sounds like too much fun to miss? Want to get on the inside? Well, you can't get in if you're not already in ("members are selected at birth," the Normals tell us, and there are "no exceptions"), but, "in order to recruit members of society willing to betray their fellow dupes to The

Joining the Web (continued)

Conspiracy, we have established Club WIRED [to] act as agents of The Conspiracy. Loyalty is assured through the heavy use of merit-based awards; for example, when a member of The Club convinces ten neighbors to watch a new Conspiracy television show, they receive a gift certificate for $5, good at any store in the shopping mall of their choice."

For more information, send e-mail to ClubWIRED@aol.com. Be sure to ask about The Conspiracy of Normals Pig. It's fatter than your average pig.

Saying that basic tenant protections have been "gutted . . . by politicians who maintained a fiction of being [in favor of] tenants' rights and by tenants themselves who lost sight of the value of stable communities," TenantNet is putting out a call for help from renters everywhere.

The service, considered the first Internet site dedicated to residential tenants, gives news and information on assorted renters' issues, tenant advocacy, a tenants' rights fact sheet, details on recent court decisions, articles on neighbors and communities, and other topics (such as "Is the Government Doing its Job?"). Also available are current and back issues of the Tenants Online newsletter.

Backers of the page note that although they are not attorneys and can't provide legal advice, "We can in some cases, and to those who are interested, suggest attorneys or tenant community organizations to contact for individual case assistance."

Much of the material on TenantNet focuses on New York City and New York State. However, the site is gathering contacts and online resources for tenant groups in other cities. At this writing, TenantNet provided links to organizations in Alaska, Arizona, California, Colorado, Florida, Illinois, Indiana, Kentucky, Maryland, Massachusetts, Michigan, Minnesota, New Jersey, Ohio, Oklahoma, Pennsylvania, Virginia, and Washington, as well as in Canada, the United Kingdom, and Australia.

If you want to be on TenantNet's mailing list, send e-mail to tenant@tenant.blythe.org with your e-mail address and real name.

Matthew Lesko's Information USA on CompuServe

Author Matthew Lesko has gained international prominence as the where-is-it answer man for finding federal and state information, and now his remarkable resources are on CompuServe. The online Information USA (enter GO LESKO on CompuServe) is based on Lesko's 1,250-page *Information USA* volume. The online service specializes in illustrating Lesko's techniques for getting questions answered, with tutorials such as "The Art of Obtaining Information from Bureaucrats."

Off the Web

This detailed resource provides phone numbers, addresses, how-to articles, tutorials, and so on. Lesko gives special emphasis to how consumers can get information out of their government. Topics covered are: where to start looking for information on agriculture and farming, arts and humanities, auctions and surplus property, books and libraries, business and industry, careers and workplace, company information and company people, consumer power, demographics and statistics, drugs and chemical dependence, economics, education, energy, environment and nature, financial help to individuals, free health care, freedom of information act, giveaways for entrepreneurs, government databases/bulletin boards, housing and real estate, international trade, international relations/defense, investments and financial services, law and social justice, lawmakers, patents, science and technology, selling to the government, taxes, trademarks and copyrights, vacations and business travel, weather and maps, and your community.

Lesko's troops also run CompuServe's Government Giveaway Forum (GO INFOUSA on CompuServe), which discusses how to get government loans, grants, and loan guarantees, and how to cash in on free services, information, and software developed by experts in many fields. The forum advises you on government offerings, such as free health care by the world's best doctors, free legal help regardless of income, and free research conducted by experts on topics from back pain to pasta. In addition, find out about hundreds of money programs that can help you start a business, travel overseas, or write a novel.

FEDERAL GOVERNMENT CONSUMER DATA

Despite budget cuts and a pull back of much of the old federal regulatory machinery, Washington still is a primary provider of consumer information. Across the Web are sites devoted to topics such as product safety, how-to manuals, information on grants, and public property for sale.

A central resource is the General Services Administration's Federal Information Center (http://www.gsa.gov/et/fic-firs/fic.htm), which was set up to answer questions about the U.S. government either directly through toll-free phone numbers or online through standing frequently asked questions (FAQ) files. The site has a database of states' and metropolitan areas' services reached by 800-numbers.

Libraries on various topics, including employment and federal jobs, Social Security issues, travel by Americans out of the country, passports, travel advisories, immunizations, Selective Service, congressional legislation, federal taxes and tax preparation, protection of intellectual property, and copyright, patents, and trademarks, are also available.

Consumer Health Information

One of the largest collections of consumer health information online—with data on everything from AIDS and cancer to foot care and alcoholism—is provided by a section of the U.S. Department of Health and Human Services.

The Consumer Health Information page (http://www.os.dhhs.gov /consumer/coninfo.html) connects you to the following resources (originators are indicated in parentheses):

- AIDS information (from the Public Health Service).
- CancerNet (from the National Institutes of Health).
- Consumer advice and information on foodborne illness, food labeling, nutrition, and seafood (from the Food and Drug Administration's Center for Food Safety and Nutrition).
- Guidelines on pain control, back problems, mammograms, and other health conditions (from the Agency for Health Care Policy and Research).

▶ Emerging infectious disease information (from the National Center for Infectious Diseases).

▶ Information for seniors on blood pressure, flu, foot care, hearing, and other problems (from the National Institute on Aging).

▶ A directory of organizations providing information or assistance on drug or alcohol abuse (from the National Clearinghouse for Alcohol and Drug Information).

▶ Immunization, parenting, and other children's health information (from Consumer Information Catalog).

Also on-site are phone numbers for the National Health Information Center; National Institutes of Health statements; technology assessment statements on important diseases and treatment methods; data on consumers, health care providers, and health plans; and a traveler's health page from the Centers for Disease Control and Prevention.

Federal Trade Commission Brochures

If you ever doubt that the federal government is one of the nation's busiest publishers on consumer issues, just swing by the Federal Trade Commission's Consumer Line (http://www.ftc.gov/bcp/conline /conline.htm), a website that provides full text of some 150 consumer and business publications. Operated by the FTC's Office of Consumer and Business Education, the site highlights its latest releases. When we were in the neighborhood, these included "Focus on Phone Leasing," "Straight Talk about Telemarketing," "Viatical Settlements: A Guide for People with Terminal Illnesses," and "Consumer Alert! Online Scams."

Any consumer will find a treasure trove of data here. Beyond the new publications, the FTC site organizes its rich resources. Along with a sampling of titles, these are the categories:

▶ General information: "66 Ways to Save Money" and "How to Resolve Consumer Disputes."

▶ Automobiles: "A Consumer Guide to Vehicle Leasing" and "New Car Buying Guide."

▶ Consumer credit: "Buying and Borrowing: Cash In on the Facts," "Credit Billing Errors," and "Credit and Older Americans."

▶ Health and fitness: "Food Advertising Claims," "Indoor Tanning," and "Varicose Vein Treatments."

▶ Home and real estate: "Home Financing Primer," "Mortgage Discrimination," and "Timeshare Resales."

▶ Investments: "Art Fraud," "A Consumer Guide to Buying a Franchise," and "Investing in Wireless Cable TV."

▶ Products: "Care Labels," "Infomercials," "Prize Offers," and "Tobacco Products."

▶ Services: "Choosing a Career or Vocational School," "Funerals: A Consumer Guide," and "Layaway Purchase Plans."

▶ Telemarketing: "Charitable Giving" and "Scams by Phone."

▶ Business: "Buying/Working at Home," "Credit Reports: What Employers Should Know about Using Them," and "Getting Business Credit."

Among other topics covered are lost or stolen credit and automatic teller cards, auto service contracts, car ads, low-interest loans and other financing offers, credit and charge card fraud, cellular telephone lottery update, the "cooling-off" rule, cosigning a loan, cosmetic surgery, electronic banking, eyewear rights and tips, food advertising claims, hearing aids, infertility services, magazine telephone scams, modeling agency scams, 900 numbers, shopping by phone or mail, truck driving schools, and unordered merchandise.

If you think you know of an instance of fraud, the site gives you details on how to report it. The FTC's home page (http://www.ftc.gov) provides commission press releases, notices and transcripts of hearings, requests for public comment, and details of recent rulings.

Consumer Products Safety Commission

The Net site of the U.S. Consumer Products Safety Commission (gopher://cpsc.gov) provides news and background on hazardous products. You can also request documents that give details on the Medical Examiners and Coroners Alert Project, Federal Register notices, information for manufacturers, retailers, and distributors, and the like. The commission maintains an e-mail list for automatic distribution of its press releases, its public calendar, and significant information and reports. To get on the mailing list, send e-mail to listproc@cpsc.gov, with no subject line. As the body of your message, type in: sub CPSCINFO-L [first name] [last name].

Social Security Benefits

Need to find out about Social Security benefits or other entitlement programs? Check out Social Security Online, the Social Security Administration's website (http://www.ssa.gov), where you'll find reports on rulings, research, statistics, legislation, and benefits.

All benefits and claims begin with someone filling out a form. In the old days, this meant a trip to the local Social Security office or at least a phone call to request that the paper forms be mailed to you. But the Web has accelerated that process by providing the most requested Social Security forms online; they can be retrieved and printed out on any laser, inkjet, or dot-matrix printer or plotter. Click on for an application for a Social Security card (in English and Spanish), a Request for Earnings and Benefit Estimate Statement, and other documents.

The "Retirement, Survivors', Disability, and SSI Program Information" section of the page links with additional online pamphlets and factsheets, including "The Social Security Handbook," a summary of all Social Security benefits and policies. You can use the "Index" or "Table of Contents" to conduct a hyperlinked search for answers to your questions about Social Security benefits. The site also has an active "Disabilities Program" section that gives information on children's disability, SSA's disability redesign activities, and new vocational rehabilitation regulations.

Consumer Information Center Catalog

The Consumer Information Center Catalog (http://www.pueblo.gsa.gov) features hundreds of government booklets and pamphlets on diverse subjects. You can download the entire catalog or selected booklets. Topics on the main menu include cars, children, employment, federal programs, food and nutrition, health, hobbies, housing, money, small business, and travel.

The site provides hot links to other related sites and invites comments from visitors. It also lists its top twenty publications. At this writing, that list consisted of:

▶ Ten free publications: "Protecting Your Privacy," "Understanding Social Security," "New Food Label Close Up," "Buying Treasury Securities," "Fly Smart," "The HUD Home Buying Guide," "An FDA Guide to Nonprescription Drugs," "Cancer Tests You Should Know About," "Top 10 Ways to Beat the Clock and Prepare for Retirement," and "The GED Diploma."

▶ Ten publications for sale: "Guide to Federal Government Sales" ($1.75), "Nine Ways to Lower Your Auto Insurance Costs" (50 cents), "Federal Benefits for Veterans and Dependents" ($3.25), "Home Inspection and You" (50 cents), "66 Ways to Save Money" (50 cents), "Discover America" (50 cents), "How to Protect Yourself" (50 cents), "Helping Your Child with Homework" (50 cents), "Swindlers Are Calling" (50 cents), and "Personal Health Guide" ($1.00).

Buying Government Property

Disseminating information about government asset sales open to the general public is the primary mission of FinanceNet (http://www.financenet.gov), a site staffed by volunteers and associated with Vice President Al Gore's National Performance Review. FinanceNet reaches across a number of government systems to provide data on the sale of all manner of assets: real property, loans, planes, boats, cars, jewelry, and just about anything that any government—federal, state, local, or international—will be offering for sale to the general public. FinanceNet, which is funded by the U.S. Chief Financial Officers Council, also offers details about newsgroups and mailing lists that will keep you further apprised of these sales. Linked to the site are pages devoted to Department of Defense public sales; General Services Administration personal property sales and public building service property disposals; Department of Housing and Urban Development asset sales; U.S. Customs public auctions; Small Business Administration sales; Canadian government sales, and the like.

FinanceNet is working with state and local governments, and their related professional associations, to offer Internet access to their public documents and asset sales notices and information. The site has a library of links to major Net resources in a number of related areas, including federal control agencies, accounting and policy resources,

Finding Grants

As part of Vice President Al Gore's National Performance Review, the Department of Health and Human Services set up GrantsNet (http://www.os .dhhs.gov/progorg/grantsnet) to assist electronic visitors in finding information on grant resources and activities. GrantsNet can find these data whether they are stored in the various agencies of the department, in other federal agencies, or in nongovernment sources.

GrantsNet is intended as a medium "for the sharing of ideas, successes, news, lessons learned, and an archival reference library of grant-related legislation, regulations, and policies," says an online statement. It also provides a yellow-pages type of directory of HHS grant offices, grants management staff, and grant program personnel. Topics covered include granting agencies and employee locators, who's who in federal grants management, grant programs and funding availability, and laws, regulations, and policies affecting federal grant programs.

The site offers an e-mail service for news of additions to its files, and it gives updates on happenings in federal grants management (such as revisions to Office of Management and the Budget Circulars). To subscribe, send e-mail to listserv@list.nih.gov. In the body of the message, write:

subscribe GNET-L [first name] [last name]

Also online are general guides, such as "How to Find Information About the Department's Grant Programs," "How to Apply for an HHS Grant," "A Researcher's Guide," and "A Teacher's Guide."

and BudgetNet, which features public financial management and accounting information and news in public budgeting.

FEDERAL BUSINESS RESOURCES

On the Web, where consumerism bumps up against business, you'll find the new U.S. Business Advisor (http://www.business.gov), a White House-backed site that President Clinton himself touts in an online statement. "I know it's hard for people in business to deal with the government," Clinton says. "Here's a step toward fixing that. We are building this website as one stop for all the services and information that government offers business."

The site is especially rich in news and information on regulatory agencies, including new information on regulations and taxes, labor, environment, safety, immigration, and communications. Users collect information either by selecting topics from on-screen lists or by searching with keywords.

The service enables business owners (and curious customers) to obtain guides and forms for complying with regulations or applying for government-backed loans and other federal assistance. Visitors can call up economic reports and journals, advice about starting a company, and recent news from dozens of federal agencies.

Incidentally, the business community helped in creating this site. A prototype was rolled out at the White House Conference on Small

Thomas Ho: Collecting the Business Links

Modestly entitled Electronic Businesses (http://webster.cadcam.iupui.edu:80/~ho/interests/commenu.html), Thomas Ho's website is one of the more comprehensive, wide-ranging directories of Internet business and consumer resources. Simply and intelligently organized, the page can point you to sites for data on advertising, economic development, company lists, electronic "storefronts," industry groups, corporate presence, individual outlets, electronic publishers, financial and professional services, and directories and clearinghouses.

Names on the Net

Ho, an Indianapolis-based computer scientist who chairs the Department of Computer Technology at the Purdue University School of Engineering and Technology, has a special interest in online commerce. His site offers a wealth of business articles from various sources, including these selections: "Electronic Commerce: A New Way of Doing Business," "The Internet and Your Business," "Internet's Your Ticket to Ride," and "Commercializing the Information Superhighway: Are We In For a Smooth Ride?"

Come here for tips on publications, conferences, research groups, news, mailing lists, and calls for professional papers.

James M. Kaplan: AuditNet Resource List

It's not exactly a newsflash that many accountants and auditors are conservatively inclined, which may explain why most of them have been reluctant to leap into cyberspace. However, with many of their clients and associates becoming naturalized Netheads, they are peeking into the Net and discovering some good news: one of their brethren has already blazed a trail.

Names on the Net

James M. Kaplan has meticulously detailed cyberspheric resources that are of interest to the business world's numbers crunchers. Kaplan's AuditNet Resource List (http://www.unf.edu/students/jmayer/arl.html) lists not only Internet features, but relevant network services such as the Accountant's Home Page (http://www.servtech.com/re/acct.html), the Accountant's Web (http://pobox.com/~accweb), various accounting newsgroups and related resources off the Web, such as CompuServe's new Accountant's Forum (GO ACCOUNTING on CompuServe), and related features on America Online.

Kaplan also stays on top of developments in government sites devoted to acquisition, efficiency, taxes, federal law, and more, and in state and international sites on related topics, such as computer security. The site has a healthy amount of information on local government resources related to accounting.

Business in the summer of 1995, but conference delegates wanted to change practically everything about the version they were shown. The government then spent the next six months working with business owners to overhaul the service.

The site is divided into five parts:

1. Common Questions: for topics like exports, the Occupational Safety and Health Administration, the U.S. Postal Service, and Social Security.

2. How-To . . . : for step-by-step guides and tools for such varied subjects as business postal forms, information on disaster assistance loans, getting a passport, and looking up zip codes.

3. Search: for online resources on particular topics available through the Internet, especially among federal data repositories.

4. Browse: for reviewing information in these sections: "Doing Business with the Government," "Finance," "General Business," "International Trade," "Labor and Employment," and "Law and Regulations."

5. News: for breaking stories that are of special interest to the business community.

Some people applaud the coming of cyber commerce, but not everyone is thrilled with the proliferation of electronic advertising, especially when it enters the message boards of the Internet newsgroups or results in electronic junk mail. Some Netheads are now fighting back with the oldest weapon in the consumer's arsenal: the boycott.

Group Attacks Online Ads with "Blacklist"

The Blacklist of Internet Advertisers (http://math-www.uni-paderborn.de/~axel/BL/blacklist.html) is a regular report that publicizes the names of those who try to sell goods and services via the newsgroups or through unsolicited e-mail. The Blacklist expects that "people who read it will punish the offenders in one way or another," says author Axel Boldt in a recent issue.

Boldt characterizes as "inappropriate commercials" ads posted to unrelated newsgroups or mailing lists or to those that traditionally don't tolerate commercial messages. "The number of complaints I receive," he added, "is also a factor. Everyone added to the blacklist gets notified so that they can correct possibly inaccurate information. As a general rule, people are taken off the list after three months unless they repeat their behavior."

Incidentally, Boldt notes that, in the blacklist business, a couple of Networthy terms have come into being. Both were borrowed from food products and stand for unwelcome behavior on the Net. In certain Internet circles, "Spam" and "Velveeta" are jargon that refer to posting of multiple copies of the same (or slightly altered) article to many newsgroups. With that type of posting, the article will be transmitted to and stored on every Usenet host multiple times—once for every newsgroup involved.

In addition to the website, the blacklist is posted regularly to several newsgroups and stored on a number of FAQ archives around the world. General tips on "netiquette" are offered.

FINDING COMPANY FACTS FROM THE SEC

We come now to Edgar, the premier Web resource for finding fundamental information about American companies and corporations. Although mainly intended as a database for investors and the stock

Dow Jones News/Retrieval: Main Name in Business Data

While America Online and CompuServe slug it out for the burgeoning home PC market, one major online service has kept itself proudly out of the running. Dow Jones News/Retrieval (DJN/R) is not interested in big, colorful graphics, or bringing rock stars and actresses online to chat it up with their modem-riding fans, or churning the pot with electronic scavenger hunts and other regular Net-based contests. Nor does it need detailed research to profile its users. Dow Jones customers are distinguished by the data they demand: business information of all kinds every day.

Off the Web

DJN/R, the only major commercial service devoted exclusively to business and commerce, is a primarily off-Web resource for the kind of information you can read in *The Wall Street Journal.* In fact, the system is the exclusive provider of the full text of the *Journal* (searchable in a database that includes today's issue and years of back issues), as well as the same-day text of *The New York Times* News Service, the *Los Angeles Times,* and the *Financial Times.* The system has more than 265 U.S. regional and local newspapers, including 8 of the top 10 and 41 of the top 50 in the United States. Five proprietary newswires are offered: (1) Dow Jones News Service, (2) Dow Jones International News Service, (3) Federal Filings, (4) Professional Investor Report, and (5) Dow Jones Capital Markets Report. An electronic clipping service called CustomClips provides news on just the companies, industries, or topics you want. (Through keyword "profiles," you file your preferences with the system in advance.) The system also provides extensive stock quote databases, resources for company and industry reports, investment analyses, and more.

Although DJN/R is a system apart from the Internet, you can contact a site (http://www.bis.dowjones.com) for details about DJN/R and other Dow Jones resources.

market community, Edgar also can be useful for consumers. Remember my mother's request, at the beginning of this chapter, and how we needed to find out whether the little-known insurance company that approached her was legitimate? A few minutes with Edgar was all it took to get our answer.

Planned as only a two-year experiment when it was started in 1994, the free Edgar database, built on the Securities and Exchange Commission's (SEC) vast library of corporate records, now has become a permanent Net fixture, following public outcry at the mere thought of losing it.

Edgar allows people to read corporate financial statements within twenty-four hours after they have been filed with the SEC. The continuation of Edgar has been jeopardized because the nonprofit groups that developed it were to lose government backing. However, SEC Chairman Arthur Levitt Jr., in the fall of 1995, announced that the commission would maintain this treasured resource. "It is a major commission priority to use electronic communications to bring clearer, faster, more complete disclosure to investors," he added.

Edgar has been a real Net success story. The National Science Foundation provided the initial two-year grant that allowed several organizations, as an experiment, to make financial documents available on the global public data network. In January 1994, the nonprofit Internet Multicasting Service of Washington, a research group exploring new technology on the Internet, started distributing records filed electronically with the SEC. They ranged from quarterly earnings reports to notices of corporate takeovers and shareholder proxy statements. The service also distributed documents filed with the Patent and Trademark Office. During the two-year experiment, an average of 16,700 documents were distributed electronically every day. Officials with Internet Multicasting Service say they have sent out 3.1 million SEC filings to individuals, Wall Street firms, and college students since the project's inception. Another 1.59 million patent documents have been distributed.

As the experiment neared its end in late 1995, several private firms offered to adopt and manage Edgar, but all planned to impose limits, such as how many documents an investor could access at once. On this, Levitt said, "Taxpayers and shareholders have already paid to compile this information. They should not have to pay again. And a

Consumer Reports on America Online, CompuServe

Consumer Reports magazine has established some major sites online to share its reviews and buying guides with the wired world.

Off the Web

On America Online (enter CONSUMER REPORTS on AOL), the magazine provides product reviews, ratings, and advice, as well as summaries of CR's tests and evaluations. Specific article collections include those on:

▶ Automobiles: reports on road tests of specific vehicles, plus a listing of recommended cars, new-car ratings, and automobile recall information.

▶ Electronics: information and recommendations on radio, television, video, and stereo equipment, services, and supplies.

▶ Appliances: recommended purchases for the home.

▶ Columns: advice on health and personal finance issues.

The feature uses three special product ratings:

1. "Best Buy": a product that is both high in quality and low in price.

2. "Check-Rating": a product judged high in quality and appreciably superior to the other products tested.

3. "Not Acceptable": a product found unsafe, defective, or clearly not capable of performing its advertised task.

On CompuServe (GO CSR), the magazine allows you to search reports prepared by the Consumers Union staff. The reports, although similar to those found in *Consumer Reports* magazine, are modified slightly for placement in this electronic database. Reports are listed in categories—such as appliances, automobiles, electronics/cameras, home—and are alphabetized in each category. The reports generally cover products and services that cost $50 or more, or lower-priced products and services that are typically bought frequently or in bulk.

Most reports are divided into introduction/overview, what to look for, recommendations, and models tested/ratings. Occasionally, other choices, such as features/specifications or article updates, are available. A guide explains ratings symbols and gives a full description of each characteristic. Generally, the ratings system is:

Consumer Reports (continued)

[*****]   Excellent

[****]   Very Good

[***]   Good

[**]   Fair

[*]   Poor

Off the Web

Of particular interest is the automobile section (GO CRAUTO on CompuServe), which covers most popular cars, small vans, and sport/utility vehicles sold in the United States. Information is taken from New-Car Ratings, Summary Judgments, Frequency-of-Repair Records, and Road Test reports developed by Consumers Union. The data are organized and presented by vehicle and make, to review all of the information currently available for an individual model. Begin a search by choosing a search criterion from this menu: (1) Model Year, (2) Make/Manufacturer, (3) Size/Type, (4) Reliability, (5) Recommended by Consumers Union, (6) Gas Mileage, or (7) Model. Narrow a search by specifying additional criteria, or broaden the search by adding criteria. The vehicle information that appears will match all criteria.

library that charges people by the page, or by the minute, is no longer a library."

Using Edgar

At this writing, the Internet Edgar Dissemination project (http://www.sec.gov/edgarhp.htm) allows you to receive any 1994 (or later) SEC filings that are available to the public. (Nonelectronic filings, filings that are not available to the public, and filings prior to 1994 are not available.)

The website offers a search field for finding reports by keywords. And, as online examples illustrate, you can use logical connectors such as SUN OR MICROSYSTEMS to find documents mentioning *either* "Sun" or "Microsystems," SUN AND MICROSYSTEMS to find those that mention both "Sun" and "Microsystems," SUN ADJ MICROSYSTEMS

("Sun" adjacent to "Microsystems"), and so on. A resulting list—providing the company name, the code for the type of report (such as "10-K," "10-Q," "8-K"), the date of the filing, and the length in bytes (characters)—might look like this:

MICROSOFT CORP	10-K	(09/27/1994)	442763 Bytes
MICROSOFT CORP	10-Q	(02/14/1994)	33028 Bytes
MICROSOFT CORP	10-Q/A	(11/16/1994)	36349 Bytes
MICROSOFT CORP	424B3	(02/28/1995)	660003 Bytes
MICROSOFT CORP	8-K	(07/29/1994)	4762 Bytes
MICROSOFT CORP	PRE 14A	(09/08/1994)	50957 Bytes
MICROSOFT CORP	S-3	(01/13/1995)	38343 Bytes

An online section of an SEC document called "A User's Guide to the Facilities of the Public Reference Room" gives details of the dozens of different corporate documents stored at the Edgar website. Here are four of the major document types:

1. 10-K: the annual report that most reporting companies file with the SEC. The report must be filed within 90 days after the end of the company's fiscal year. Seek out this report to get a comprehensive overview of the registrant's business. (This was my primary source of information when I researched my mother's question, in the earlier example.)

2. 10-Q: filed quarterly by most registered companies. The report must be filed for each of a company's first three fiscal quarters and is due within 45 days of the close of each quarter. This is a valuable source for seeing how a business is doing. It includes unaudited financial statements and provides a continuing view of the company's financial position during the year.

3. 8-K: the "current report" used to narrate the occurrence of any material events or corporate changes that are of importance to investors or securities holders and have not been previously reported by the registrant. The 8-K provides more current information on certain specific events than would the 10-Q or 10-K. The document must be filed within 15 days of any event it describes.

4. 18-K: used for the annual reports of foreign governments or political subdivisions of foreign governments.

The Edgar database also generates indexes each day. The company index contains a list, sorted by company name, of each submission and the associated file name. Online instructions provide details. Other indexes are generated with the same data but sorted by form type.

Chapter 8

Let 'em Know What You Think—By E-Mail, Fax, and Phone

Even lacking late 20th-century jargon to describe it as such, our country's founders created an interactive nation. Our participatory democracy depends on data flowing in both directions, to and from the governing and the governed. Telling officeholders how to do their jobs is an American passion, as you'd expect in a land born of dissent and protest. Along with town meetings, petitions, and demonstrations, our letters to our elected officials are as American as Apple computers. Electronic mail is just the latest medium in a long tradition of citizens' talking back to the government.

But e-mail does much more than simply pick up where the typewriter, the ballpoint pen, and the feathered quill left off. Ubiquitous, instant, and easy, e-mail is unlike any medium the world has known. Not only can it transmit words and images around the world in seconds, but it also can be sent to fax and telex machines, or transmitted to print sites where it is transformed automatically into paper mail for traditional U.S. Postal Service delivery, or sent with binary files such as graphics, spreadsheets, and programs.

To get the most out of your e-mail—not to mention your phone calls and your faxes—you need to know *where to send them,* and that is the focus of this chapter. For instance, we'll see:

▶ Where to find the World Wide Web's directories for government officials. Resources include e-mail and street addresses, phone and fax numbers for elected and appointed federal representatives. And, as we noted in the previous chapter, since consumerism has become America's Little-P politics, we have similar resources for finding businesses.

▶ How to search electronic phone books. Telephone numbers for literally tens of millions of American residents and businesses now can be searched in seconds online. The same resources can serve you whether you're looking for a distant business associate, a long-lost love, an old college roommate, an Army buddy, or a missing relative.

▶ How to locate e-mail addresses for your fellow Net surfers, through a new breed of specially designed Web-based search utilities. We'll show you the first efforts being made to create a universal directory for our modem nation.

Along the way, we'll see some cool new e-mail technology. All Internet service providers and commercial online services these days offer their own electronic mail features for subscribers, but the real cutting-edge mail technology is being developed on the Net itself. Net sites are further automating the e-mail capability. Imagine dropping by a Web page, selecting from an online list the name of the specific officeholder(s) to whom you wish to write, composing your message in a box provided on the same page, and then simply clicking on the Send button and letting the site handle the details of delivering your message. That kind of innovation has already arrived on the Net. Never has the rattling of official cages been so easy—or so much fun.

KNOCKING ON THE FEDS' FRONT DOOR

Thirty-eight-year-old computer consultant Steve Moyer says he has two homes, in Vermont and New Zealand. Not long ago, he returned from the latter with the idea of doing "something special" for the former, and for the rest of his U.S. homeland.

The result was E-mail Democracy (http://www.entrepreneurs.net /solutions/emaildem.htm), a website that automates the process of sending e-mail to elected officeholders in the federal government. The page can be used to write letters to the individual members of the Senate and House of Representatives. The names of possible recipients are listed alphabetically by state; you need only click on your addressees' names, and then compose your message. Or, you can enter your zip code in a query box and let the site find your area's representatives for you.

"Why waste paper, time, and money?" Moyer says. "Communicate electronically with your representatives. It's the way of the 21st century and it's available now!" As of mid-February 1996, 81 of the 100 U.S. senators and 176 of the 435 members of the U.S. House of Representatives had e-mail addresses supported by the page.

Similar—with a wider, though less comprehensive collection of electronic addresses—is Interactive Democracy (http://www.cgx.com /id.html), from the Conservative Generation X online publication. The site automates e-mail delivery to any of a selection of government officials (Clinton, Gore, Gingrich, Kennedy, and so on), media talk show hosts (Limbaugh, Liddy, and others), TV network news operations (All Things Considered, NBC Nightly News, CSPAN, and so on), and magazines and newspapers (*TIME, Newsweek, U.S. News and World Report, Rolling Stone, Mother Jones, Forbes, Business Week, The Washington Post,* and *USA Today.*

Finding Federal Addresses, Phone, and Fax Numbers

E-mail addresses are the essential connection points for cyber-denizens, but the rest of world still requires certain *other* numbers for communications—phone numbers, fax numbers, U.S. Postal Service addresses ("Snail-Mail" is our smarmy Net-speak term for it)—and the Net can provide them as well.

Not long ago, Juan E. Cabanela, an astrophysics PhD candidate at the University of Minnesota, took time out from his academic pursuits to create the Contacting the Congress page (http://ast1.spa.umn.edu /juan/congress.html), a valuable, yet unpretentious site that provides multiple means for reaching most members of the U.S. Senate and House of Representatives. Using this site, you'll find e-mail addresses, fax machines, and phone numbers in the members' Washington offices and in their home states. Congress members' names are links to their

CompuServe's Congressgram Automates Federal Mail

CompuServe's mail feature (GO MAIL on CompuServe) includes Congress-grams—personalized, hard-copy letters you can send electronically from CompuServe to members of the U.S. Senate, the U.S. House of Representatives, the president, or the vice president. Con-gressgrams are delivered by the U.S. Postal Service and carry a $1.00 surcharge for each letter.

Off the Web

When using the feature, you are prompted to enter the recipient's name and title (senator, representative, president, or vice-president), the text of your message, the subject, your name, and your postal address. CompuServe Mail will automatically enter the recipient's address, the salutation, and the closing.

Web or gopher home pages, when available. To use the page, click on the name of the state you are interested in, and the feature builds a table of all relevant data it has available.

Says Cabanela, "I hope you can use this information to counter-act some of the idiocy going on in Washington, whatever you consider 'idiocy' to be. Keep in mind that every fax or voice call is interpreted by your congressperson as equal to the opinion of many more con-stituents who don't call. You can make a difference."

Cabanela even has suggestions on *how to construct* an effective, concise Congress-bound e-mail message. He suggests online letters should be no longer than one page—two brief paragraphs are best—and that you identify yourself (by name, not a hide-behind moniker), and give your affiliation and your major concern in the first paragraph. In the second paragraph, he suggests, describe why the concern is im-portant and worthwhile. End with your postal address, so someone on the senator's or representative's staff can reply.

Other sources for congressional connections include:

▶ U.S. House of Representatives directory of its 435 members (http://www.house.gov/Whoswho.html) will give you the name of each member and his or her phone numbers and addresses. Each committee has members from the majority and minority parties. Each full committee and its subcommittees, along with their phone numbers and addresses, are listed. If members and committees have public e-mail addresses, they are also there.

▶ U.S. Senate page (www.senate.gov) provides specifics on its members and on key committees, such as the Democratic and Republican policy committees, the Small Business Committee, the Committee on Aging, and others. E-mail addresses are included if they exist.

Receiving the *Federal Register* by E-mail

Among all the collections of federal contacts, nothing quite beats the *Federal Register*. Every proposed rule, final rule, and notice from

---

Highway 1 is a not-for-profit corporation formed by a number of major high-tech firms—including Apple, AT&T, IBM, Novell Inc., and Quantum Corp.—to promote innovative uses of new technologies in the legislative environment and in the democratic process.

The project's website (http://www .highway1.org) says it intends to provide an opportunity for members of Congress, their staffs, other government executives, and members of the public interested in the leg-

Highway 1 Seeks to Improve Government Communications

islative process to become more familiar with the latest information technologies and communication tools.

In addition, "Highway 1 will enable visitors to view and use applications of digital/audio/video/photography, advanced voice-processing systems, online communications, remote access to multimedia databases and CD-ROM authoring."

Come here to get details and registration information on upcoming seminars and panel discussions on current technology, including e-mail management systems, Net security, and home page creation. An online form enables you to request Highway 1 brochures, press clippings, and seminar schedules.

the more than 140 executive branch agencies is, by law, published in the daily *Federal Register.*

A service from a Cambridge, Massachusetts, company called Counterpoint Publishing now offers some e-mail magic to help you keep tabs on this important publication, which stays on top of the overwhelming number of new Environmental Protection Agency proposals, Housing and Urban Development Department rules, grant opportunities, or any of the thousands of other government decisions and actions that are published daily in its pages.

Counterpoint's E-mail Federal Register (http://www.counterpoint .com/emailfr) enables you to receive notification of articles that conform to your research criteria. The service is targeted to the major government e-mail crowd, including anyone who has a concern with regulatory or legal compliance, grant seekers, environmental engineers, federal–state liaisons, attorneys, or anyone else who follows the processes of the federal government.

Federal Numbers on America Online, CompuServe

On America Online, Washington Week in Review Online (enter WWIR on AOL) is an electronic extension of public television's longest-running public affairs program. Its focus is on government and Washington (DC) information. Browse through the "Capital Facts" area. Inside, you'll find federal departments and agencies, the House of Representatives, and the Senate listed alphabetically with addresses and phone numbers. Find biographies of the justices and a schedule of hearings in the "Supreme Court" folder. Look in "Washington News Bureaus" for a list of major print and broadcast media located in the Washington area. If you plan to travel to Washington, check out "Visitor Information" for places to see and things to do when you visit.

Off the Web

On CompuServe, a Members of Congress database provides the names of congressional representatives, the president, and the vice president (enter GO FCC-1 on CompuServe). This service provides a state-by-state listing of all members of the House of Representatives and the Senate. Each listing includes the name, party affiliation, Washington telephone number, hometown, and committee memberships.

The stereotype image of stodgy government bureaucrats and business moguls resisting new technology is a fallacy, at least when it comes to electronic mail.

A survey by Louis Harris and Associates Inc. found that, by the spring of 1995, 83 percent of federal workers and 65 percent of state government employees were using electronic mail. Those figures put government workers ahead of employees at the biggest 2,000 companies, who came in third (60 percent) in e-mail use. The survey indicated that, in government, 57 percent of e-mail systems were linked to the Internet; in companies, less than 50 percent were.

Government and Business Workers Are Quick to Embrace E-mail

The Harris pollsters also found relatively little electronic communication between government and companies. Among companies doing business with the government, only 6 percent of that business was done electronically. However, business representatives believed that percentage would change. Of those polled, 71 percent said they expected to be doing business with the government electronically within two years, and they predicted that the percentage of transactions done via computer will nearly triple, to 16 percent.

Writing in *The Washington Post,* reporter Kathleen Day noted the survey was financed by Control Data Systems Inc., a computer company based in Arden Hills, Minnesota, and 505 people were questioned at federal and state agencies and at companies.

If you're looking for business connections around the country, you might want to turn to the commercial agency that has always been in the business of business: the Chamber of Commerce. Access the Chamber through:

▶ A Directory of Chambers of Commerce (http://chamber-of-commerce.com), which lists addresses, phone numbers, and names of personnel in chamber organizations across the country. Search options let you look for contacts by state, by city, or by keyword.

▶ The home page of the U.S. Chamber of Commerce (http://www.uschamber .org/chamber), which provides directory data plus news, statements, alerts, and bulletins from the national headquarters, and text of the "Voice of Business Weekly"—radio addresses by Chamber President Richard Lesher. During our visit in mid-March 1996, topics included "Clinton's Favorite Tax Cheats," "Quack Medicine," and "Congressional Overtime." The page has material publications and programs for local chambers, and details on seminars, conferences, and related activities.

Here's how it works. You provide Counterpoint with a list of the topics you want the feature's computer to search for you daily in the *Federal Register*. Your instruction could be as simple as "All new Environmental Protection Agency articles" or as specific as "Any new FDA final rule concerning biologics" or "any article with the words calcium carbonate." Each day, Counterpoint searches the full text of the *Federal Register* for your topics. You get an e-mail message listing the article titles that match your criteria. You then check a box next to each article you want, and you return the message using the "Reply" feature. The service will send your articles to you as e-mail messages.

To order the service, send e-mail to info@counterpoint.com with your method of payment (credit card or a request to be billed) and your search criteria. For more details, visit the firm's home page (http://www.counterpoint.com).

Netheads interested in the *Federal Register* might also want to check out the Federally Funded Research in the United States (http://cos.gdb.org/best/fed-fund.html), which includes names and addresses of principal investigators, grant titles, abstracts, and keywords associated with grants funded by federal departments and agencies. At this writing, the site had details on funding contacts at the National Institutes of Health, the National Science Foundation, Small Business Innovation Research, the U.S. Department of Agriculture, and the Advanced Technology Program.

PHONE BOOKS

Back in the 1980s, when the word "videotex" was widely used to describe computer communications and online services, France's Minitel system generally was cited as the beginning of it all. And at the heart of Minitel was a national telephone directory.

Considering the massive storage capacity online and the speed of search facilities, the Net *still* seems like an ideal vehicle for phone books, and some publishers are beginning to catch on. Aided by court decisions and federal legislation that have broadened their options for competition, regional phone companies now are beginning to bring their yellow pages online. Others are creating searchable files of the white pages and of specialized resources, such as the AT&T 800-number directory.

Switchboard—White Pages Online

Your computer keyboard might be the ultimate tracer of missing persons. Have you lost contact with old friends and colleagues over the years? Do you ever wonder whether there is any way to locate them again? Try checking with Switchboard.

Switchboard (http://www.switchboard.com) is an exciting new electronic white-pages directory that enables you to locate phone numbers and street addresses from among 93 million residential listings and 11 million businesses throughout the United States. At this writing, it's free. Brought online by a Westboro, Massachusetts, software company, Banyan Systems Inc., and its new Internet division, called Coordinate.com, this remarkably fast, easy resource uses data licensed from Database America, a major compiler of names and demographic information. To use it, simply enter the name of the person you are seeking, and his or her hometown. In seconds, Switchboard provides the phone numbers and U.S. Postal Service mailing addresses you requested.

That service alone would be enough to make most Net travelers stop and take notice, but Switchboard has much more planned for itself than being merely a superfast national phone book. The people at Banyan Systems are hoping their site—launched in early 1996—will become a true Internet directory as well. The company offers a free "Registration" option online, enabling you to *personalize* and update your own phonebook entry. You can add your e-mail address, your occupation, affiliations, and other professional contact information, additional phone numbers, and a description of yourself and your interests. Later, you can modify your listing if you wish, or you can use your "Registration" option to remove your entry from the directory altogether.

An innovation called "KnockKnock" will be a boon to online privacy. Once you register your account, you can use "KnockKnock" to make yourself accessible on the Net without a risk of exposing your actual e-mail address to unwelcome correspondence. "KnockKnock" lets you place "privacy screens" on your listing, shielding your e-mail address but allowing others to contact you (using Switchboard as an intermediary). In other words, Switchboard delivers the message and includes the sender's entire Switchboard listing. After reading the message and reviewing the information about the sender, you can decide whether to

**Decoder to Unlock
Phone Number Data**

You come back to the office to find you've received a phone call from an area code you don't recognize. Before returning the call, you might like to know where you'll be calling. If it's on the other side of the continent, it might affect how long you choose to speak or when you opt to call. The solution: Make your first call to the Web.

The AmeriCom Long Distance Area Decoder (http://www.xmission.com/~americom/aclookup.html) lets you find codes anywhere in the world. To look up an area code (known as a "city code" outside the United States and Canada), enter the city, state, and/or country, and click on the SUBMIT button. To look up a city or country, enter the area code and/or country code and press SUBMIT. (You may enter city codes in the area code field, to look up cities outside the United States and Canada.) And don't worry about spelling accuracy. The decoder has a rather liberal outlook on spelling and usually can automatically figure out what you mean.

reply. Only then will the sender see your e-mail address. Switchboard is a kind of "Caller ID" version of e-mail.

At this writing, Switchboard's database is limited to data about U.S. residents. However, Banyan says it receives many requests to include Canada and is considering expanding northward and heeding the suggestion to include registrations from users in other countries.

Other Phone Books

Also of interest are these online phone book projects:

▶ New York's Nynex Interactive Yellow Pages (http://www.niyp .com), which offers searching for information about businesses, products, and services in the Northeast. You can search "Business Name" or "Business Category" features, or you can visit the site's "Top 25 Headings."

▶ AT&T's directory of toll-free 800-numbers across the country (http://www.tollfree.att.net/dir800) does its searching by keyword. Database logical operators (AND, OR, and NOT) are available for more complex searching. The site also has a useful section that gives answers to frequently asked questions, details on how to have a company's number added to the directory, and how to get a printed version of the data.

INTERNET DIRECTORIES

Picture a community where the population doubles every few years. Now imagine the worst clerical job you could possibly have in that boom town: putting together the most needed book in town—the phone book—with its constant flow of incoming new data. Painting a

---

You join the campaign staff, and your first assignment is to do something cool with the call-in phone lines for the headquarters. Instead of a plain old phone number, you want a sexy and upbeat word-and-number combination for the ads—something easy to remember, like "Dial 555-WINS" or "Dial BAG-DEMS" or "Dial WHO-KNOWS." PhoNETic (http://www.soc.qc.edu /phonetic) stands ready for the challenge.

Creating Names from Numbers

Offered by the Queens College Sociology Department in New York City, PhoNETic converts a telephone number into all combinations of the telephone keypad letters. If you're unfamiliar with the concept, look at a telephone dial and notice that the letters A, B, and C are associated on the "2" key; D, E, and F are on the "3" key, and so on. The call letters can be used to form words that can help in remembering numbers, and the website can help you find the words.

The program begins by asking you to enter the phone number you are using (include the area code *only if* you want it to be included in the coding). You then specify the minimum number of letters to consider meaningful (that is, how many contiguous numbers should be converted into letters); minimum is two, maximum is ten. After a moment, the system produces a list of words and near-words that can be created on a phone dial with those numbers.

The site has background on the phone number/letter system, how to get the most out of PhoNETic, and related topics. The site also can convert an existing phoNETic telephone number into numeric digits.

The CoolBoard: Wiring Web With-it-ness

There are directories and then there are DIRECTORIES, and who wouldn't want to be included on a list called Who's Cool in America (http://www.getcool .com/~getcool)! You can seek admission, but, as an online statement points out, "To be officially cool, someone else must determine this for you." Enter the CoolBoard, sponsor of this website, "a group of people who do nothing but evaluate, cogitate and pontificate on this subject. (These are individuals who would have appeared on the lecture circuit at any major university, but were too cool to show up.)"

Names on the Net

The site adds, "Because all boards need a purpose, the CoolBoard is pleased to announce that our new mission statement includes the desire to fund scientific DNA research into discovering and isolating the 'coolness gene' and through genetic engineering make 'coolness' available to everyone." The page offers downloadable membership cards for those who feel a need to certify their coolness.

The road to recognition begins with an online form in which you write, in a hundred words or less, why you think you're so cool. Your case then is reviewed by the coolness cartel and it's hard to predict just what they will like. "My entry," confesses *Arizona Republic* newspaperman Bill Goodykoontz, "included the following: 'I'm cool because I would rather spend the evening eating chicken wings and drinking beer . . . than filet mignon and red wine at a swank restaurant with red-velvet wallpaper. I floss sometimes . . . .' Hey, cut me a break," Goodykoontz adds. "It was late!"

But, guess what—it worked.

Not just *everybody* gets accepted. For instance, site creators Steve Morris and Warden Minor have shared one of their rejected applications, which read: "I drive a Ford Escort wagon, gray in color. I live with my parents in an apartment over their garage . . . ." Sad, but true. And, alas, too uncool.

All this suggests to the lads a continuing need for the rulings of the CoolBoard.

Cool, says Morris, is "like being handsome—it only counts if someone else makes the determination."

moving car would be easier. A similar problem exists on the Net these days. The most frequently heard question from each new wave of Internet immigrants is: "Where do I find the directory of all the e-mail addresses?" And then comes the most frequently shared response from the leaden-eyed locals: "In your dreams, pilgrim."

A number of noble efforts—the Switchboard site described above, and the projects mentioned in this section—are trying to get a commonly accepted Net directory going. However, as of this writing there is no single source for finding folks on the Net. Be patient, and watch the Web. The need for such a resource is so great, so universally understood (if you don't know a person's e-mail address, there is no central place where you can look up that person's online mailing address), that even as you read these words, someone, somewhere out in cyberspace, is turning to friends and saying, "Whoa! Hey! I've got an idea . . . !"

The Four11 Directory (http://www.four11.com) boasts of being the Internet's largest "White Page Directory," claiming at this writing more than 5 million listings. Named in honor of the traditional telephone-company directory-assistance number (411), the online directory offers all users a free listing and free searching. The directory gets listings from three sources: (1) voluntary registrations (some 100,000 at this writing), (2) public sources (primarily, the message headers in Usenet newsgroups), and (3) automatic registration (usually via selected Internet service providers).

Offered by Larry Drebes and Mike Santullo's SLED (Stable-Large-E-mail-Database) Corporation, of Menlo Park, California, the directory can be searched by first name, last name, location, and interests. You can search for free, but you yourself must be listed in the directory in order to use the search feature. A particularly nifty option is the directory's list of "Group Connections" (interests), intended to allow searchers to look for connections through various categories, including current organization, books/movies/music, interests/hobbies/sports, Net hangouts, research topics, past high school, past college/university, past organizations, past location/residence, past military service, and more.

All Four11 users enter a custom listing of the information they want included. The administrators do not require unnecessary personal information; directory features that rely on more personal information are optional. Also, at any time, users can access the site to update their own listings. Once signed up, you can search the directory immediately;

Finding Addresses on America Online, CompuServe, and Prodigy

All commercial information services have databases for searching "local" user IDs to verify users of that specific service.

Off the Web

On America Online, the Member Directory (enter DIRECTORY on AOL) enables you to search for people who share your interests. You can search the directory by the member's full profile, which contains personal information (screen name, real name, and location), occupation, hobbies and interests, and more. To do that, simply type in the search phrase and click on the SEARCH option. In a moment, a menu containing the name or names that meet your search criteria appears and you can then select names from the list and read those members' profiles. You also can add your own profile to the Member Directory. All information is optional. You can include just your screen name and city, or you can include sex, marital status, a personal quote, and so on. You can change your profile at any time.

On CompuServe, the Member Directory (enter GO DIRECTORY on CompuServe) is searchable by name. The state and city may be used as search criteria to narrow a name search. You may omit the first name, state, or city responses by entering a blank line (that is, pressing RETURN). However, if you omit any of these, there is a good chance the resulting list will be too large to be displayed. If that happens, you will be prompted again for the omitted information. The feature has an option that lets you include or exclude your own user ID number in the directory. Any change you request will take a week to be effective.

On Prodigy, the directory assistance option is built into the Prodigy Mail (enter just the Jump Word MAIL on Prodigy). Click on the "Member List" option on the main Mail menu, and follow the screen instructions.

a Four11 password will be sent to your e-mail address so you can log in to Four11 in the future. (Note: Passwords are not selected online; they are generated randomly by the system for e-mailing to your mailbox. Once your account is established, you can change your Four11 password using an online Web change form.)

For those who pay a membership upgrade fee, Four11 provides a "Sleeper Search" option—a request that is stored in the site's system and run against all new directory entries and changes. Whenever a match is found, an e-mail notification is sent to the customer's e-mail address. This is a great way to have the system keep on the lookout for members of specific organizations, certain interests, specific family names, and so on.

Another interesting effort at creating a Net directory is the Internet Phonebook (http://www.iag.net/~impt/index.html), intended primarily for finding Net surfers in specific regions of the world. It opens by asking the visitor to click on one of the listed regions. The system then displays a linked continental map to get more details, by searching states or districts. A form allows visitors to add their own entries. The system prompts for name, e-mail address, country, state, and city, and the Web address of a personal home page, if any. Entries can appear with photos, and usually include interests, comments, hometown, favorite Net activities, and similar data.

E-MAIL CAN COME BACK TO HAUNT YOU

Try this true-or-false pop quiz:

1. Privacy of all electronic mail is guaranteed by law.
2. Once you have deleted an electronic letter from your mailbox, it's gone, caput, vanished, like it never *was*.
3. The content of all private e-mail between two people is inadmissible in court.

The answer to all three of these teasers is a resounding, sobering "false." Does that give you something to think about when you begin to type what goes after "Dear John" in your next e-mail, especially if you're at the office when you're writing it?

Electronic mail, like most computer communications, seems so confidential, so personal that many Net travelers begin to think that all their e-mail is private. However, if that e-mail is being generated from an office or other work site, watch out. Federal law allows employers to literally monitor their workers' e-mail. And, even if the boss isn't looking in routinely, all e-mail generated from a company computer is fair game in court suits. In other words, if someone sues a company, the rules of discovery demand that the company must produce all relevant business records, and that can include the e-mail records.

But what if you deleted it? Isn't it gone? It may be gone to your eyes, but files that were deleted long ago often survive on backup tapes. In many business operations, the systems department routinely backs up data every night. And if lawyers come with subpoenas, they will be looking for those backup tapes.

Here are some general tips for safe and happy e-mailing:

- Don't write anything you wouldn't want repeated. E-mail can be forwarded to hundreds of people, inside and outside the company.

- Work out problems face-to-face, not in e-mail. Remember that electronic mail can leave a permanent—if sometimes inaccurate, incomplete, or uncomplimentary—record.

- Say to yourself, at least once a day: "Would I want a jury to read this e-mail?"

- If in doubt, don't write it. At a minimum, consult with your company's human resources director or legal counsel to get further clarification on these tips.

Chapter 9

The Future: Web of Wonder, Web of Woe

To some seers, cyberspace is more than something to venerate or to vilify, much more than a medium that needs to be regulated or needs to be left alone to grow and evolve on its own. To these social scientists and new modemocratic philosophers, the Net is no less than The New Gutenberg—and perhaps a harbinger of the next great social revolution.

The *first* Gutenberg (Johannes, c. 1400–1468) ended Europe's Dark Ages when his development of printing from movable type enabled mass circulation of books. He brought on quite an upheaval. Literacy and education were no longer controlled by the royalty and the clergy. General distribution of Bibles led to the Protestant Reformation, the rise of secular society, and the city-state (and to some of the fiercest, bitterest wars in history). As the world turned itself upside down and inside out, newspapers, journals, and philosophical papers spread new ideas, including cries for democracy and for the toppling of kings and emperors.

Suddenly, people had another way to keep score. In the constant contest between Us and Them, power began to accrue to those who controlled the press. Publishers acquired influence and authority that used to center only on wealthy aristocrats. In the early going, governments grabbed that power for themselves, reserving for the kings and queens the exclusive right to say who could and couldn't publish, and what could

297

be printed. Eventually, rebellions by common citizens, such as those in America and France in the 18th century, created governments founded on freedom of the press.

But, because the mechanics of printing were expensive, private-enterprise media moguls ascended to power, and they laid out a field of journalism where they could train the information gatekeepers. Today's reporters, editors, and news directors are direct descendants of those first gatekeepers. They determine what information is "news-worthy"—that is, of enough interest to warrant news coverage that will satisfy their subscribers or sponsors and still share the facts with the rest of us.

For the 500 years since the first Gutenberg, almost anyone with something to say to the world has had to first say it to publishers and hope to impress them enough so that they would print the message. But no more. With the rise of the Internet, we live in exciting times. At the very least, we are witnessing a worldwide explosion in self-publishing and free expression. Is it more than that? Is the Net the first step in a global realignment of power? Who knows? It's hard to get a vantage point from which to see our own history being made while we're living it. That's why historians will always have jobs. But one thing is certain: because of the Net, fascinating changes are afoot all around us. Cyber-space is challenging existing laws and customs, and governments are wondering whether to regulate the Net—and if so, how?

As we conclude our journey together, this chapter identifies some techno-ideological hot spots, and, by asking the questions we're all struggling to answer, erects a few imaginary signposts along the way. Each one reads: "Watch this space: History may be happening here."

COMING TO A WORLD NEAR YOU: EVERYMAN AS PUBLISHER

Geoff Huston smells revolution in the air. This Australian technology expert predicts that the social impact of cyberspace will be enormous, for two very simple reasons: (1) Everyone can publish what he or she wants to publish, and (2) the publication can be done instantly.

"You and I can be as big a content provider as media moguls Rupert Murdoch or Kerry Packer, just with you and your machine," Huston, the technical manager of the Australian Academic and Research Network, told an international academic conference in Sydney in the summer of 1995. And, unlike publishing in the past, sharing your ideas with the world is no longer an expensive undertaking. Paper, ink, printing presses and trained technicians to run them aren't required. Huge amounts of information can be made available online at almost no cost, and, with the new technology, it takes only seconds for us to electronically throw our voices around the globe. Even when we need to talk to each other about the information, the data flow doesn't have to stop. "In the past," Huston noted, "you needed to meet or you slowed the process down to interchange letters, but Internet says you don't have to slow it down."

You also don't have to rely on speculation if you want to think about how the speed and accessibility of data will establish a new global platform for ideas. Rather than endorse supposition, we need only read the day's news to see how cyberspace is becoming an open stage for anyone who knows how to use it. Judging from the international reports, some of the first persons who are stepping up to this new electronic lectern are those who cannot always be heard at home.

Consider the Zapatista rebels. They operate in Chiapas, Mexico's most backward state, where the nearest telephone might be fifty miles away. However, assisted by supporters in other parts of Mexico as well as in other countries, the rebel peasants are making their case in cyberspace. Their online statements are regularly posted and forwarded by church and human rights groups. Barbara Pillsbury, a 24-year-old Yale graduate from New York City, translates and posts news and analysis about Chiapas on the Net from her Mexico City office at Equipo Pueblo, a rural development organization. Pillsbury, who first saw army tanks headed into the Chiapas jungle when she was on a family vacation in 1994, says that some of the news she sends goes to congressional staffers in the United States, because "it's clear that a lot of things that affect Mexico get decided in Washington." Her boss, Carlos Heredia, says, "The Mexican government can deal with critics who write newspaper columns, but once you get on Internet and American TV, they can't control it." Routinely, soldiers physically block reporters from entering war zones, so news within Chiapas itself travels slowly, but once the information reaches computers in Mexico City, it moves across the wires within minutes. And the contact work is getting results: The electronic communication has brought the people who monitor human rights in Chiapas together with organizations that lobby the government in the Mexican capital.

Or consider how Carlos Andres Perez has used the cybersphere to thwart house arrest, which used to be the ultimate way to give someone a low profile. His confinement didn't stop him, in the autumn of 1995, from inviting the world to drop in for a chat. Perez, the charismatic two-time Venezuelan president accused of misappropriating $17 million in public funds, sat down in the company of his lawyers and talked with online computer users around the world about his ongoing trial. His message also reached people in his own country—the opportunity created such interest that information highways into Venezuela were jammed. Groups of up to seventy people clustered around megascreens in Venezuela to watch two and a half hours of Internet banter.

On the other side of the planet, Asia is coming under the scrutiny of the Net community. When Vietnamese dissident/writer Ha Si Phu was arrested in early 1996, the local news media were silent and the international press corps carried only brief reports, because the government critic was little known outside his own country. However, Internet discussion groups spread the news of his incarceration internationally in hours. Online, those with the greatest interest in the ongoing activities in Vietnam were prompted by the reports to begin calls for political reform and to launch a heated debate about the one-party Communist rule in the country.

Elsewhere, the Net is now being used by those already in power. To explain unpopular decisions or complex issues, to generate attention for new projects and campaigns, or just to influence international opinion, world leaders are beginning to sit down at a keyboard, after sidestepping the traditional news gatekeepers, to speak to an open—albeit sometimes rowdy—global audience.

Following 1995's embarrassing election fiasco in Haiti (more than 100,000 people were unable to vote because ballots arrived late or never arrived at polling stations), Haitian President Jean-Bertrand Aristide took to the Net to try to repair his island nation's reputation among its neighbors. After first answering questions from journalist Charlayne Hunter-Gault of PBS's "MacNeil-Lehrer NewsHour," Aristide invited other people participating in an online chat room to have a crack at interviewing him on what Americans could do to help Haiti. As the Aristide conference demonstrated, access does not necessarily mean answers. The first question from the cyber-public audience following the journalist's interview was: "Mr. President, will Haitians living in the United States be returning to Haiti soon?" Like many others, that query by the anonymous participant went unanswered. Silence is still silence, even in cyberspace.

Meanwhile, in the Middle East, RAND Corporation analyst Jerrold D. Green admits he is somewhat puzzled by the ease with which governments there are giving up their monopoly on the dissemination of information. Speaking at Washington's Georgetown University, at a summer 1995 symposium on the commercial, cultural, and political dimensions of the information revolution in the Arab world, Green said that, in contrast to the tight control over satellite-TV dishes that governments such as Saudi Arabia's and Iran's have imposed, "these places are wide open" with regard to telecommunications and computer technologies.

"The information revolution cannot be blocked," Green said. "It's like the air—or the dust in Cairo."

"Information Poverty" Threatens Some Parts of the World

But don't misunderstand. The World Wide Web is not yet truly worldwide. For one thing, the Net is largely an English-speaking medium with little, so far, to offer people of other tongues. And third-world countries generally have been slow to reach cyberspace, prompting some observers to fear a rise of data elitism among information-rich peoples.

Others are quick to point out that, even in regions where the technology has arrived, access to the Net does not automatically translate to a cyber-literate community. For instance, very few Arabs actually are *using* the Net, even though connections are widely available at Middle Eastern educational and research institutions. There, as in many parts of the world, the information highway continues to be a tool of the intelligentsia, which limits the Net's effectiveness as a means of social and political change. Even with wider use of the Net in the Middle East, many technology watchers are skeptical of its lasting impact. The spread of the information revolution, they say, will not necessarily lead to a political upheaval. On the contrary, new technologies could as easily serve only to further legitimize political elites as to enable challenges to their standing.

"Just having access to this stuff doesn't necessarily make you a Western liberal democrat," RAND's Jerrold Green notes, scoffing at those who believe authoritarian governments will automatically fall if "we airdrop Apples."

Nonetheless, without the basic hardware and software—air-dropped or otherwise—many developing countries currently face near-certain "information poverty" because, so far, the Internet, for all its boasts of being global, is concentrated in the richer countries.

"There is a danger of a new information elitism, which excludes the majority of the world's population," says a new study by Europe's Panos Institute, a nongovernmental organization funded largely by Scandinavian countries. Researchers found poor countries already are being left behind because of the high cost of computer equipment and their low literacy rates. Some 70 percent of computers linked up to the Internet in 1995 were in the United States; only ten (or fewer) African countries were connected. The study found 3.4 million host computers hooked up to the Net in the United States in 1995, and just over 500,000 in western Europe. Africa had only 27,100 hosts, Central and South America 16,000, and the Middle East 13,800.

"The technology could actually increase the gap between rich and poor," says study author Mike Holderness. Adding to the problem, the price of equipment differs greatly in various countries. A modem costs almost four times more in India than in the United States, and a new computer costs about six months' worth of unemployment benefits paid to a jobless Briton or several years' wages for an "underemployed" Indonesian. Holderness suggests not only stepping up existing literacy campaigns in the developing world, but also relaxing trade constraints that have made computer equipment so expensive in underdeveloped nations.

Some world-watchers would add at least one more item to the Net's to-do list: Don't be just multicultural; become multilingual as well. The nearly imperial presence of English on the Net has begun to rankle many of Cyberia's non-English-speaking citizens. "For me," says Alain Caris-tan of INRIA, a French computer research institute, "the Internet is the theater of a new colonial war. Anglophones created the Internet. They're at the heart of its growth. There's a danger it'll stay that way."

It is true that the popular "search engine" utilities for finding material on the Web are virtually all in English. To balance this situation, non-English speakers have begun creating search engines in other languages. A group of French researchers has put together the first all-French search engine, called Lokace (http://www.iplus.fr/lokace), and German users have been drawn to Cinetic (http://cinetic.de) to search for material in that language.

But that's only a small step, and some think the drive for a multilingual Net will have far-reaching consequences. "The French-speaking world's future is at stake," a French language support group called Francophone Agency for Higher Learning and Research commented in a recent statement. "It's fair to say the very existence of a language will be threatened if it isn't computerized." Talk about social revolution! To this organization, the impact of the global computer network "is comparable to civilization's passage from oral language to written language."

IS OBJECTIVITY AN ENDANGERED SPECIES?

Let's back up to the image of information gatekeepers and see what effect the Net has on *truth*.

Australian network expert Geoff Huston's prediction of a social revolution on the order of Gutenberg is only partially founded on the fact that the Net enables us all to become our own publishers. Also significant to the upheaval he foresees is the cybersphere's "international gossip network," that is, the Net's ease in lending itself to the sharing of sensationalism and propaganda globally in seconds.

Some even say that the very speed and distribution of digital data ultimately might influence whether we view the things we see online as "true" or not. The notion isn't too far-fetched. Most of us grew up thinking that something must be *true* if it was in the newspaper or on the evening news. Even if we were alone as we read the newspaper or watched the television, we were inclined to *believe* information when we were aware that it was being told to thousands of us at the same time. Then what happens to our perception of truth in the gatekeeper-free cybersphere, where what Huston calls the "gossip model" of communications prevails?

Startling, unchallenged observations are being forwarded everywhere instantly, raising yet more important questions to ponder:

▶ How can we tell what is true on the Net?

▶ What kind of future do we have without our familiar gatekeepers checking and rechecking the facts before disseminating the news to us?

▶ Will the Information Age be chaos if the truth and accuracy of the information itself are constantly in question?

A Little Journalistic History

We need to put these questions in historical perspective by realizing that the objectivity we hold in such high regard is a relatively *recent* enhancement of journalism. In fact, it is a child of the Industrial Age.

When America's founders spoke of freedom of the press, they weren't thinking of such modern media sovereignties as *The New York Times, The Washington Post,* and *The Wall Street Journal,* none of which existed at the time of the Revolution. Instead, the press that the founders meant to protect was, by and large, what today we might call "tabloid journalism," hundreds of small, local, fiercely opinionated, independent, often salacious and downright vindictive rags. Few of them had any interest in accuracy or fairness. Instead, their editors selected articles based on whether the stories would please the papers' owners, who were often political parties or groups that had established the papers to smear specific candidates. (Those who bemoan the venomous politicking of today ought to look at Thomas Jefferson's 1804 reelection bid, which was one of the nastiest campaigns in our history because of the opposition press.)

Only after the innovations of the Industrial Age in the mid-1800s could news-gathering become a national business. With the stringing of the country's telegraph wires, national news services (still called *wire* services because of their one-time reliance on the telegraph) could sell news reports over great distances. However, early in their new enterprise, the news services learned that, in order to avoid offending the local sensibilities and attitudes of their far-flung clients, they needed to remove opinion and commentary from their news accounts. In other words, objectivity originated from a marketing decision rather than from high-minded journalistic ethics. Fairness was good business.

Over the past century and a half, that early Industrial Age business decision completely altered news gathering. Opinion and commentary, which once filled every inch of a newspaper in Jefferson's agrarian era, began its retreat to designated inside pages (editorial, op-ed, the comics, movie reviews, and large slices of the sports section). Today, the idea of balanced reporting is so ingrained in our collective consciousness that most casual news readers, listeners, and viewers seem to think objectivity is a requirement, a footnote to the First Amendment. It is not.

And now—as we leave the Industrial Age, which mandated objectivity, and enter an age in which everyone can be his or her own publisher with an instant, international audience—we have to wonder: Will fairness survive the trip?

Two Scenarios

That may be the biggest question facing the fledgling Information Age. It goes to the very heart of the new era's raw material: quality control of the data. No one knows the answer—that's what makes it such a swell question—but two optimistic scenarios come to mind.

1. *What if objectivity's profit motive is still alive and rides in to save the day?* The scene would go like this. The Web is a model of a frontier town, with the exhilaration and the confusion of any other outpost of civilization in the wilderness. As the online immigration continues and the cyber-population grows, the initial zeal for all that F*R*E*E! information begins to cool. New leaden-eyed Web wanderers begin to find that, waaaay too often, free data are worth every penny you pay for them. Their frustration over the difficulty of sifting fact from rumors and from outright lies happens to coincide with the arrival of commercial ventures in the neighborhood. Among the newcomers are several bright-eyed entrepreneurs who see in these disheartened data hunters a base of potential customers willing to hire old-fashioned news gatekeepers to collect and verify the news of the

day in a guaranteed controlled setting, free from tampering. *Voila!* Accuracy is again marketable.

2. *What if data overload ultimately alters the human psyche, and ordinary people begin to evolve into their own gatekeepers?* Regardless of what editors and reporters might tell you, they are not a breed apart. They have *learned* the century-old process by which unbiased news accounts are developed. Their time-tested technique may seem ridiculously slow and cumbersome in an age of instant data. Trained reporters laboriously verify with independent sources facts that are then challenged again by editors before being submitted for distribution by a publisher who has a vested (usually commercial) interest in his or her reputation for accurately delivering information on a regular basis. However, after being bitten by one too many pieces of bad data, a growing number of nonjournalist cyber-citizens might see the sense in the arduous procedure and adopt some of the same techniques for verifying facts. Actually, it's not so much an urge to imitate journalists as a reaching back to our pool of shared tribal wisdom ("Don't believe everything you read." "Nurture your skepticism."). After a generation or two, Cyberian children might even be born with built-in bunk detectors.

Variations and combinations of the scenarios also are possible— *more than* possible: they're already starting. As we saw on our travels together in this book, traditional commercial news providers are beginning to stream to the Web, where they're being met by competition from Net-based originals, all vying to become the computing public's premier paperless newspaper. And, while we all probably are just a tad too close to the subject to see any real evolutionary changes in *ourselves*, it's fair to say that, in this age of computer networks, 24-hour news on TV and radio, nonstop talk shows, phone-line data services, fax, cable-TV, and satellite dishes, we are no longer informational innocents.

Meanwhile, for some of our fellow citizens, a social revolution/evolution against the technology itself has already begun. Reeling from information overload—or just tired of hearing about computers every day—they have become resistant to the Net. Are they hungry for a more naturally oriented, less technology-dependent lifestyle? Or perhaps just repulsed by chaotic images they see and hear from the darker side of cyberspace?

DARKER VIEWS OF OUR DIGITAL DESTINY

Our future in a networked world can sound so darned charming. The Global Village, where Granny Smith is jacked into an online chat room for a quick cyber-visit with her babies around the world, while husband Farmer Bob lopes onto the Net to download the day's data on sow bellies and soybean prices. It's an odd, but unthreatening image of "Modem Mayberry." Our other terms for this wired community are equally pastoral. "Cyberspace" and "The Information Superhighway" link to images of freedom and the open road, of a binary Big Sky Country where everyone's got plenty of growing room and we all just mind our own business.

Not everybody's having the same digital daydreams. For some observers, our data-based future seems much darker indeed. Futurists say the breaking up of old geopolitical boundaries is inevitable as the Information Age bursts upon us. Some foresee digital democracy; others see only chaos.

"Hell is a loss of privacy, and nothing brings us closer to hell than telecommunications technology," groans American attorney Delbert Smith. "We will all end up consumers with no privacy in a technological world with no protections." Speaking in Osaka, Japan, at a summer 1995 conference of the British-based International Institute of Communications, Smith added, "The telecommunications revolution is all about control and power."

He is hardly alone in this worry. All of France seemed caught up in a Net privacy issue for the first few weeks of 1996. It started when French courts, citing concerns for a famous family's privacy, banned the printing of a book called *Le Grand Secret* (which detailed late President François Mitterrand's previously undisclosed battle with cancer). However, within hours of the court decision to restrict the book's publication, a café owner named Pascal Barbraud, in the eastern French town of Besançon, thumbed his nose at the state censors. Obtaining a copy of the controversial book (it had been printed in a limited edition before the court's ruling to ban its further distribution), he transcribed all 190 pages on his computer and placed them into his World Wide Web site on the Internet. Word spread quickly, and thousands of people inside and outside of the country were soon reading for free the book that the courts in France had outlawed. At this writing, the case is dragging on in court, and the French government—angered by the whole incident—was urging its European partners to draft international rules for the Internet, saying that today, online data go across national borders in a legal vacuum.

Others would say "vacuum" is a much too mild word. In the debate that ended that three-day Japanese telecommunications conference of some 100 telecommunications experts from 23 countries, participants abandoned a proposed motion to say the telecommunications revolution would usher in an era of "heaven on earth." Far from it, the participants said. In place of the originally proposed motion, conference attendees decided to go on record as saying that, although the coming telecommunications era would improve access to information, it also probably would destroy jobs, isolate women, eliminate time for quiet contemplation, and possibly drag the entire world into total anarchy.

How Ending the Cold War Gave Citibank a Headache

Others fret over what the Net will do to our money. Wall Street still gets the willies just thinking about what happened to Citibank in 1995. That's when a young Russian computer user named Vladimir Levin, working from an ordinary computer in St. Petersburg, allegedly broke into the massive New York bank electronically and successfully transferred more than $10 million before he was stopped. Citibank ultimately recovered all but $400,000 and, with the help of the FBI and Russian police, tracked down the 24-year-old mathematics graduate and several alleged cohorts.

Nonetheless, the incident is unnerving to anyone with a stake in the status quo. Many observers say more Citibank-like capers are to come. And the case chillingly illustrates that, despite all the good reconnaissance by our futurists and philosophers, we are not going to be able to anticipate all the political, economic, and social ramifications of the Big Events in our new Information Age.

Who expected the end of the Cold War to threaten the biggest bank in the world? Yet, in retrospect, the connection is clear. First, some background. Someday historians, probably will declare that the collapse of the Soviet Union was one of the first major political developments in the Information Age. It had been anticipated for a while in some quarters. For decades, high-tech seer and writer Arthur C. Clarke had been saying that the Iron Curtain and other societies hostile to the free flow of information simply would not withstand the effects of communications satellites, international computer networks, and other manifestations of the new telecommunications era.

What was *not* anticipated was that the fall of the old order also would set loose a whole new breed of predators on the electronic highways. Post-Soviet Russia has spawned some of the world's most ruthless, daring crime gangs, and many of them are now allying themselves with that country's thousands—perhaps tens of thousands—of idle but quite gifted computer programmers. Russia has always had some of the world's best programmers, in part because of the old Soviet Union's emphasis on math and science education. Ironically, the computer savvy also is a byproduct of backward Soviet technology. Because the Soviets didn't make very good computers, programmers there had to do more with less, and had to compete with each other for time on shared systems. Like athletes building up muscle through strenuous daily activity and hardship, that constant scrapping for shared computer resources enabled the Russian programmers to hone the very skills they later could use in prowling the Net and sometimes invading supposedly secure systems.

Now shift forward in time to the collapse of the Soviet Union and the related fall of all the institutes and industries where those clever, hungry programmers had been working. Suddenly, thousands of them were left to stream back to Russia from newly independent countries like Kazakhstan, Tajikistan, or the Baltics. "Many of these people are entering into the illicit markets," Russian organized-crime expert Louise Shelley, at American University in Washington, comments, "because they've come back with no money, no apartments, no way of earning money legitimately."

And for that reason, Shelley says, the Citibank break-in "is just the beginning."

Smut, Hate, and Bomb: Natural Net Byproducts?

Would you prefer to worry about smut, hatred, and bombs?

In early 1996, the Anti-Defamation League (ADL) released a disturbing report. More than ever, hate groups are using the Internet to bring racist and anti-Semitic messages into millions of American homes.

Peddling hate is not new, but, says ADL National Director Abraham Fox-man, "being confronted with it as you sit in your home or office brings it to a new level. This is hate up close and personal; it is technology per-verted." What is particularly troubling is the frequent online appeal that some of these groups have to the young. Says Foxman, "Newcomers to the propagation of prejudice and hatred, initially independent of an or-ganization, are college students who have unlimited access to the Inter-net through school facilities established to encourage the exchange of knowledge."

However, those who want to answer online hatred with online censorship are likely to bump heads with free-speech advocates. That's what happened in January 1996, when the Simon Weisenthal Center, a leading Jewish human rights group, began sending hundreds of letters to Internet access providers asking them to refuse to carry messages that promote racism, anti-Semitism, mayhem, and violence. The appeal was quickly met with fire from civil libertarians and cyber rights groups. Arguing that public debate is the way to defeat hate, Mike Godwin, staff counsel for the Electronic Frontier Foundation (EFF), said the Internet allows users to "show the whole world what's wrong about what the hate speakers are saying."

And do we want to see free-speech debates become even more volatile? Stir in some "cyberporn." That is the term coined by the news media in the mid-1990s to describe what some say is the Net's obses-sion with sex. In fact, says UK computer expert Harold Thimbleby, if we are talking about a global village, "most of it is a heavily used red-light district." In remarks at a prestigious annual Newcastle, England, science festival of the British Association, Thimbleby added, "Some people see the Internet and the World Wide Web as an important step toward democracy, education and peace, and of benefit to everyone from children to entire nations. They see Utopia . . . . The reality is rather different from the vision. The Internet brings pornography and computer viruses; it tells you how to take drugs and make bombs." He added that his research found the top eight most frequently used "search words" on the Net relate to pornography. More than 10 percent of Net shops sold erotica and some 10 percent of Net bulletin boards accessed in a random sample were pornographic, in his judgment.

Similar concerns over online pornography—especially sexually explicit images accessible to Net-surfing youngsters—have sparked international incidents. In December 1995, federal prosecutors in Germany ordered CompuServe, the U.S.-based commercial online service that has a growing business in Europe, to stop providing German users with access to 200 of the 15,000 or so Internet newsgroups (or bulletin boards) that German prosecutors decided were offensive because of their strong sexual content. Caught by surprise by the order, CompuServe said its technology did not enable it to block access *only* to its 200,000 German users; to comply, it had to close down access to the disputed newsgroups for its entire 4-million-plus subscriber base. The subsequent global outcry—with accusations of censorship levied directly at both CompuServe and the German government—lasted for more than a month. Finally, CompuServe restored access to all but the five newsgroups found most objectionable, and at the same time announced it would be offering a "parental control" feature on the system, enabling adults to prevent certain materials from reaching the family computer.

At this writing, Germany has taken no further action against CompuServe, but a German parliamentary commission has called for international Internet controls against material harmful to children. Similar debates over sex and politics on the Net have surfaced in Hong Kong, Australia, Vietnam, and Indonesia. Particularly incensed is China, which now has gone so far as to require all Internet users in the country to register with the government and threatens prosecution of those accused of transmitting to the Net any state secret or other information deemed "harmful to national security or public order," especially pornography.

Back in the United States, fears of cyberporn spurred the U.S. Congress, in February 1996, to include the controversial "Communications Decency Act" in a massive law that overhauled the country's telecommunications industry. Making it a crime punishable by $250,000 in fines and two years in prison to transmit on the Net "indecent" material that could be viewed by a minor, the Act immediately was targeted in a free-speech suit from the American Civil Liberties Union (ACLU) and some two dozen organizations and businesses, including all the major online services. The suit contended that the Act was so broad and vague that it would outlaw transmission of legal speech, including even passages from famous literature such as J.D. Salinger's 1951 novel, *The Catcher in the Rye,* not to mention present-day rap music lyrics, profane conversations, and descriptive information about abortion. At this writing, a Net-wide protest, complete with its own symbol—a digital image of a blue ribbon—was urging the courts to overturn the new federal decency Act. Protesters argue that a better alternative to government regulation is existing software that enables parents to block certain materials from appearing on the family computer screen. The ACLU suit is being tried by a panel of three federal judges in Philadelphia. However, lawyers on both sides of the dispute are predicting that, regardless of the panel's ruling, the case probably is headed eventually for the U.S. Supreme Court.

Can Technology Be Neutral?

Let's step back from the specifics of these hot-button issues and see whether we can get a long view of a bigger question: Do these incidents point up a basic, fatal flaw in our modern nation, or are they only anomalies? In other words, if you were an ace cyberspace police reporter, would you be inclined to see that Russian Citibank caper, for instance, as an isolated event, simply a 1990s update on the bank jobs of old, with modems and computers replacing shotguns and masks? Or do such incidents have greater significance? Are they one more disturbing intimation of how a world of have-nots will be settling its scores from now on, perhaps throughout the rest of our lives? If so, what responsibility does the technology itself bear, if any?

John Eger, communications and public policy professor at San Diego State University, says technology cannot remain aloof, above the fray. "The first response is that new technologies are simply tools," he says, "and whether they help or harm society depends on the wisdom of those who use them. However, in the eyes of the resistance [to technology] this is the fundamental error. Technology is never neutral."

Nothing is inherently wrong with new technology, but, Eger says, humankind has been misusing technology for centuries now and probably will continue to do so. Furthermore, citing the divide between rich and poor, Eger says current political, ethnic, and cultural differences in Ireland, Canada, Nigeria, and other countries, as well as religious, linguistic, and tribal conflicts elsewhere around the globe, *all* have been fuelled to some extent by the spread of new telecommunications technology.

"Is this what technology gave birth to?" he asks. "Is this the potential reversal we will witness in the wake of the communications revolution? This is the problem we must do something about if we are to succeed and survive in the new global information economy and society."

WHAT IS THE "SOMETHING" WE CAN DO . . . AND HOW DO WE DO IT?

Identifying the *something* we are to do is the first problem. There may not *be* a magic bullet, a single "something" that can reverse the negative impact of technology.

Are judges' rulings the answer? Enforcement of court orders might be a problem. Those hoping for judicial regulation of the Net must find it disheartening to reflect on how, as we've seen, the French court's ban of that controversial book about François Mitterrand was undermined in hours by a café owner's Web page.

What about giving the courts more ammunition by producing tougher new laws? Fear of cyberporn is producing the social laboratory for that approach. As we've seen, lawmakers, from China and South Korea all the way to the floor of the U.S. Congress, have been addressing the issue of Net smut, and the U.S. Supreme Court may soon be asked to wade into the battle. But how does the United States, or any one nation, hope to regulate something as global, fluid, and largely anonymous as the Net, particularly considering that so much of the objectionable data originate outside individual nations' jurisdictions? Gerry Berman, director of the Center for Democracy and Technology, testified at the U.S. District Court trial over the disputed Communications Decency Act that as much as a third of the pornography on the Internet appears to originate overseas.

Lawmakers might have better luck trying to legislate the rain and wind or to outlaw lust and hate. At least one national government has even acknowledged that the Net probably can't be regulated by legislation. Ian Taylor, Britain's science and technology minister, surprised some attendees at a London conference early in 1996 by concluding that laws in themselves cannot control the burgeoning content of the

Internet. He cited as evidence Germany's failure to make CompuServe restrict newsgroup access.

More hopeful—though hardly guaranteed—are the efforts by the online industry to regulate *itself,* particularly in concert with the new brand of software that allows users to actively block receipt of potentially offensive material on their specific screens. Software is also the primary weapon on the business front: the commercialization of the Web demands security for credit card numbers, bank accounts, and other financial data. There is something fitting and elegant in our assigning software the responsibility of protecting us against the rogue programmers who roam the Net. At the same time, logic requires us to remember that no software solution is bullet-proof. Each new security scheme launched on the Net is like a clarion call to rally the world's hackers, who then begin chipping away at it—some in hopes of personal gain, but many more motivated simply by the irresistible attraction of the hunt.

Is There an Old Answer to These New Problems?

No wonder some people get nervous just looking at the Net. It is so big and unrestrained.

But perhaps we're approaching this challenge from the wrong direction. Maybe we would feel more comfortable about it if we were to deemphasize this notion that we can regulate or discipline the Net. And it might help to stop referring to the Net as a *virtual* community and to start thinking of it, instead, as a real community, full of individuals with all kinds of intentions, good and bad; a community with some of the same opportunities and dangers found in New York, London, or Tokyo. Perhaps we could approach the Net with the same cautious enthusiasm that tourists and immigrants bring every day to the large, exciting—and potentially dangerous—cities in the Real World.

The road to making peace with the Net may not lead to the Big-P Politics of government regulation, but to the Little-P politics of individual initiative and consumer-oriented self-interest. Futurists from John Naisbitt to Alvin and Heidi Toffler all say our destiny is in just such decentralization, not in big, old-fashioned Industrial Age government bureaucracies.

The digital age even may be heralding a fundamental change in how we define "activism." Perhaps we are shifting away from a passive reliance on government regulations and assorted agencies to protect us, evolving into an active, involved public that uses its new information connections to learn how to protect itself. Maybe the answer to civilizing cyberspace is not in new laws, but in education. Can the new online citizenry teach itself how to avoid the digital dangers? And what do you want to bet the rules of the road for the information superhighway won't be so terribly unfamiliar to us after all? They're probably the same basic clan customs we have learned from our mothers. "Be friendly and helpful, but temper your openness with a healthy skepticism." "Don't believe everything you read." "Respect yourself; let the world know you value your name and reputation." "Don't act like a victim." "Trust your instincts. And don't accept rides from strangers."

Whither Anarchy?

In the end, what are we to make of these fears that the Information Age will have us Net surfing our way right into global anarchy? If we define "anarchy" as simple a state of society without government or law, then the Net *already is* such an anarchy; it has been for more than twenty years. Born lawless, it remains so, as lawless as any other frontier.

But that does not necessarily mean disorder. On the contrary, the birth and prosperity of the highly sociable, potentially profitable Web over the past five years illustrates what always seems to happen in the wilderness: Life seeks structure.

The great historian Will Durant once observed, "Custom rises out of the people, whereas law is forced upon them from above. Law is usually a decree of the master, but custom is the natural selection of those modes of action that have been found most convenient in the experience of the group."

Cyberspace is more than a place. It is an experience from which new customs may arise to shape our society in the next century.

Alphabetical Listing of Websites

A Basic Citizen's Definitive Electronic Freedom Guide
    (http://www.dakota.net/~pwinn/abcdefg)
Abortion Rights Activis
    (http://www.cais.com/agm/index.html)
Accomplishments of the Clinton Administration
    (http://whitehouse.gov/Accomplishments.html)
Accountant's Home Page
    (http://www.servtech.com/re/acct.html)
Accountant's Web
    (http://pobox.com/~accweb)
Activist's Oasis
    (http://www.matisse.net/~kathy/activist)
Activist Toolkit
    (gopher://gopher.well.sf.ca.us:70/11s/Politics/activist.tools
        /how .to.win/)
Aether Madness: An Offbeat Guide to the Online World
    (http://www.aether.com/Aether/limbaugh.html)
AFL-CIO
    (http://www.aflcio.org)
African American Haven
    (http://www.auc.edu/~tpearson/haven.html)
African American Interest
    http://www.earthlink.net/~anthony/african.html)
Afro-American
    (http://www.afroam.org/afroam)
Agriculture Department
    (http://www.usda.gov)
AIDS and Related Topics
    (http://www.actwin.com/aids/vl.html)
AIDS Patents Project
    (http://patents.cnidr.org)

All Politics
    (http://allpolitics.com)
Alliance for Public Technology
    (http://apt.org/apt/index.html)
Alta Vista
    (http://www.altavista.digital.com)
Amendments
    (http:www.house.gov/Constitution/Amend.html)
Amendments considered but not ratified
    (http:www.house.gov/Constitution/Amendnotrat.html)
America's Job Bank
    (http://www.ajb.dni.us)
American Association of Retired Persons' '96 Voters Guide
    (http://www.electionline.com/AD/AARP/home.cgi)
American Life Leagu
     (http://www.ahoynet.com/~all/index.html)
American Reporter
    (http://www.clickshare.com:9999)
Americans for Tax Reform
    (http://www.Emerald.Net/ATR)
AmeriCom Long Distance Area Decoder
    (http://www.xmission.com/~americom/aclookup.html)
Amnesty International
    (http://www.traveller.com/~hrweb/ai/ai.html)
A Monument to the Clinton Presidency
    (http://www.clark.net/pub/jeffd/cgi-bin/dodger.cg:.html)
Animal Health, Well Being and Rights
    (http://www.tiac.net/users/sbr/animals.html)
Animal Rights Resource Site
    (http://envirolink.org/arrs/index.html)
Anti-Rush
    (http://www.cjnetworks.com/~cubsfan/rush/antirush.html)
Asian American Resources
    (http://www.mit.edu:8001/afs/athena.mit.edu/user/i/r/irie
    /www/aar.html)
Assault Prevention
    (http://galaxy.einet.net/galaxy/Community/Safety
    /Assault-Prevention/apin/APINindex.html)
AT&T's toll-free number
     (http://www.tollfree.att.net/dir800)
AuditNet Resource List
    (http://www.unf.edu/students/jmayer/arl.html)

Banned Books
    (http://www.cs.cmu.edu/Web/People/spok/banned-books.html)
Berkeley Republican Club's Grand Old Page
    (http://www.berkeleyic.com/conservative/index.html)

Black/African Related Resources
      (http://www.african.upenn.edu/African_Studies/Home_Page/mcgee
        .html)
Black Avenger
      (http://www.globaldialog.com/hamblin)
Blacklist of Internet Advertisers
      (http://math-www.uni-paderborn.de/~axel/BL/blacklist.html)
Blacksburg Electronic Village
      (http://www.bev.net)
Bootcamp from WCBS NewsRadio88
      (http://www.pulver.com/bootcamp)
BosniaLINK
      (http://www.dtic.mil/bosnia/index.html)
Boston University's Violence Site
      (gopher://software.bu.edu/11/Things%20You%20Should%20Know
        /Safety%20Resources/Safety%20Issues/Domestic%20Violence)
Brett Kottmann
      (http://www.erinet.com/bkottman/reagan.html)
Bureau of Justice Statistics
      (gopher://uacsc2.albany.edu/11/newman)
Bureau of Labor Statistic
      (http://www.dol.gov)

California Abortion Rights Action League
      (http://www.caral.org)
Campus for Choice
      (http://ux5.cso.uiuc.edu/~hindin/choice)
Capitol Steps
      (http://pfm.het.brown.edu/people/mende/steps/index.html)
CapWeb
      (http://policy.net/capweb/congress.html)
CapWeb's Political Page
      (http://policy.net/capweb/political.html)
Car Loan Calculator
      (http://www.motorcity.com/site/MC/AutoLoan.html)
Carter Center
      (http://www.emory.edu/CARTER_CENTER)
Cato Institute
      (http://www.cato.org/main/home.html)
CBS
      (http://www.cbs.com)
Center for the Advancement of Paleo Orthodoxy
      (http://www.usit.net/public/CAPO/capohomne.html)
Center for Democracy and Technology
      (http://www.cdt.org)
Centers for Disease Control and Prevention
      (http://www.cdc.gov)

Center for World Indigenous Studies Information
(http://www.halcyon.com/FWDP/cwisinfo.html)
Central Intelligence Agenc
(http://www.odci.gov)
Chicago Tribune's Career Finder
(http://www.chicago.tribune.com)
Chicano/LatinoNet
(http://latino.sscnet.ucla.edu)
Child Quest Internationa
(http://www.childquest.org)
Children Now
(http://www.dnai.com/~children)
Choice Net Report
(gopher://gopher.well.sf.ca.us/11s/Politics/Abortion)
Christian Broadcasting Network
(http://the700club.org)
Christian Coalition
(http://www.cc.org)
Christlib
(http://www.teleport.com/~bruceab/xlib.html)
Chuck Shepherd
(notw-request@nine.org)
Cinetic
(http://cinetic.de)
Citizens Committee for the Right to Keep and Bear Arms
(http://www.ccrkba.org)
ClariNet e.New
(http://www.clarinet.com/index.html)
Clinton Exposé
(http://www.en.com/users/bthomas/expose.htm)
Clinton Watch
(gopher://dolphin.gulf.net:3000/hh)
Clinton, Yes!
(http://www.av.qnet.com/~yes)
Club WIRED
(ClubWIRED@aol.com)
CMP Publishing's TechWeb
(http://techweb.cmp.com/techweb)
CNN Interactiv
(http://www.cnn.com)
Code of Federal Regulations
(http://www.pls.com:8001/his/cfr.html)
Commerce Department
(http://www.doc.gov)
Commerce Department's Economic Conversion Information Exchange
(http://ecix.doc.gov)

Commodity Futures Trading Commission
(http://www.clark.netpub/cftc)

Communications for a Sustainable Future
(http://csf.Colorado.EDU/homeless)

Computer Professionals for Social Responsibility
(http://cpsr.org/home)

Computer Underground Digest
(http://www.eff.org/pub/Publications/CuD)

Congressional Quarterl
(gopher://gopher.cqalert.com)

Conservative Generation X
(http://www.cgx.com)

Conservative Link
(http://www.portcom.com/BmDesign/cicg/cicghome.html)

Consumer Health Information
(http://www.os.dhhs.gov/consumer/coninfo.html)

Consumer Information Center Catalog
(http://www.pueblo.gsa.gov)

Contacting the Congress
(http://ast1.spa.umn.edu/juan/congress.html)

Cornell University Law School
(http://www.law.cornell.edu/supct/classics/410us113.ovr.html)

Corporation for National Service
(http://www.whitehouse.gov/White_House/EOP/cns/html/cns-index
.html)

Cost-of-living adjustment
(http://www.ssa.gov/OACT/95COLA/FR.sum.html)

Council of Better Business Bureaus
(http://www.bbb.org/bbb)

Council of State Governments
(http://www.csg.org)

Countdown on the Clinton Presidency
(http://www.acs.ncsu.edu/~nsyslaw/scripts/rawdeal-nsyslaw)

Counterpoint
(http://www.counterpoint.com)
(info@counterpoint.com)

Counterpoint's E-mail Federal Register
(http://www.counterpoint.com/emailfr)

Counter Revolution Resources
(http://nyx10.cs.du.edu:8001/~nmonagha/arc.html)

Court TV
(http://www.courttv.com/library/supreme)

Court TV Law Center
(http://www.courttv.com)

Court TV Legal Center
(http://www.courttv.com/legalhelp)

Cyber-Republicans
(http://www.rpi.edu/~scotta/republican.html)
Cybergrrl!
(http://www.cybergrrl.com)
CyberWire Dispatch
(majordomo@cyberwerks.com)
Cypherpunks
(http://www.csua.berkeley.edu/cypherpunks/Home.html)

Data Maps
(http://www.census.gov/stat_abstract/profile.html)
DeathNet
(http://www.IslandNet.com:80/~deathnet)
Debt Calculator
(http://www.uclc.com/consumer/debtcalc.html)
Declaration of Independence
(http:www.house.gov/Declaration.html)
DefenseLink
(http://www.dtic.dla.mil/defenselink)
DeMOCKracy
(http://www.clark.net/pub/theme/demockracy)
Democratic Party Activists
(http://www.digitals.org/digitals)
Democratic Senatorial Campaign Committee
http://www.dscc.org/d/dscc.html)
Democratic Socialists of America
(http://ccme-mac4.bsd.uchicago.edu/DSA.html)
Democrats
(http:www.democrats.org)
Department of Health and Human Services
(http://www.os.dhhs.gov)
Department of Transportation
(http://www.dot.gov)
Department of Treasury
(http://www.ustreas.gov/treasury/homepage.html)
DIANA, An International Human Rights Database
(http://www.law.uc.edu/Diana)
DiploNet
(http://www.clark.net/pub/diplonet/DiploNet.html)
Directory of Chambers of Commerce
(http://chamber-of-commerce.com)
Directory of Human Rights Resources
(http://www.igc.apc.org/igc/hr)
Disability Resources
(http://www.disability.com)
Distance Server
(http://gs213.sp.cs.cmu.edu/prog/dist)

Diversity
      (http://latino.sscnet.ucla.edu/diversity1.html)
Divorce
      (http://www.primenet.com/~dean)
Doonesbury Electronic Town Hall
      (http://www.doonesbury.com)
Dow Jones News/Retrieval
      (http://www.bis.dowjones.com)
Drudge Report
      (http://www.lainet.com:80/~drudge)
DV Resources
      (http://marie.az.com/~blainn/dv/index.html)
Dwight D. Eisenhower Library
      (http://gopher.nara.gov:70/1/inform/library/eisen)

Earth First!
      (gopher://gopher.igc.apc.org/11/orgs/ef.journal)
EarthWatch
      (http://gaia.earthwatch.org)
Econet
      (http://www.igc.apc.org/econet)
Economy
      (http://www.census.gov/econ.html)
Editor & Publisher Interactive
      (http://www.mediainfo.com/edpub)
Education Department
      (http://www.ed.gov)
EFF
      (http://www.eff.org)
Election '96
      (http://dodo.crown.net/~mpg/election/96.html)
ElectionLine
      (http://www.electionline.com)
Electronic Bunker
      (http://rainbow.rmii.com/~tph/bunker.html)
Electronic Businesses
      (http://webster.cadcam.iupui.edu:80/~ho/interests/commenu.html)
Electronic Embassy
      (http://www.embassy.org)
Electronic Frontier Foundation
      (http://www.eff.org)
Electronic Newsstand
      (http://www.enews.com)
E-mail Democracy
      (http://www.entrepreneurs.net/solutions/emaildem.htm)
Embassy of Norway page
      (http://www.norway.org)

Environmental News Network
   (http://www.enn.com)
Environmental Protection Agency
   (http://www.epa.gov)
EnviroWeb
   (http://envirolink.org:/start_web.html)
ESPNET SportZone
   (http://espnet.sportszone.com)
EText Archives
   (http://www.etext.org)
Ethical Spectacle
   (http://www.spectacle.org)
E-Zine List
   (http://www.meer.net/~johnl/e-zine-list/index.html)

Facts for Families
   (http://www.psych.med.umich.edu/web/aacap/factsFam)
FatherNet
   (gopher://tinman.mes.umn.edu:80/11/FatherNet)
Fathers' Resource Center
   (http://www.parentsplace.com/readroom/frc/index.html)
Fathers' Rights and Equality Exchange
   (http://www.vix.com/pub/free/index.html)
FBI
   (http://www.fbi.gov/homepage.htm)
FBI ten most wanted
   (http://www.fbi.gov/toplist.htm)
Federal Communications Commission
   (http://www.fcc.gov)
Federal Court Locator
   (http://ming.law.vill.edu/Fed-Ct/fedcourt.html)
Federal Deposit Insurance Corporation
   (http://www.fdic.gov)
Federal Emergency Management Agency
   (http://www.fema.gov)
Federal Judicial Center
   (http://www.fjc.gov)
Federally Funded Research in the United States
   http://cos.gdb.org/best/fed-fund.html)
Federal News Service
   (http://www.fednews.com)
Federal Trade Commission
   (http://www.ftc.gov)
Federal Trade Commission's Consumer Line
   (http://www.ftc.gov/bcp/conline/conline.htm)
FedWorld
   (http://www.fedworld.gov)

FEMA Global Emergency Management System
    (http://www.fema.gov/fema/gems.html)
Feminism and Women's Resources
    (http://www.ibd.nrc.ca/~mansfield/feminism.html)
Feminist Mailing List
    (http://www.lm.com/~lmann/feminist/feminist.html)
Feminist Science Fiction, Fantasy & Utopia
    (http://www.uic.edu/~lauramd/sf/femsf.html)
54 Ways You Can Help the Homeless
    (http://ecosys.drdr.virginia.edu/ways/54.html)
FinanceNet
    (http://www.financenet.gov)
Firearm
    (http://bronze.ucs.indiana.edu/~wwarf/firearm.html)
    (http://ramcad2.pica.army.mil:80/~rjd/guns)
    (http://www.portal.com/~chan)
Firearms, Individual Rights, and Politics
    (http://www.cs.cmu.edu:8001/afs/cs.cmu.edu/project/nectar/member
        /karl/html/firearms/firearms.html)
Firearms and Liberty
    http://www.cica.indiana.ed/hyplan/scotto/firearms/firearms.html)
Flummery Digest
    (http://jasper.ora.com/sierra/flum)
Food and Drug Administration
    (http://www.fda.gov/fdahomepage.html)
Foreign Affairs
    (http://www.enews.com/magazines/foreign_affairs)
Four11 Directory
    (http://www.four11.com)
Franklin D. Roosevelt Library
    (http://gopher.nara.gov:70/1/inform/library/fdr)
Freedom Network
    (http://www.aclu.org)
Freethought
    (http://freethought.tamu.edu/freethought)

G. Gordon Liddy
    (http://www.rtis.com/nat/pol/liddy)
    (potent@aol.com)
General Accounting Office
    (gopher://dewey.lib.ncsu.edu/11/library/disciplines/government
        /gao-reports)
General Services Administration
    (http://www.gsa.gov)
General Services Administration's Federal Information Center
    (http://www.gsa.gov/et/fic-firs/fic.htm)

Geography
(http://www.census.gov/geog.html)
Gerald R. Ford Presidential Library and Museum
(http://www2.sils.umich.edu/FordLibrary)
(http://gopher.nara.gov:70/1/inform/library/ford)
Gingrich
(http://www.house.gov/mbr_dir/GA06.html)
(georgia6@hr.house.gov)
Global Fund for Wome
(http://www.ai.mit.edu/people/ellen/gfw.html)
Goldwater
(http://www3.dive.com/GoldWeb/GoldwaterHome.html)
Government Information Locator Service
(http://info.er.usgs.gov/gils/index.html)
GrantsNet
(http://www.os.dhhs.gov/progorg/grantsnet)
(listserv@list.nih.gov)
Grass Roots
(http://www.uwsa.com:8972/uwsa)
Green Parties of North America
(http://www.rahul.net/greens)
Greenpeace
(http://www.greenpeace.org)
GulfLINK
(http://www.dtic.mil/gulflink)

Hard Response
(http://turnpike.net/emporium/H/HR/index.htm)
Harnessing the Internet
(http://www.trincoll.edu/harnessing/home.html)
Harvard Salient
(http://www.salient.org/Salient)
Highway 1
(http://www.highway1.org)
Historical Text Archive
(http://www.msstate.edu/Archives/History/index.html)
Homeless
(listserv@csf.colorado.edu)
Homeless News Service
(gopher://csf.Colorado.EDU:70/11/psn/homeless.HNS)
Hospital
(http://demOnmac.mgh.harvard.edu/hospital.html)
House Democratic Leadership
(http://www.house.gov/democrats)
House of Representatives
(http://www.house.gov)

House Republican Conference
    (http://www.house.gov/gop/HRCHome.html)
HUD
    (http://www.hud.gov)
Human Rights
    (http://www.traveller.com/~hrweb/hrweb.html)

IanWeb
    (http://www.pitt.edu/~ian/ianres.html)
In His Own Words, Broken Promises from the President
    (http://www.umr.edu:80/~umrcr/lies.html)
    (http://www.winternet.com/~ssarazin/clinton.draft.html
Indian Health Service
    (http://www.tucson.ihs.gov)
Individual's NewsPage
    (http://www.newspage.com)
Infobahn Political
    (http://www.cs.cmu.edu/~jab/politics.html)
Information = Power. Queer Resource Center
    (http://www.actwin.com/queerindex.html)
Information about the Queer Nation
    (http://www.cs.cmu.edu/Web/People/mjw/Queer/MainPage.html)
Institute for Global Communications ConflictNet
    (http://www.conflictnet.apc.org/conflictnet)
Institute on Global Conflict and Cooperation
    (http://irpsbbs.ucsd.edu/igcc/igccmenu.html)
Interactive Democracy
    (http://www.cgx.com/id.html)
Interactive King of All Media Newsletter
    (http://haven.ios.com/~koam)
Interactive Week
    (http://cyberwerks.com:70/cyberwire.cwd)
Interior Department
    (http://info.er.usgs.gov/doi/doi.html)
Internal Revenue Service
    (http://www.irs.ustreas.gov)
Internet Edgar Dissemination projec
    (http://www.sec.gov/edgarhp.htm)
Internet Green Marketplace
    (http://envirolink.org/products)
Internet Hourly News
    (http://www.RealAudio.com/contentp/abc.html)
Internet Phonebook
    (http://www.iag.net/~impt/index.html)
Internet Radio Nexus
    (http://www.nexus.org/Internet_Radio)

Internet Solutions Inc.
    (http://www.internetsol.com)
Investigative Report on Domestic Violence
    (http://www.ultranet.com/newstandard/projects/DomVio
    /domviohome.HTML)
iRock
    (http://www.irock.com)

Jesse Helms
    (http://www.nando.net/sproject/jesse/helms.html)
Jimmy Carter Library
    (http://gopher.nara.gov:70/1/inform/library/carter)
John Birch Society
    (http://www.primenet.com/~tevans/jbs.html)
John F. Kennedy Library
    (http://gopher.nara.gov:70/1/inform/library/kennedy)
Just Say Yes
    (http://www.actwin.com/aids/jsIndex.html)
Justice Department
    (http://justice2.usdoj.gov)

Keep Right
    (http://www.crl.com/www/users/jm/jmcraven)
KidsPeace: The National Center for Kids in Crisis
    (http://good.freedom.net/kidspeace)
KlaasKids
    (http://klaaskids.inter.net/klaaskids)

LaborNet
    (http://www.labornet.org/labornet)
Latin American Network Information Center
    (http://info.lanic.utexas.edu)
Lawyer Search
    (http://www.counsel.com/lawyersearch)
LC Online Systems
    (http://lcweb.loc.gov/homepage/online.html)
LCMARVEL database
    (gopher//marvel.loc.gov)
Left On
    (http://www.winternet.com/~tulley/left.html)
Left Side of the Web
    (http://paul.spu.edu/~sinnfein/progressive.html)
Libertarian
    (http://www.libertarian.com/wwlp)
Libertarian Party Documents
    (http://lydia.bradley.edu/campusorg/libertarian/lpdocs/index.html)

Libertarian Party Headquarters
    (http://access.digex.net/~lphq)
    (lphq@digex.net)
Libertarian Web
    (http://w3.ag.uiuc.edu/liberty/libweb.html)
Library of Congres
    (http://thomas.loc.gov)
    (http://lcweb.loc.gov/homepage/lchp.html)
Library of Congress's Country Studies/Area Handbook Program
    (http://lcweb.loc.gov/homepage/country.html)
LifeLinks
    (http://www.nebula.net\,maeve\lifelink.html)
Links from the Underground
    (http://www.links.net)
LOCIS system
    (telnet://locis.loc.gov)
Lokace
    (http://www.iplus.fr/lokace)
Lycos
    (http://query2.lycos.cs.cmu.edu)
Lyndon B. Johnson Library
    (http://gopher.nara.gov:70/1/inform/library/johnson)
    (gopher//ffp.cc.utexas.edu:3003/11/pub/lbj-library)

Meanderings
    (http://www.webcom.com:80/~sppg/meanderings/me.html)
Mecklermedia iWorld
    (http://www.iworld.com)
Men's Issues
    (http://www.vix.com/pub/men/index.html)
Mercury Center
    (http://www.sjmercury.com)
Militia Watch
    (http://paul.spu.edu/~sinnfein/progressive.html)
Minnesota Attorney General Hubert Humphrey III
    (http://www.state.mn.us/cbranch/ag)
Minnesota Higher Education Center Against Violence and Abuse
    (http://www.umn.edu/mincava)
Modern Times
    (http://www.columbia.edu/cu/mt/mt.html)
MoJo
    (http://www.mojones.com)
Mortgage Calculator
    (http://www.majon.com/majon/estate.mort.html)
Mother Jones Supplement on Newt Gingrich
    (http://www.mojones.com/mojo_magazine.html)

Multimedia Newsstan
  (http://mmnewsstand.com)

National Aeronautics and Space Administration
  (http://www.nasa.gov)
National AIDS Clearinghouse of the Centers for Disease Control
  (gopher://cdcnac.aspensys.com:72/11)
National Archives and Records Administration
  (http://www.nara.gov)
National Center for Missing and Exploited Children
  (http://www.scubed.com/public_service/missing.html)
  (webmaster@scubed.com)
National Child Rights Alliance
  (http://www.ai.mit.edu/people/ellens/NCRA/ncra.html)
National Coalition of Free Men
  (http://www.liii.com:80/~ncfm2)
National Coalition for the Homeless
  (http://www2.ar:.net/home/nch)
National Endowment for the Humanities
  (http://ns1.neh.fed.us)
National Firearms Act and Other Gun Laws
  (http://www.cs.cmu.edu/afs/cs.cmu.edu/user/wbardwel/public
  /nfalist/index.html)
National Fraud Information Center
  (http://www.fraud.org)
National Institutes of Health
  (http://www.nih.gov)
National Organization for Women
  (http://now.org)
National Performance Review
  (http://www.npr.gov)
National Public Radio
  (http://www.realaudio.com/contentp/npr.html)
National Rifle Association
  (http://www.nra.org)
National Science Foundation
  (http://stis.nsf.gov)
National Security Agency
  (http://www.nsa.gov:8080)
National Technology Transfer Center
  (http://www.nttc.edu)
National Trade Data Bank
  (http://www.stat-usa.gov)
Native American Internet Information
  (http://hanksville.phast.umass.edu/defs/independent
  /ElecPath/elecpath.html)

Native Web
    (http://kuhttp.cc.ukans.edu/~marc/native_main.html)
Natural Law Party
    (http://www.fairfield.com/nlpusa)
    (info@natural-law.org)
NBC
    (http://www.nbc.com/news/index.html)
NBC Dateline
    (tdmned@cityview.com)
NBC Nightly News
    (newsroom@cmonitor.com)
Net fraud complaints
    (http://www.fraud.org)
New England Online
    (http://ftp.std.com/NE)
News Briefings from the ANC
    (http://minerva.cis.yale.edu/~jadwat/anc)
NewsLink
    (http://www.newslink.org)
NewsView
    (http://www.fyionline.com)
Newsweek
    (letters@newsweek.com)
NewtWatch
    (http://www.cais.com/newtwatch)
New York Time
    (http://nytimesfax.com)
    (webmster@nytimes.com)
New York's Nynex Interactive Yellow Pages
    (http://www.niyp.com)
Non-Violence International
    (http://www.igc.apc.org/ni)
NOW and Abortion Rights/Reproductive Issues
    (http://now.org:80/issues/abortion/abortion.html)
Nuclear Regulatory Commission
    (http://www.nrc.gov)

Office of Technology Assessment
    (http:www.ota.gov)
Official Bob Dole for President
    (http://www.dole96.com)
Oliver North
    (http://www.north.inter.net/north)
ONE
    (http://www.clark.net/pub/conquest/one/home.html)

Online Intelligence Projec
    (http://www.icg.org/intelweb/index.html)
Online News Service
    (majordomo@democrats.org)
OpenNet
    (http://apollo.osti.gov/home.html)
    Out.com (http://www.out.com)

Pacific Northwest Travel
    (http://www.shore.net/~adfx/2398dir/pntp.html)
Pathfinder
    (http://www.pathfinder.com)
Pat Paulsen
    (http://www.amdest.com/Pat/pat.html)
Peace Corps
    (http://www.peacecorps.gov)
PeaceNet
    (http://www.peacenet.apc.org/peacenet)
Peaceweb
    (http://www.ottawa.net/~peaceweb)
Perspectives
    (http://hcs.harvard.edu/~perspy)
Pharmaceutical Information Network
    (http://pharminfo.com)
PhoNETic
    (http://www.soc.qc.edu/phonetic)
Piper Resources' State and Local Government on the Net
    (http://www.piperinfo.com/~piper/state/states.html)
Political Prisoners
    (http://www.xs4all.nl/%7Etank/prison.htm)
Political Scientist's Guide to the Internet
    (http://www.trincoll.edu/pols/home.html)
Politics USA
    (http://PoliticsUSA.com)
Population and Housing Data
    (http://www.census.gov/pop.html)
President's Council on Physical Fitness
    (http://www.whitehouse.gov/WH/PCPFS/html/fitnet.html)
Prison Issues
    (http://www.igc.apc.org/prisons)
    (majordomo@igc.apc.org)
Prison Legal News
    (http://www.synapse.net/~arrak:s/pln/pln.html)
Progress and Freedom Foundation
    (http://www.pff.org)
Progressive Business
    (http://envirolink.org/products/pbw.html)

Progressive Pages
  (ftp://ftp.crl.com/users/ro/grossman/progress.html)
Progressive Review
  (http://www.princeton.edu/~progrev)
Project Censored
  (http://zippy.sonoma.edu/ProjectCensored)
Project Vote Smart
  (http://www.vote-smart.org)
Pro-Life Encyclopedia
  (http://hebron.ee.gannon.edu/~frezza/plae/contents.html)
Pro-Life News
  (http:/hebron.ee.gannon.edu/~frezza/AboutPLN.html)
Propaganda Analysis
  (http://carmen.artsci.washington.edu/propaganda/home.htm)
Proponents at the Center to Prevent Handgun Violence
  (http://bianca.com/lolla/politics/handguns/handgun.html)
Public Technology Inc.
  (http://pti.nw.dc.us)

Queer Resources Directory
  (http://vector.casti.com/QRD/.html/QRD-home-page.html)

Radio Show
  (http://www.mcp.com/people/rwaring/rush.html)
Railroad Retirement Board
  (http://www.mcs.net/~taxation)
RealAudio from Progressive Networks
  (http://www.realaudio.com)
Relocation Calculator
  (http://www.homefair.com/homefair/cmr/salcalc.html)
Republican National Committee
  (http://www.rnc.org)
  (majordomo@rnc.org)
Retirement Planning Calculator
  (http://www.altamira.com/altamira/rrsp_calc.html)
Richard M. Nixon Library and Birthplace
  (http://www.chapman.edu/nixon)
  (http://gopher.nara.gov:70/1/inform/library/nixon)
Right to Keep and Bear Arms
  (http://iquest.com/~fitz/politics/rkba)
  (http://sal.cs.uiuc.edu/rec.guns/rkba.html)
Right Side of the Web
  (http://www.clark.net/pub/jeffd)
Robert F. Kennedy Progressive Democrats
  http://www.webcom.com/~albany/rfk.html)
Ronald Reagan
  (http://www.dnaco.net/~bkottman/reagan.html)

(http://www.asc.oakland.edu/~djsussma/stuff/reagan.html)
Ronald Reagan Library
    (http://gopher.nara.gov:70/1/inform/library/reagan)
Rush
    (http://www.rtis.com/nat/pol/rush)
Rush Limbaugh
    (70277.2502@compuserve.com)

SafetyNet
    (http://www.cybergrrl.com/dv.html)
Seamless WEBsite: Law and Legal Resources
    (http://seamless.com/index.html)
Second Amendment Foundation
    (http://www.CCRKBA.org:80/saf.org)
Secular Web
    (http://freethought.tamu.edu)
Securities and Exchange Commission
    (http://www.sec.gov)
Self-Help Law Center
    (http://gnn-e2a.gnn.com/gnn/bus/nolo)
Senate
    (http://www.senate.gov)
Senate Republican Conference
    (ftp://ftp.senate.gov/committee/repub-conf/general/src.html)
Sexual Assault Information
    (http://www.cs.utk.edu/~bartley/saInfoPage.html)
Small Business Administration
    (http://www.sbaonline.sba.gov)
Smithsonian Institution
    (http://www.si.edu)
Socialist Party USA Cybercenter
    (http://sunsite.unc.edu/spc/index.html)
Social Security Administration
    (http://www.ssa.gov)
Solidarity Group Political Prisoners
    (http://www.xs4all.nl/%7Etank/english.htm)
Southeast Information Depot
    (http://www.southeast.org)
Southwest Scou
    (http://www.swscout.com)
Spamily's Politics
    (http://www.io.org/~spamily/SocPolEnv.html)
Stanford Netnews Filtering Service
    (http://woodstock.stanford.edu:2000)
State Department's Bureau of Public Affairs
    (http://dosfan.lib.uic.edu/dosfan.html)

State Department's Foreign Affairs Network
    (http://dosfan.lib.uic.edu/dosfan.html)
State Government Information Servers
    (http://www.trincoll.edu/pols/us/states.html)
StateSearch
    (http://www.state.ky.us/nasire/nasireEmain.html)
Stop F.T.R
    (http://www.mcs.com/~dougp/stopftr.html)
Stop Prisoner Rape
    (http://www.ai.mit.edu/people/ellens/SPR/spr.html)
Stop Violence Against Women
    (http://www.io.org/~irishg/mainpage.html)
StreamWorks from Xing Technology Corp.
    (http://www.xingtech.com)
Supreme Court data
    (gopher://marvel.loc.gov/11/federal/fedinfo/byagency/judiciary)
Switchboard
    (http://www.switchboard.com)

Tarja Black
    (yes@qnet.com)
TenantNet
    (http://tenant.blythe.org/TenantNet)
    (tenant@tenant.blythe.org)
Thomas Jefferson
    (http://www.mit.edu:8001/activities/libertarians/ask-thomas-jefferson
        /jefferson.html)
    (gopher://gopher.vt.edu:10010/11/106)
TIME Magazine
    (timeletter@aol.com)
Trincoll Journal
    (http://www.trincoll.edu/tj/trincolljournal.html)
Truth Fears No Questions
    (http://www.teleport.com/~stiltman/Politics)
Turn Left
    (http://www.cjnetworks.com/~cubsfan/liberal.html)

United Nations
    (http://undcp.or.at/unlinks.html)
U.S. Agency for International Development
    (http://www.info.usaid.gov)
U.S. Bureau of Labor Statistics
    (http://stats.bls.gov/blshome.html)
U.S. Bureau of Transportation Statistics
    (http://www.bts.gov)

U.S. Business Advisor
    (http://www.business.gov)
U.S. Census Bureau
    (http://www.census.gov)
U.S. Chamber of Commerce
    (http://www.uschamber.org/chamber)
U.S. Code
    (http://www.pls.com:8001/his/usc.html)
U.S. Constitution
    (http:www.house.gov/Constitution/Constitution.html)
U.S. Consumer Products Safety Commission
    (gopher://cpsc.gov)
    (listproc@cpsc.gov)
U.S. Copyright Office
    (http://lcweb.loc.gov/copyright)
U.S. Federal Courts
    (http://www.uscourts.gov)
U.S. Federal Government Agency Directory Scope
    (http:www.lib.lsu.edu/gov/fedgov.html)
U.S. Government Printing Office
    (http://www.access.gpo.gov)
U.S. House of Representatives
    (http://www.house.gov/Whoswho.html)
U.S. Information Agency
    (http://www.usia.gov)
U.S. International Trade Commission
    (http://www.usitc.gov)
U.S. News Online
    (http://www2.USNews.com/usnews)
U.S. Postal Service
    (http://www.usps.gov)
U.S. Senate Republican Policy Committee
    (ftp://ftp.senate.gov/committee/repub-policy/general/rpc.html)
U.S. State Department's Travel Advisories
    (http://www.stolaf.edu/network/travel-advisories.html)
Universal Black Pages
    (http://www.gatech.edu/cgi-bin/ubp-find)
Universal Press Syndicate
    (http://www.nine.org/notw/archive.html)
University of Maryland's Sexual Harassment Resources
    (http://inform.umd.edu:86/Educational_Resources
        /AcademicResourcesByTopic/WomensStudies/GenderIssues
        /SexualHarassment)
University of Michigan's Geographic Name Server
    (telnet://martini.eecs.umich.edu:3000)
Unofficial Bob Dole
    (http://www.seas.upenn.edu/~lapple/bobdole.html)

Unofficial Rush Limbaugh
    (http://mail.eskimo.com/~jeremyps/rush)
USA CityLink Project
    (http://www.usacitylink.com/citylink)
USA Today
    (http://www.usatoday.com)
    (usatoday@clark.net)
US News & World Report
    (71154.1006@compuserve.com)
UWSA Headquarters
    (http://www.uwsa.org)
UWSA Newsletter
    (http://www.telusys.com/uwsa.html)

Vanderbilt's Television News Archive
    (http://tvnews.vanderbilt.edu)
Vibe
    (http://metaverse.com/vibe)
Vietnam Era Prisoner of War/Missing in Action Database
    (http://lcweb2.loc.gov/pow/powhome.html)
Villanova Center for Information Law and Policy
    (http://www.law.vill.edu)
Virtual Library's Electronic Journals Lists
    (http://www.edoc.com/ejournal)
Virtual Sisterhood
    (http://www.igc.apc.org/vsister/vsister.html)
Voice of America
    (gopher://gopher.voa.gov/1)
Voices of Women
    (http://www.voiceofwomen.com/VOWworld.html)

Wall Street Journal
    (http://wsj.com)
Washington Post Digital Ink project
    (http://www.att.com/bnet/services/dink.html)
Washington Weekly
    (http://dolphin.gulf.net/Gingrich.html)
We the People
    (http://www.hia.com/hia/wtp)
Welcome to the White House: An Interactive Citizens' Handbook
    (http://www.whitehouse.gov)
Well
    (http://www.well.com/Community/comic)
    (tomorrow@well.com)
What's Newt: Keeping Track of Newt Gingrich
    (http://www.wolfenet.com/~danfs/newt.html)

White House Fellows
  (http://www.whitehouse.gov/White_House/WH_Fellows/html
    /fellows1-plain.html)
White House for Kids
  (http://www.whitehouse.gov/WH/kids/html/home.html)
Who's Cool in America
  (http://www.getcool.com/~getcool)
Wilderness Society
  (http://town.hall.org/environment/wild_soc/wilderness.html)
Women Leaders Online
  (http://worcester.lm.com/women/women.html)
WomensNet
  (http://www.igc.apc.org/women/feminist.html)
  (http://www.igc.apc.org/womensnet)
World Health Organization
  (http://www.who.ch)
World's Smallest Political Quiz
  (http://lydia.bradley.edu/campusorg/libertarian/wspform.html)
WWW Virtual Library of State Government Servers
  (http://www.law.indiana.edu/law/states.html)

Xerox PARC Map Server
  (http://pubweb.parc.xerox.com/map)

Yahoo
  (http://www.yahoo.com)
Yankee Web Explorer
  (http://www.tiac.net/users/macgyver/ne.html)
Youth Bill of Rights
  (http://www.ai.mit.edu/people/ellens/NCRA/rights.html)

Ziff-Davis Publishing
  (http://www.ziff.com)

Index